CLIMATE RISKS REPORTING PRACTICES AND ASSURANCE

ADVANCES IN ENVIRONMENTAL ACCOUNTING & MANAGEMENT

Series Editor: Olayinka Moses and Ven Tauringana

Recent volumes:

Volume 12:	Sustainable and Resilient Supply Chain: Environmental Accounting and Management Focus, 2024
Volume 11:	Green House Gas Emissions Reporting and Management in Global Top Emitting Countries and companies, 2023
Volume 10:	Environmental Sustainability and Agenda 2030: Efforts, Progress and Prospects, 2022
Volume 9:	Environmentalism and NGO Accountability, 2020
Volume 8:	Environmental Reporting and Management in Africa, 2019
Volume 7:	Sustainability Accounting: Education, Regulation, Reporting and Stakeholders, 2018
Volume 6:	Advances in Environmental Accounting & Management: Social and Environmental Accounting in Brazil, 2017
Volume 5:	Accounting for the Environment: More Talk and Little Progess, 2014
Volume 4:	Sustainability, Environmental Performance and Disclosures, 2010
Volume 3:	Environmental Accounting: Commitment or Propaganda, 2006
Volume 2:	Advances in Environmental & Management, 2003
Volume 1:	Advances in Environmental Accounting & Management, 2000

ADVANCES IN ENVIRONMENTAL ACCOUNTING & MANAGEMENT VOLUME 13

CLIMATE RISKS REPORTING PRACTICES AND ASSURANCE

EDITED BY

AHSAN HABIB
Massey University, New Zealand

DIMU EHALAIYE
Massey University, New Zealand

AINUL ISLAM
Victoria University of Wellington, New Zealand

AND

SEDZANI MUSUNDWA
University of South Africa, South Africa

emerald PUBLISHING

United Kingdom – North America – Japan
India – Malaysia – China

Emerald Publishing Limited
Emerald Publishing, Floor 5, Northspring, 21-23 Wellington Street, Leeds LS1 4DL

First edition 2025

Printed and bound by CPI Group (UK) Ltd, Croydon, CR0 4YY

British Library Cataloguing in Publication Data
A catalogue record for this book is available from the British Library

ISBN: 978-1-83662-193-5 (Print)
ISBN: 978-1-83662-192-8 (Online)
ISBN: 978-1-83662-194-2 (Epub)

ISSN: 1479-3598

CONTENTS

ABOUT THE EDITORS

Dr Ahsan Habib is a Professor of Financial Accounting at Massey University, Auckland. His main areas of research interest include but are not limited to capital market-based accounting research, the interface between corporate governance and accounting information, and corporate social responsibility. He has published extensively in prestigious journals like *Accounting & Business Research, ABACUS, The British Accounting Review, Business & Society, Corporate Governance: An International Review, European Accounting Review, International Journal of Accounting, International Review of Financial Analysis* and *Journal of Accounting Literature*. He is widely cited as evidenced by his Google Scholar citations statistic of 9,850. Ahsan has been ranked among the top 2% of the world's scientists each year since 2022 published by Stanford University and Elsevier. He is a Deputy Editor of Accounting & Finance, an Associate Editor of Advances in Accounting and Spanish Accounting Review and serves on several journals as an editorial board member.

Dr Dimu Ehalaiye BSc, MBA, PhD, CA, FHEA, is a Senior Lecturer in Accounting at the School of Accountancy, Massey University, Palmerston North, New Zealand. He is very involved in research including doctoral supervision and has authored several journal publications, book chapters and commissioned reports. His current research interests focus on financial accounting and reporting, auditing, accounting standards setting, climate risks reporting and assurance, accounting in emerging markets and public sector accounting. His research has been published in prominent journals like *Financial Accountability & Management, The International Journal of Accounting, Meditari Accountancy Research, Pacific-Basin Finance Journal, Applied Economics, Public Money and Management, International Journal of Accounting and Information Management, Australian Accounting Review and Pacific Accounting Review.* He is also a member of the Chartered Accountants Australia and New Zealand (CA ANZ) and currently serves on the local committee of CA ANZ in the Manawatu region.

Dr Ainul Islam is a Senior Lecturer at the School of Accounting and Commercial Law, Victoria Business School, Victoria University of Wellington, New Zealand. He is a member of Chartered Accountants Australia and New Zealand (CA ANZ) and a member of the Certified Practising Accountants (CPA) in Australia. Ainul's research broadly covers the area of financial reporting, auditing and corporate governance. He has published in reputable accounting and business journals.

Dr Sedzani Musundwa is a Senior Lecturer in Financial Accounting at the University of South Africa (UNISA). A Chartered Accountant (CA(SA)) with a PhD in Accounting Sciences, her research spans accounting education and social sciences, specializing in sustainability, diversity, equity and inclusion. With a prosperous career in academic leadership, she has served as Head of the Department of Financial Accounting (UNISA) and is a member of the Ethics Review Board. An internationally recognized scholar, Dr Musundwa's work is published in highly ranked journals. She has delivered keynote addresses on issues of inclusion, decolonization and sustainable development. She also serves as a reviewer and editor for international journals. She is a dedicated mentor, an advocate for systemic transformation and a passionate educator committed to redefining the accounting profession through critical research and innovative teaching. Dr Musundwa's impact extends beyond academia, shaping the future of accounting in South Africa and beyond.

LIST OF REVIEWERS

Adrian Kubata	*University of Luxembourg, Luxembourg*
Thomas Kaspereit	*University of Luxembourg, Luxembourg*
Muhammad Nadeem	*University of Queensland, Australia*
Dinithi Ranasinghe	*University of Otago, New Zealand*
Sudipta Bose	*University of Newcastle, Australia*
Dr Adeyemi Adebayo	*University of South Africa, South Africa*
Radiah Othman	*Massey University, New Zealand*
David Hay	*University of Auckland*
Olayinka Moses	*Victoria University of Wellington, New Zealand*

ABOUT THE CONTRIBUTORS

Lourens Erasmus is a Professor in the Department of Financial Governance at the College of Accounting Sciences at the University of South Africa (UNISA). His fields of academic interest are in public sector financial governance and internal auditing. Lourens is a Commissioner of the Financial and Fiscal Commission of South Africa, the chairperson of the Education Committee of the Southern African Institute of Government Auditors (SAIGA) and Treasurer of the Research Ethics Committee Association of Southern Africa. Lourens is a rated researcher and Editor-in-Chief of the *Southern African Journal of Accountability and Auditing Research* (SAJAAR). He is an Associate Editor of the Scopus-listed, *South African Journal of Accounting Research* (SAJAR) and project leader of the registered Engaged Scholarship projects, Continuous Auditing in Public Sector Internal Auditing (CAPIA) and Research on Audit Committees South Africa.

Lindie Grebe (CA)SA is an academic and part of the executive management team of the Good Governance Academy of Professor Mervyn King, where she leads global research initiatives on corporate governance and sustainability. She also teaches governance at undergraduate and postgraduate levels and supervises higher degree candidates in the field of governance and sustainability. Her recent publications focus on the development of a corporate reputation reporting framework and a book chapter on digital transformation in corporate reputation, among others.

Muhammad Nurul Houqe is an Associate Professor of Accounting at the School of Accountancy, Massey University, New Zealand. His main areas of research interest include but are not limited to capital markets, accounting policy reforms, financial reporting, sustainability reporting and corporate governance.

Thomas Kaspereit is an Associate Professor of Financial Accounting at the University of Luxembourg, whose research interests lie at the intersection of corporate sustainability and capital markets. He had the privilege of serving as a visiting scholar at the University of Cagliari in December 2022 and again in June 2024. This chapter applies methods developed as part of the project 'On the Business and Regulatory Implications of Local Air, Soil, and Water Pollution: The Case of Europe and Québec'.

Su Li recently completed his PhD in Accounting at Victoria University of Wellington in 2023. He was also awarded his first PhD degree in Financial Management in 2008 from Southwestern University of Finance and Economics. He has extensive research interests, including valuation, climate risk, accounting conservatism, asset pricing, monetary policy, compensation and performance evaluation. He currently works in the general areas of capital markets research in accounting but with a particular focus on climate change. In addition to his previously published papers, one of his recent papers won the best paper award at a renowned accounting conference in the world and has been published in a leading academic journal.

Olayinka Moses teaches sustainable decision-making and control, accounting technologies and systems management and strategy at the Wellington School of Business and Government, Victoria University of Wellington, New Zealand. His research focuses on the intersection of accountability, management accounting and sustainability reporting, with his work published in several top-tier academic journals. Yinka also holds influential editorial positions, contributing to the dissemination of new knowledge and the advancement of the accounting profession. He is an Executive Member and Vice President of the African Accounting and Finance Association (AAFA) and holds a Professor Extraordinarius appointment at the University of South Africa, Pretoria. He is a Fellow of both Chartered Accountants Australia and New Zealand and CPA Australia. As Chair of the Environmental, Social and Governance (ESG) Committee for CPA Australia's New Zealand division, Yinka leads initiatives to equip members with sustainability skills critical to the evolving accounting profession.

Innocent Okwuosa is a Visiting Associate Professor of Accounting at Pan Atlantic University, Lagos. He holds a PhD in Accounting from Henley Business School, University of Reading, UK. Dr Okwuosa is currently the Chairman/CEO of the Nigerian Integrated Reporting Committee (NIRC), an organization supporting the Financial Reporting Council (FRC) of Nigeria with IFRS S1 and S2 implementation in Nigeria. He is a member of the African Integrated Reporting Council (AIRC) and has served as a board member of the Association of Accountancy Bodies in West Africa (ABWA), Pan African Federation of Accountants (PAFA), International Panel on Accounting Education (IPAE) of International Federation of Accountants (IFAC). His research interest is in the area of financial, sustainability and integrated reporting both in the private and public sector as well as the professional accountant and accountability. He is the Immediate Past President of the Institute of Chartered Accountants of Nigeria.

Nives Botica Redmayne, MInstD, PhD, MSc, BSc, AFAANZ, CAANZ, is a Professor at Massey University Business School, Palmerston North. She is also a Fellow of the Chartered Accountants of Australia and New Zealand (CAANZ) and the Past CAANZ President. Nives is the current President (NZ) of the Accounting and Finance Association of Australia and New Zealand (AFAANZ). She is a board member of the Comparative International Governmental Accounting Research (CIGAR) Association. She was a member of the New Zealand External Reporting Board – Accounting Standards Board, and she is a current member of the New Zealand Financial Market Authority Audit Oversight Committee. Her main area of research and expertise is assurance, in particular, the economics and production of assurance services. Nives' other area of research and expertise is in financial reporting and assurance, in particular, financial reporting in for-profit and not-for-profit/public sectors, assurance services and market regulation.

Fasilat Aramide Sanusi, School of Accountancy, Massey University, Private Bag 11222, Palmerston North, New Zealand, is a PhD candidate in Accounting at the School of Accountancy, Massey University, Palmerston North, New Zealand, investigating the quality of universities' sustainability reporting practices. Fasilat has several publications in accounting and business journals. Her research experience and interests focus on financial and sustainability reporting, environmental accounting, human resource management, climate reporting and assurance practices, particularly by universities. Fasilat completed her undergraduate studies with a Bachelor of Technology in Accounting Management at Ladoke Akintola University of Technology, Nigeria, and a Master's degree in International Accounting at the University Utara Malaysia. Her work has been recognized with the award of the Graduate Assistantship Merit Award for 2022 at University Teknologi PETRONAS, and she has presented research findings at several conferences and symposiums.

Joseph Tinarwo's research interests are around financial governance, particularly public sector auditing and sustainability reporting. Joseph holds a PhD in Public Management and Governance from the University of Johannesburg in South Africa. Over the years, Joseph has been consulting and supporting the Government of Zimbabwe, development partners and NGOs on development-related projects. Dr Tinarwo is a Postdoctoral Research Fellow at the University of South Africa. Previously, Joseph was a Postdoctoral Research Fellow at the Queen Mary University of London and held different full-time and consultancy positions in several non-governmental organizations including UNICEF Zimbabwe, Clinton Heath Access, International Medical Corps and OXFAM Great Britain, among others. Joseph collaborates with many international researchers and is currently a co-investigator of a project that focuses on the implementation of international public sector accounting standards in developing countries.

Tony van Zijl is an Emeritus Professor of Accounting and Financial Management at Victoria University of Wellington, and he is the past Director of the Centre for Accounting, Governance and Taxation Research. His research interests are in the impact of financial reporting on capital markets. He is a Certified Securities Analyst Professional and a Fellow Chartered Accountant. He is a life member of both Chartered Accountants Australia and New Zealand and of the Accounting and Finance Association of Australia and New Zealand. Tony is a former Chair of the Financial Reporting Standards Board, a foundation member of the Accounting Standards Review Board, a member of the XRB External Reporting Advisory Panel and the Valuation and Property Standards Board of the New Zealand Property Institute. He is a Consulting Director of Sapere Research Group Limited and a Director of Financial Analysis Consulting Group Limited.

Roger Willett is a Professor in the Wellington School of Government and Business, Victoria University of Wellington. Roger was awarded his PhD by the University of Aberdeen in Scotland in the United Kingdom. Roger's work focuses on the theory, application and practice of accounting measurement in the modelling of economic and social systems. Roger has published in international journals on topics ranging across mathematical theories and models of accounting measurement, applied econometric analysis of capital markets, auditing, statistical modelling of operational systems in management and cultural and religious aspects of international accounting. His sponsored research includes collaboration with engineers, statisticians, management academics and professionals and includes studies of the legal aid system and the management of medical funding in Queensland. Roger has also been involved in projects relating to the pressing problems of waste management. Roger is the founder and lifetime member of the International Society of Engineering Asset Management.

ACKNOWLEDGEMENT

Ahsan Habib dedicates this book to his wife Rehena and his children Fariha and Farjad.

EDITORIAL CHAPTER: CLIMATE RISKS REPORTING PRACTICES AND ASSURANCE

Ahsan Habib[a], Dimu Ehalaiye[a], Ainul Islam[b] and Sedzani Musundwa[c]

[a]*Massey University, New Zealand*
[b]*Victoria University of Wellington, New Zealand*
[c]*University of South Africa, South Africa*

ABSTRACT

The intensifying climate crisis has raised the importance of climate risk reporting and assurance as a key priority for academics, practitioners and other key stakeholders. Climate risk, which includes both physical and transition risks, has significant repercussions for businesses, economies and societies. Although regulatory initiatives are on the rise, climate risk reporting remains predominantly voluntary and inconsistent across different jurisdictions and sectors, posing challenges for stakeholders who seek comparable, reliable and decision-useful disclosures. Furthermore, the assurance of climate-related disclosures remains underdeveloped, characterized by inconsistent standards and limited research on its effectiveness. This issue explores the evolving domain of climate risk reporting and assurance, highlighting major challenges, emerging trends and regulatory developments. The collective research in this issue addresses critical gaps in current practices, offering insights into stakeholder responses, the quality of reporting and challenges related to assurance. By fostering enhanced transparency and comparability in climate risk disclosures and assurance practices, this issue strengthens existing practices and contributes to advancing global sustainability goals.

Keywords: Climate risk reporting; assurance practices; regulatory initiatives; global sustainability goals; stakeholders

INTRODUCTION

The exacerbating climate crisis and its profound implications for businesses, economies and societies have intensified the focus on climate risk reporting and assurance practices (CRRAP) (Moses & Hopper, 2022; Tauringana & Moses, 2023). Climate risk has been considered a long-term risk factor (Krueger et al., 2020), with consequential implications for the global economy and financial capital markets (Bolton & Kacperczyk, 2023; Hsu et al., 2023). Climate risk is broadly categorized into physical climate risk and transition climate risk. Physical climate risk refers to financial losses and disruptions caused by climate change-related events, such as extreme weather conditions and rising sea levels. In contrast, transition climate risk emerges from the economic and regulatory costs associated with transitioning to a lower-carbon economy, driven by evolving climate policies and regulatory frameworks.

As sustainability and environmental, social and governance (ESG) considerations continue to gain global momentum, the demand for transparent, accurate and credible disclosures on climate-related risks has become increasingly critical (Ehalaiye, Moses, Laswad, et al., 2025; Freedman & Jaggi, 2009). This is not merely an issue impacting corporate responsibility but a fundamental necessity for fostering stakeholder trust, enabling informed decision-making and promoting sustainable business practices in an era of heightened regulatory and societal accountability. Understanding the current landscape of climate risk reporting, including its key drivers and broader implications, is imperative for enhancing disclosure quality and ensuring that businesses effectively manage and appropriately communicate their climate-related financial risks (DiSalvio & Dorata, 2014).

However, a significant challenge in credible climate risk reporting is the absence of uniformity in sustainability disclosure standards. Despite notable advancements, such as establishing the International Sustainability Standards Board (ISSB) in 2021 and the release of Sustainability Disclosure Standards (IFRS S1 and IFRS S2) in 2023, climate risks and ESG-related reporting predominantly remain voluntary. This voluntary nature exacerbates inconsistencies, reduces comparability and ultimately diminishes the reliability of disclosures, leaving stakeholders to navigate a fragmented and often opaque reporting landscape. Empirical research suggests that mandatory climate-related risk disclosure enhances the quality and reliability of reporting compared to voluntary approaches (Bolton & Kacperczyk, 2021; Ehalaiye, Moses, Laswad, et al., 2025). Yet, in the absence of stringent regulatory requirements, organizations and accounting professionals face mounting pressure to align their reporting practices with evolving societal and regulatory expectations. The challenge of navigating these complexities is profound, requiring firms to balance transparency, compliance and strategic risk management in an increasingly scrutinized business environment.

Transparent climate risk reporting is essential, as it plays a critical role in maintaining stakeholder confidence and reinforcing corporate accountability. By providing clear and verifiable disclosures, organizations enable stakeholders to assess their resilience to climate risks and their alignment with global sustainability objectives. However, in the absence of credible assurance, concern about greenwashing and misleading corporate signalling persist, ultimately undermining trust in sustainability-related disclosures. Empirical evidence suggests that audited ESG reports are perceived as more reliable, reinforcing the value of independent assurance in enhancing disclosure credibility (IFAC, 2022; Zhou, 2022). Assurance practices enhance and not only strengthen stakeholder confidence but also shield companies from reputational risks associated with misleading sustainability claims. Despite these benefits, the assurance landscape remains fraught with challenges, including inconsistent assurance standards and a lack of comprehensive research into how assurance practices influence both reporting quality and investor perceptions. To address these knowledge gaps, further exploration of the role of assurance in reinforcing the credibility of ESG disclosures is essential. A more standardized and rigorous assurance framework would help mitigate inconsistencies, enhance comparability and ensure that sustainability disclosures meaningfully contribute to informed decision-making and long-term corporate accountability.

DEEPENING CLIMATE RISKS REPORTING PRACTICES AND ASSURANCE KNOWLEDGE

This volume offers novel insights into the evolving landscape of CRRAP. Drawing on contributions from scholars and industry experts worldwide who employ diverse methodologies, it enhances our understanding of these critical areas. In this emerging research field, the extant literature has largely focused on the nature of climate change risks (Braasch & Velte, 2023; Daddi et al., 2018; de Grosbois & Fennell, 2022; Estrada & Botzen, 2021), the need to report the financial impact of these risks (Borghei et al., 2024; Ehalaiye, Moses, Laswad, et al., 2025; Tsang et al., 2023; Zhou, 2022) and the prospects for assuring information related to these risks (Boiral et al., 2019, 2020; Bouten & Hoozée, 2025; Datt et al., 2018, 2020; Dutta & Dutta, 2021). However, there remains a significant gap in understanding how firms and organizations report climate-related risks, particularly given the non-uniformity of standards and the mostly non-mandatory nature of reporting these risks. Similarly, the assurance of climate-related information is neither standardized nor mandatory in most jurisdictions. Hence, it is important to seek evidence on current practices on climate risks reporting and assurance, to foster a deeper understanding of the benefits, challenges and future directions of these practices. Collectively, the research contained in this issue addresses these research gaps and contributes to the discourse on climate risks reporting and assurance in several ways.

Firstly, the volume examines various practices of climate risks reporting in different jurisdictions and sectors, across developed and developing markets and corporate to the public sector, providing a broad range of perspectives on how various firms and organizations are approaching climate risks reporting. Secondly, the volume documents stakeholder actions and responses to new standards/regulations such as IFRS S1 and S2, in concert with existing reporting frameworks such as the Global Reporting Initiative (GRI) and the Carbon Disclosure Project (CDP). Thirdly, it highlights, challenges in assurance processes for climate-related information and reflects on prominent concerns to consider in facilitating credible practice for the assurance of climate-related information to be beneficial to stakeholders. Finally, by offering insights into current practices, this volume deepens our understanding and supports the progress of the Sustainable Development Goals (SDGs), particularly SDG 13, which emphasizes the need for collective efforts to take urgent action against climate change and its effects (Moses & Tauringana, 2022).

CONTRIBUTIONS TO THE SPECIAL ISSUE

This volume's research documents important findings about climate risks reporting practices and assurance across multiple jurisdictions. Seven chapters were accepted for this issue, with two quantitative papers using data from the United States, two papers from New Zealand, two from South Africa (with one's scope covering Sub-Saharan African) and one from Nigeria. Fig. 1 maps out the papers by region and methodology employed.

Key summaries from each of the contributions in the volume are discussed next.

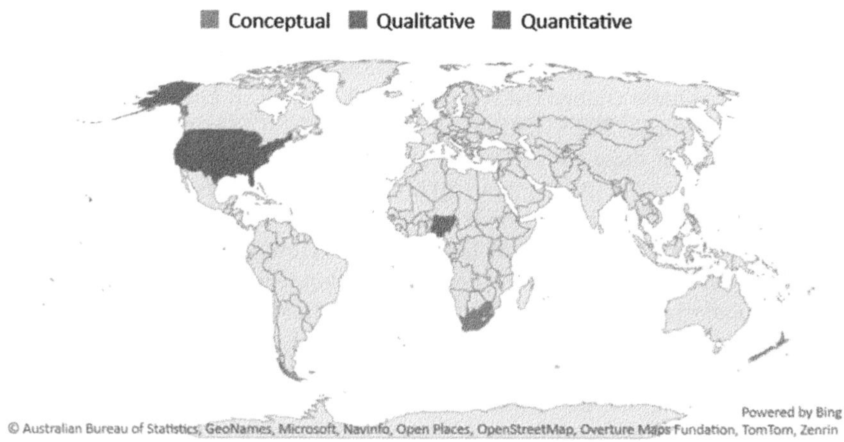

Fig. 1. Submission Analytics.

Sanusi et al. (2025) open the volume. This work provides key insights into CRRAP, focusing on its significant aspects, emerging issues, and evolving trends. It explores how CRRAP drives investments in green assets and infrastructure, highlighting its potential to mitigate the impacts of climate change and support a sustainable global economy. The study adopts a conceptual approach, drawing on academic research, case studies and global reporting standards to comprehensively understand CRRAP. It examines historical developments, regulatory frameworks and theoretical perspectives to present a detailed analysis of these practices and their implications. This chapter contributes to the literature by offering a comprehensive exploration of CRRAP, situating it within historical, regulatory and theoretical contexts. Additionally, it identifies gaps in current practices and suggests pathways to improve transparency, comparability and accountability in climate risk reporting and assurance.

Grebe (2025) explores the need for a contextualized, stakeholder-oriented approach to environmental reporting. Its primary aim is to identify the specific stakeholder groups the organizations report to and determine the extent to which organizational and stakeholder perspectives converge. The chapter seeks to address gaps in inclusivity by proposing a framework for generating environmental reports that meet the varied expectations of distinct stakeholder groups. The study employs a conceptual framework grounded in stakeholder theory, supported by an analysis of existing sustainability standards and reporting frameworks, such as IFRS S1 and S2, the GRI and the CDP. It also references industry and academic insights to outline practical implications for improving stakeholder-inclusive environmental reporting. This chapter contributes to the literature by proposing a stakeholder-focused approach that bridges the gap between standardized reporting frameworks and the specific needs of stakeholders. Furthermore, it provides a research agenda for advancing methods to identify and address stakeholder-specific concerns in environmental reporting.

Okwuosa (2025) investigates the quality of climate-related performance disclosures by early adopters of IFRS S2 in Nigeria and examines the motivations behind their decision to adopt the standard early ahead of their peers. It aims to assess compliance with IFRS S2 metrics and targets and explores how these early adopters signal their commitment to climate-related sustainability practices. A qualitative research design was employed, involving content analysis of sustainability reports from four early adopters of IFRS S2 and seven semi-structured interviews with sustainability officers, accountants and consultants. The study provides the first empirical evidence on the quality of climate-related disclosures by IFRS S2 early adopters in Africa. It highlights the need for capacity building and regulatory support to improve disclosure practices and foster successful adoption. The research also contributes to the literature on the motivations behind early adoption, demonstrating how companies use IFRS S2 as a strategic tool to signal leadership and attract investment while exposing gaps in actual performance.

Ehalaiye, Moses, and Botica Redmayne (2025) examine the development and effectiveness of New Zealand's climate-related assurance standards for Climate Reporting Entities (CREs). The primary objective is to evaluate the progress made in establishing assurance mechanisms under the country's climate-related disclosure regime and to provide reflective insights into how these regulatory expectations can be successfully realized within New Zealand's professional and regulatory landscape. The study adopts a conceptual approach, analysing various regulatory documents. It also reflects on recent developments, including consultation processes and amendments proposed by the External Reporting Board (XRB). The chapter synthesizes these findings to assess the readiness of CREs and the assurance market. This chapter contributes to the discourse on sustainability assurance by critically evaluating New Zealand's climate-related disclosure regime. It underscores the importance of balancing regulatory timelines with the need for consistent and high-quality assurance practices. The findings offer valuable insights for policymakers, preparers and assurance providers seeking to enhance the credibility and reliability of climate-related disclosures.

Erasmus et al. (2025) systematically review CRRAP within sub-Saharan Africa's public sector. It aims to assess challenges, including materiality and cost–benefit constraints, while proposing a conceptual framework to enhance these practices. The broader goal is to advance responsible governance and align public sector efforts with global sustainable development targets. The chapter employs a systematic literature review and highlights significant barriers to climate risk reporting and assurance in the sub-Saharan African public sector. This chapter offers a valuable contribution by presenting a conceptual framework tailored to sub-Saharan Africa's unique challenges and opportunities in climate risk reporting and assurance. It underscores the need for robust legal frameworks, multi-stakeholder partnerships, capacity building and financial investment to enhance reporting practices.

Kaspereit (2025) introduces a comprehensive, survivorship bias-free dataset of firms committed to or having set Science Based Targets (SBTs). SBTi is a collaborative effort that helps firms set emission reduction targets aligned with the Paris Agreement. Once firms commit to setting targets, they immediately appear on the SBTi dashboard. While the SBTi dashboard provides no updates when a firm submits its targets, it acknowledges the final setting of targets. Since February 2023, firms failing to submit or get targets approved within 24 months are flagged as 'commitment removed' rather than being silently removed from the dashboard, as was the case before. The author considers this to be an interesting research setting: regime shift from a silent removal process to a transparent 'name-and-shame' approach. Since the SBTi does not provide historical archives of its dashboard, this poses a major challenge for research aimed at understanding why firms fail to meet their commitments. The main contribution of this chapter is the construction and description of a dataset based on monthly snapshots from the Internet Archive of the SBTi dashboard, dating back to its inception in September 2015 and extending up to September 2024. The author expects that this dynamic and survivorship bias-free view on the target-setting process will enable researchers to address a wide range of relevant questions.

Li et al. (2025) examine whether climate risk influences accounting-based equity valuation by observing how investors adjust their relative valuation weights on different accounting variables when facing climate risk. The authors use a log-linear valuation model with the valuation weights measured by the elasticities of market prices with respect to the book value of equity and earnings. The authors use the annual global anomaly temperature as a proxy for climate risk. Using a large sample of US firms, the authors find the association of climate risk with the elasticity of book value is positive but the association with the elasticity of earnings is negative. The authors also find that the association varies across industries and appears to be long-run rather than short-run. This chapter contributes to the climate finance literature by documenting the important role of accounting information in valuing climate risk. This chapter further contributes to the literature on the value-relevance of accounting information by identifying climate risk as one of the potential underlying economic drivers.

CONCLUSION

As climate risks continue to reshape global businesses, economies and societies, the stakeholders are asking for robust, transparent and credible climate risk reporting that is appropriately assured. By reporting on practices across multiple jurisdictions and sectors, this issue highlights the fragmented nature of current disclosure practices, the ongoing challenges of voluntary and inconsistent reporting standards and the limited but growing role of assurance in enhancing the credibility of climate-related information. While regulatory initiatives such as IFRS S1 and S2 represent steps towards greater standardization, significant gaps remain in ensuring comparability and reliability across jurisdictions.

The research presented in this volume underscores the critical role of climate risk disclosures in guiding sustainable business practices and supporting global sustainability efforts. It also identifies the pressing need for further empirical research on the assurance of climate-related disclosures, particularly in developing markets where regulatory oversight is still evolving. By addressing these challenges, the studies contribute to the broader discourse on accountability and transparency in climate risk reporting, paving the way for future advancements in standard-setting and assurance practices.

REFERENCES

Boiral, O., Heras-Saizarbitoria, I., & Brotherton, M. (2019). Assessing and improving the quality of sustainability reports: The auditors' perspective. *Journal of Business Ethics*, *155*, 703–721.

Boiral, O., Heras-Saizarbitoria, I., & Brotherton, M. (2020). Professionalizing the assurance of sustainability reports: The auditors' perspective. *Accounting, Auditing & Accountability Journal*, *33*(2), 309–334.

Bolton, P., & Kacperczyk, M. (2021). Do investors care about carbon risk? *Journal of Financial Economics*, *142*(2), 517–549.

Bolton, P., & Kacperczyk, M. (2023). Global pricing of carbon-transition risk. *The Journal of Finance*, *78*(6), 3677–3754.

Borghei, Z., Linnenluecke, M., & Bui, B. (2024). The disclosure of climate-related risks and opportunities in financial statements: The UK's FTSE 100. *Meditari Accountancy Research*, *32*(3), 1031–1063.

Bouten, L., & Hoozée, S. (2025). How sustainability assurance work gets done: Assurors' sensemaking, socialization and interactions with clients. *Accounting, Auditing & Accountability Journal*, *38*(1), 143–173.

Braasch, A., & Velte, P. (2023). Climate reporting quality following the recommendations of the task force on climate-related financial disclosures: A focus on the German capital market. *Sustainable Development*, *31*(2), 926–940.

Bua, G., Kapp, D., Ramella, F., & Rognone, L. (2024). Transition versus physical climate risk pricing in European financial markets: A text-based approach. *The European Journal of Finance*, *17*, 2076–2110.

Daddi, T., Todaro, N. M., De Giacomo, M. R., & Frey, M. (2018). A systematic review of the use of organization and management theories in climate change studies. *Business Strategy and the Environment*, *27*(4), 456–474.

Datt, R., Luo, L., & Tang, Q. (2020). Corporate choice of providers of voluntary carbon assurance. *International Journal of Auditing*, *24*(1), 145–162.

Datt, R., Luo, L., Tang, Q., & Mallik, G. (2018). An international study of determinants of voluntary carbon assurance. *Journal of International Accounting Research*, *17*(3), 1–20.

de Grosbois, D., & Fennell, D. A. (2022). Determinants of climate change disclosure practices of global hotel companies: Application of institutional and stakeholder theories. *Tourism Management*, *88*, 104404.

DiSalvio, J., & Dorata, N. T. (2014). *SEC guidance on climate change risk disclosures: An assessment of firm and market responses. Accounting for the environment: More talk and little progress* (pp. 115–130). Emerald Publishing Limited.

Dutta, P., & Dutta, A. (2021). Impact of external assurance on corporate climate change disclosures: New evidence from Finland. *Journal of Applied Accounting Research*, *22*(2), 252–285.

Ehalaiye, D., Moses, O., & Botica Redmayne, N. (2025). The state of play of climate risks assurance in New Zealand. *Advances in Environmental Accounting and Management*, *13*.

Ehalaiye, D., Moses, O., Laswad, F., & Botica Redmayne, N. (2025). Local government enterprises climate action: An exploration of New Zealand container seaports' climate-related disclosure practices. *Financial Accountability and Management*, *41*(1), 60–88.

Estrada, F., & Botzen, W. W. (2021). Economic impacts and risks of climate change under failure and success of the Paris Agreement. *Annals of the New York Academy of Sciences*, *1504*(1), 95–115.

Freedman, M., & Jaggi, B. (2009). *Global warming and corporate disclosures: A comparative analysis of companies from the European Union, Japan and Canada. Sustainability, environmental performance and disclosures* (pp. 129–160). Emerald Publishing Limited.

Grebe, L. (2025). Towards stakeholder inclusive environmental reporting practice. *Advances in Environmental Accounting and Management*, *13*.

Hsu, P., Li, K., & Tsou, C. (2023). The pollution premium. *The Journal of Finance*, *78*(3), 1343–1392.

IFAC. (2022). *The state of play in reporting and assurance of sustainability information: Update 2019–2020 data & analysis*. https://www.ifac.org/knowledge-gateway/contributing-global-economy/publications/state-play-reporting-and-assurance-sustainability-information-update-2019-2020-data-analysis. Accessed on July 25, 2023.

Kaspereit, T. (2025). A dynamic view on science based targets—Research opportunities. *Advances in Environmental Accounting and Management*, *13*.

Krueger, P., Sautner, Z., & Starks, L. T. (2020). The importance of climate risks for institutional investors. *Review of Financial Studies*, *33*(3), 1067–1111.

Li, S., van Zijl, T., & Willett, R. (2025). Valuation, accounting, and climate risk. *Advances in Environmental Accounting and Management*, *13*.

Moses, O., & Hopper, T. (2022). Accounting articles on developing countries in ranked English language journals: A meta-review. *Accounting, Auditing & Accountability Journal*, *35*(4), 1035–1060.

Moses, O., & Tauringana, V. (2022). Environmental sustainability and the progress towards agenda 2030. In *Environmental Sustainability and Agenda 2030: Efforts, Progress and Prospects* (pp. 1–9). Emerald Publishing Limited.

Okwuosa, I. (2025). Climate-related risk disclosure practices: Evidence from IFRS S2 early adopters in Nigeria. *Advances in Environmental Accounting and Management*, *13*.

Sanusi, F. A., Hoque, N., & Ehalaiye, D. (2025). Navigating climate risks: Reporting practices and assurance for a sustainable future. *Advances in Environmental Accounting and Management*, *13*.

Tauringana, V., & Moses, O. (2023). *Greenhouse gas reporting and management in top emitting countries and companies. Greenhouse gas emissions reporting and management in global top emitting countries and companies* (pp. 1–9). Emerald Publishing Limited.

Tinarwo, J., & Erasmus, L. J. (2025). A critical review of public sector climate-risk reporting and assurance practices—A pathway towards responsible governance in sub-Saharan Africa. *Advances in Environmental Accounting and Management*, *13*.

Tsang, A., Frost, T., & Cao, H. (2023). Environmental, social, and governance (ESG) disclosure: A literature review. *The British Accounting Review*, *55*(1), 101149.

Zhou, S. (2022). Reporting and assurance of climate-related and other sustainability information: A review of research and practice. *Australian Accounting Review*, *32*(3), 315–333.

NAVIGATING CLIMATE RISKS: REPORTING PRACTICES AND ASSURANCE FOR A SUSTAINABLE FUTURE

Fasilat Aramide Sanusi, Muhammad Nurul Houqe and Dimu Ehalaiye

Massey University, New Zealand

ABSTRACT

There has been increasing global attention on climate-related risk management in relation to environmental, social and governance (ESG) initiatives. This includes the recently established International Sustainability Standards Board (ISSB) to deliver a comprehensive framework on climate-related disclosures. With this development, interest in climate-risk reporting and assurance is growing to enhance users' confidence in sustainability and non-financial reporting. Therefore, this book chapter provides key insights into climate-risk reporting practices and assurance (CRRPA). It covers subject matters related to climate-related information. This chapter identifies significant aspects of CRRPA and highlights key trends and evolving issues. Hence, CRRPA can increase organizations' investment in green assets and infrastructure as an opportunity to mitigate the adverse impacts of climate change for a sustainable global economy.

Keywords: Climate; climate change; assurance; reporting practices; risks

1. INTRODUCTION

In the present climate change–constrained world, organizations are implementing active climate-risk management and assurance procedures to mitigate potential risks, embrace climate change opportunities and improve resilience to gain the trust and confidence of stakeholders (Sebos et al., 2023). Climate-risk reporting

Climate Risks Reporting Practices and Assurance
Advances in Environmental Accounting & Management, Volume 13, 1–23

Published under exclusive licence by Emerald Publishing Limited
ISSN: 1479-3598/doi:10.1108/S1479-359820250000013003

practices and assurance (hereafter CRRPA) is the identification, assessment, management and reporting of climate change risks and their impacts on organizations and the global community. Assurance practices are the process of validating or giving assurance to concerned stakeholders that businesses or organizations disclose actions related to climate risks in an accurate, transparent and reliable manner. Typically, it is a statement of proof that information disclosed as climate risk is of good quality and authentic after the climate-related information, data, processes and controls have undergone independent assessment and verification (Zhou, 2022). This will enhance the trust and credibility of the CRRPA (Braasch & Velte, 2023).

However, CRRPA evolved in response to the increased recognition of the impacts that climate change can have on economies, businesses, the environment and society at large. This development can be traced to several key responses, like increased awareness of climate change impacts, industry initiatives and standards, a shift in the regulatory landscape, stakeholder vs investor pressure on the need for environmental, social and governance (ESG) investment and increased demand for transparency and accountability.

Moreover, climate-risk reporting practices are crucial for stakeholders like governments, communities, investors and organizations in decision-making on various issues (Acharyya et al., 2019; Borghei et al., 2024; Garg et al., 2023). These practices are briefly explained as follows:

Government: Climate reporting agencies and policymakers use climate-risk reports or information to set targets and monitor progress towards climate goals. These reports inform regulations and policies to reduce carbon emissions and promote sustainability practices.

Communities: Climate-risk reporting practice and assurance can guide local communities and organizations in understanding the potential impacts of climate change on their livelihoods, environment and overall well-being. This also helps in increasing their efforts to adapt to unavoidable climate change impacts.

Investors: CRRPA enable better investment decisions by providing significant insight into climate change risks and opportunities. Hence, investors can assess the sustainability and long-term impacts of climate change on their investments. In recent times, climate-risk reporting is a key factor that prompt investors to focus on green investment (Borghei et al., 2024).

Organizations: CRRPA help businesses develop strategies to mitigate climate change risks and capitalize on opportunities that promote business continuity and resilience. Therefore, CRRPA are crucial for informed decision-making across diverse corporate sectors. The quality of the information reported directly influences the effectiveness of strategies to address climate change and its impacts.

Over the years, studies have shown and provided overwhelming evidence about the threat of climate change to the ecological system and social and economic lives. The negative effects of climate change are increasingly evident in the growing global environmental, social and economic crises. For example, the recent rise in biodiversity loss is linked to climate change, which is causing shifts in species of living organisms, some of which are on the brink of extinction-posing a great danger to the global ecosystems. The rise in sea levels, driven by the rapid melting of the Antarctic and Greenland ice sheets, and the swift increase in global temperature compared to the 19th century are particularly concerning. This leads to widespread droughts and heatwaves globally. From an ecological point of view, the rise in temperature is also threatening global food security (Estrada & Botzen, 2021; Fernandez & Trasande, 2024).

Other examples of climate change impacts include floods, wildfires, water scarcity and the displacement of communities leading to the destruction of livelihoods. These events disproportionately affect vulnerable populations, with significant social and economic repercussions. Economic costs associated with climate change also include damage to infrastructure, food shortages/increases in food prices and a decline in the global standard of living. These examples indicate the urgent need for comprehensive action to mitigate climate change and protect our ecological, social and economic well-being (De Grosbois & Fennell, 2022).

This has prompted calls for increased transparency and accountability in how businesses are addressing climate change-related risks (Fernandez & Trasande, 2024). This also includes a series of changes in the climate-related regulatory landscape, in which countries have mandated both environmentally sensitive and non-environmentally sensitive industries to disclose carbon emissions and climate-related risks, including strategies for mitigating these risks (Kryk & Kożuch, 2024; Thai et al., 2022). However, the rate of compliance and penalty could differ based on the gravity of the damage caused to the ecological system. An example is the Task Force on Climate-Related Financial Disclosures (hereafter TCFD), established by the Financial Stability Board (FSB), which developed voluntary frameworks for businesses to publish climate-related financial reports (Ehalaiye et al., 2025; Garg, 2023). As a result of this development, some countries have implemented mandatory sustainability reporting of climate impacts including actions taken to mitigate them (Karamaneas et al., 2023; Katirtzidou et al., 2023; Ruane et al., 2024).

In addition to this, there is an era of increasing transparency and accountability, where stakeholders are pressuring businesses to account for the risks, they face from climate change and the efforts they make to address them in an open and honest manner. This will demonstrate a commitment to sustainability and responsible business practices. In practice, CRRPA promotes green investment both in assets and infrastructure, as it allows investors to assess and analyze their exposure to climate-related risks and opportunities and integrate findings into their investment decisions.[1] As a result, investors have developed an interest in ESG-related factors in their climate-related investments (Comoli et al., 2023; Comyns, 2018).

The industry-led efforts and standards created to direct organizations in reporting on climate-related risks and opportunities are another intriguing and new development in the CRRPA. One such platform is the Carbon Disclosure

Project (CDP), which allows companies to reveal their greenhouse gas emissions and risks associated with climate change (Bedi & Singh, 2024). Among these is the Global Reporting Initiative (GRI), which offers standards for reporting sustainability and the effects of climate change (Giannarakis et al., 2023). Perhaps, due to the urgent need to address climate change and its consequences on people's socio-economic conditions, these practices are vital in supporting businesses with their climate-risk reporting and assurance procedures. These practices represent a paradigm shift in sustainability and resilience in business processes (Hazemba, 2024; World Health Organization, 2022).

2. AN OVERVIEW OF THE HISTORY OF CRRPA

The history and evolution of CRRPA may be linked to the urgency of climate research in the late 19th and early 20th centuries, which significantly advanced scientific understanding of climate change. This improves the early identification of climate change as a serious worldwide problem (Malik & Ford, 2024). Subsequently, this led to the development of frameworks, standards and recommendations for regulations that addressed the risks associated with climate change. The CRRPA programme, which encourages assessments of climate effects and opportunities as well as measures to lessen its threat, is one of the current developments in the field. Nonetheless, awareness of the impact of greenhouse gases on both humans and the environment started to emerge in the late 1800s. By the 20th century, researchers had laid important groundwork for understanding the origins and effects of climate change (Cointe & Guillemot, 2023).

The 1992 Rio Earth Summit, also known as the United Nations Conference on Environment and Development (UNCED), is another important turning point in the history of the CRRPA. It is recognized as a turning point in the field of global environmental governance. The United Nations Framework Convention on Climate Change (UNFCCC), which aims to lower greenhouse gas emissions in the atmosphere and avoid harmful human interference with the ecosystem, was adopted during this summit (Wright et al., 2023).

The Kyoto Protocol of 1997, an international environmental management agreement governed by the UNFCCC, came next. It set legally binding emission reduction objectives for industrialized (developed) nations. Frameworks for projects including the Clean Development Mechanism (CDM) and carbon trading were also established under the treaty. The Kyoto Protocol emphasized that participating nations must disclose greenhouse gas emissions and environmental efforts in a transparent manner (Susilowati et al., 2024; Wright et al., 2023).

Nevertheless, in the late 20th century, corporate environmental reporting gained famous recognition for stressing the importance of environmental impacts and performance disclosure by corporate organizations. The concept of corporate environmental reporting begins as a voluntary initiative to an advanced structured standard like the GRI, which provides frameworks for reporting on climate-related issues, sustainability to be specific (Giannarakis et al., 2023; Ivanova, 2012). Meanwhile, the concept of the 'Triple Bottom Line' (TBL) was introduced by John Elkington in 1994 to challenge organizations to focus on social and environmental performance rather than solely on profit maximization. The following are some of the early milestones for environmental reporting:

John Elkington's Book (1997): Elkington's book on TBL was published in 1997, and it was named The TBL of 21st Century Business. It emphasizes the need for organizations to account for the social, environmental and economic impacts of their operations within their communities. It sets the tone for promoting the TBL framework.

The Global Reporting Initiative (GRI) (1997): The GRI was established in 1997 to create a standardized framework for sustainability reporting. It allows businesses to measure and communicate their environmental, economic and social performance to the stakeholders.

United Nations and International Council for Local Environmental Initiatives (ICLEI) (2007): Another significant milestone in TBL development came in 2007 with the United Nations and the ICLEI. This collaboration integrated TBL into public sector accounting and established standards for metropolitan and public accounting on sustainable TBL practices. These standards have laid the foundations for shaping sustainability reporting practices.

Moreover, the Intergovernmental Panel on Climate Change (IPCC) assessment reports were established in 1990. Their purpose is to publish climate change assessment reports and summaries of the latest scientific research findings on climate change. The report serves as a foundation for information dissemination for businesses, policymakers and the public about the science of climate change and its potential impacts (Scott et al., 2023).

In addition, the TCFD was established in 2015 by the FSB to develop voluntary frameworks for disclosing climate-related financial information. The TCFD recommendations provide guidelines for businesses to disclose information about their climate-related risks, opportunities, governance, strategy and metrics. This is closely aligned with CRRPA (Braasch & Velte, 2023; Garg, 2023).

Nonetheless, in the present 21st century, the concept of regulatory development arises, where governments around the world have implemented various regulatory frameworks to enforce climate-risk reporting. For example, the European Union (EU) introduced the Non-Financial Reporting Directive (NFRD), requiring environmentally sensitive companies to disclose non-financial information and environmental and social issues in their annual reports (Turzo et al., 2022). Countries like New Zealand, Australia and Canada have also introduced mandatory reporting requirements for climate-related risks (Ehalaiye et al., 2025). Also, the growing amount of investors focusing on ESG factors in investment decisions in the 21st century marked a historical development in CRRPA. In recent times, investors have incorporated ESG factors into their investment decisions. This has led to a greater demand for transparency in climate-risk disclosures from businesses (Comoli et al., 2023).

Another historical development in CRRPA in the 21st century is the establishment of assurance services, which promotes a wide recognition of CRRPA. Assurance services verify the accuracy and reliability of climate-related information. This involves the responsibility of audit firms and specialized sustainability consultants tailored to climate-risk reporting (Pizzi et al., 2024).

Thus, the evolution of reporting standards and frameworks is an ongoing initiative for climate-risk reporting as it evolves in response to changing stakeholder expectations, regulatory requirements and expectations for best practices. In recent times, agencies like the GRI, CRRPA, CDP and Sustainability Accounting Standards Board (SASB) have played key roles in developing and promoting reporting standards for climate-related issues. Therefore, the history of CRRPA reflects the growing recognition of climate change as a material business matter that has critical roles of risk management, transparency and accountability in addressing climate-related risks and opportunities.

3. THE PARIS AGREEMENT AND CRRPA

The Paris Agreement is a recognizable international treaty on climate change established in December 2015 at the 21st Conference of the Parties (COP21) to the UNFCCC. It is a landmark achievement in the global effort to address the urgent problems of climate change by encouraging countries to take desirous actions to limit global warming and reduce its impacts (Andersen, 2024; Estrada & Botzen, 2021).

However, the scientific agreement that global warming exceeding 2 degrees Celsius (°C) above pre-industrial levels could have severe and irreversible consequences for people and the planet is a major concern for the global goals of the Paris Agreement. Meanwhile, one of the significant aims of the Paris Agreement is to limit global temperature thresholds to 1.5°C. Based on this reason, each member country is required to submit a nationally determined contribution (NDC), which highlights its climate action plan and commitments to reducing greenhouse gas emissions and should be subjected to periodic review (Estrada & Botzen, 2021). Hence, the agreement stipulates the need for transparency and accountability to ensure that the participating countries fulfil their commitments by regularly reporting emissions mitigation progress in line with NDC guidelines (Chai et al., 2017).

The agreement also establishes a mechanism for five-yearly assessments called global stock take to review progress on climate actions on emissions reductions, the financial support provided and received in the cause of climate change treatment mitigation, and adaptation efforts. Part of these efforts is climate finance, where developed countries mobilize both public and private financiers to provide annual climate assistance funds to developing nations to finance climate mitigation and adaptation efforts. Adaptation efforts focus on adapting to climate impacts by vulnerable communities, including loss and damage that cannot be prevented or adapted to. The agreement also recognizes the benefit of technology in capacity building to support developing countries in their climate mitigation and adaptation efforts (Chai et al., 2017; Wright et al., 2023). Although there has been debate over which developed or developing countries are to blame for climate change and which country should be more responsible for kerbing emissions?

Developing countries accused developed countries of emitting more greenhouse gases, saying developed countries should carry the burden due to their enormous industrial growth. The United States was found to be the number one emitting country, followed by the EU (Friedrich et al., 2023). Since the Paris Agreement, climate experts have concluded that countries' pledges are not ambitious enough and will not be enacted quickly enough to limit global temperature rise to 1.5°C. Therefore, the Paris Agreement represents a historic global treaty that sets the framework for international cooperation to address climate problems. Meanwhile, its success depends on the ambitious and coordinated efforts of participants and other stakeholders to reduce greenhouse gas emissions and build resilience to climate impacts (Chai et al., 2017). As of 2023, 194 countries, including the EU, have agreed to and ratified the Paris Agreement, representing over 98% of the consensus to kerb global greenhouse gas (GHG) emissions. This includes China and the United States which are the major global carbon emitters. However, some countries are neither committed nor validate this agreement and thereby backtracked on their pledges. An example is the United States, under the Trump administration, Trump formally withdrew from the Paris Agreement in 2020, although it was later ratified under the Biden administration. Countries, like Türkiye and Russia were criticized for setting unambitious targets on carbon emissions. Also, it was reported that many countries are not doing enough to meet the global 2030 emission reduction targets (Borghei et al., 2024; Braasch & Velte, 2023).

4. STATE-OF-THE-ART BETWEEN THE PARIS AGREEMENT AND THE CRRPA

The Paris Agreement and the concept of the CRRPA are intricately linked, indicating increasing recognition of the need for transparency and accountability and effort in addressing climate change. The interconnection between the Paris Agreement and the CRRPA is through the objectives of promoting transparency and accountability, risk management, investors' and stakeholders' expectations, financial stability and resilience in kerbing climate change including policy alignment and support (De Grosbois & Fennell, 2022). Considering similarities in the aspects of *transparency and accountability*, both the Paris Agreement and the CRRPA recognized efforts to mitigate climate change with truth and honest commitment. In terms of financial support received and provided in the cause of mitigating climate change, emissions reporting, mitigation efforts and adaptation efforts, the CRRPA has extended its commitment to transparency and accountability to corporations and financial institutions, requiring them to report and publish their exposure to climate change and opportunities and how they are managing the risks involved (Estrada & Botzen, 2021; Zhou, 2022).

Another area of similarity between the Paris Agreement and the CRRPA is *risk management and assessment*; hence, both emphasize the importance of assessing and managing climate-related risks to promote adaptation and mitigation efforts. Both the Paris Agreement and the CRRPA require businesses to identify, assess and disclose exposure to transitional and physical climate-related risks and liabilities associated with climate change.

Similarity related to investor and stakeholder expectations: While the Paris Agreement enlightens the global community on the influence of investors and stakeholders in addressing climate change, stakeholders are increasingly demanding transparency and disclosure regarding climate-related risks and opportunities in the CRRPA. Both provide a framework for meeting these expectations by offering guidelines and the best methods to assess and disclose climate-related risks.

Similarity related to financial stability and resilience: The Paris Agreement's goals are to enhance the resilience of participating countries to climate change impacts and transition to green energy economies. While CRRPA helps businesses identify and address risks to their financial stability and resilience. This can foster the achievement of the Paris Agreement goals. In addition, international organizations like the IPCC and the Network for Greening the Financial System (NGFS) have concluded that climate change poses significant risks to the resilience and financial stability of businesses (Scott et al., 2023).

Policy alignment and support: Both the Paris Agreement and the CRRPA provide standard frameworks and measures for assessing and reporting climate-related risks, which enhance the implementation of climate change policies at national and international levels. They also provide an opportunity to review climate policies and strategies to meet long-term objectives and adjustments in line with the change in climate conditions. Overall, the alignment between the Paris Agreement and the CRRPA will contribute to global efforts to address climate change and achieve sustainable development.

5. WHAT IS CLIMATE RISK?

Climate risk refers to the potential negative impacts that climate change and extreme weather events can have on society, the economy and the environment. These risks can manifest as physical risks such as damage to infrastructure from storms or rising sea levels; transition risks such as regulatory changes or shifts in market preferences impacting businesses and liability risks such as legal action against companies for non-compliance with climate regulations (Nobanee & Nghiem, 2024; Thai et al., 2022). Climate risk affects different sectors and regions differently, depending on geographical location, socio-economic conditions and adaptive capacity. Addressing climate risk often involves assessing vulnerabilities, implementing mitigation and adaptation strategies and incorporating climate considerations into decision-making processes across different levels of society, from individual households to national governments and international organizations (Zhou, 2022).

Climate risk results from potential problems caused to societies or ecosystems by the impacts of climate change. Understanding climate risk involves the assessment or analysis of the consequences, likelihoods and responses to the impacts of climate change. The 20th and 21st industrial evolutions come with societal constraints, such as greenhouse gas emissions released into the atmosphere in metric tons of carbon dioxide (CO_2) annually by different industrial sectors (see Figs. 1 and 2). This shapes our ecological adaptation and environmental conditions, which in turn creates adverse consequences for humans and entire ecological systems. This includes impacts on lives and means of livelihoods, health and well-being, social and cultural heritage, economics and investments, infrastructure, ecosystems and species (Acharyya et al., 2019). Climate risk can be defined as a hazard related to physical events that cause damage and loss to both human and material resources (Estrada & Botzen, 2021; Scartozzi, 2024).

Electricity and heat production are the major contributors to global emissions (See Fig. 2). However, these emission contributions can vary based on the country. According to Climate Watch (2024), in the United States, for example, transport is a major contributor compared to the global average. While in some countries, most emissions come from agriculture, oil & gas companies, manufacturing and construction companies (Climate Watch, 2024).

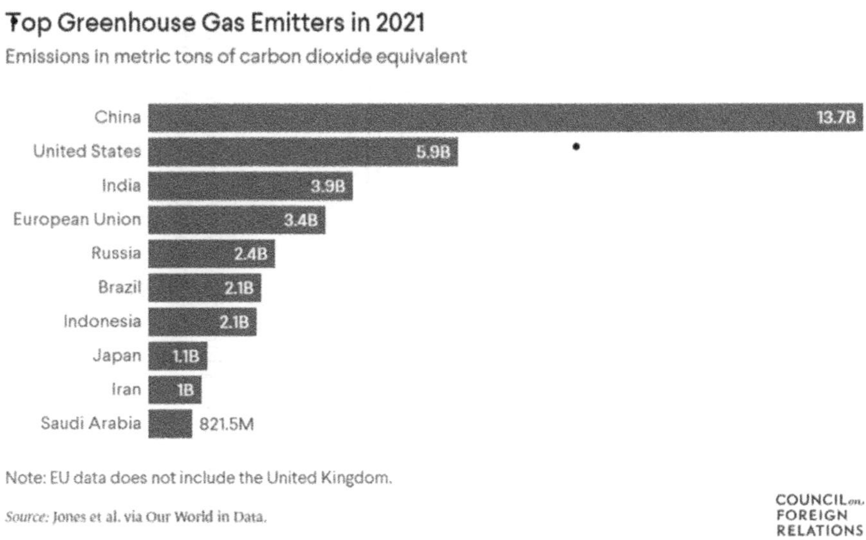

Fig. 1. Top Greenhouse Gas Emitters. *Source:* Our World in Data (2023). https://ourworldindata.org/ *Note:* The graph above shows emissions of CO_2 in metric tons across major selected countries in the world. This can be measured by the level of industrial growth.

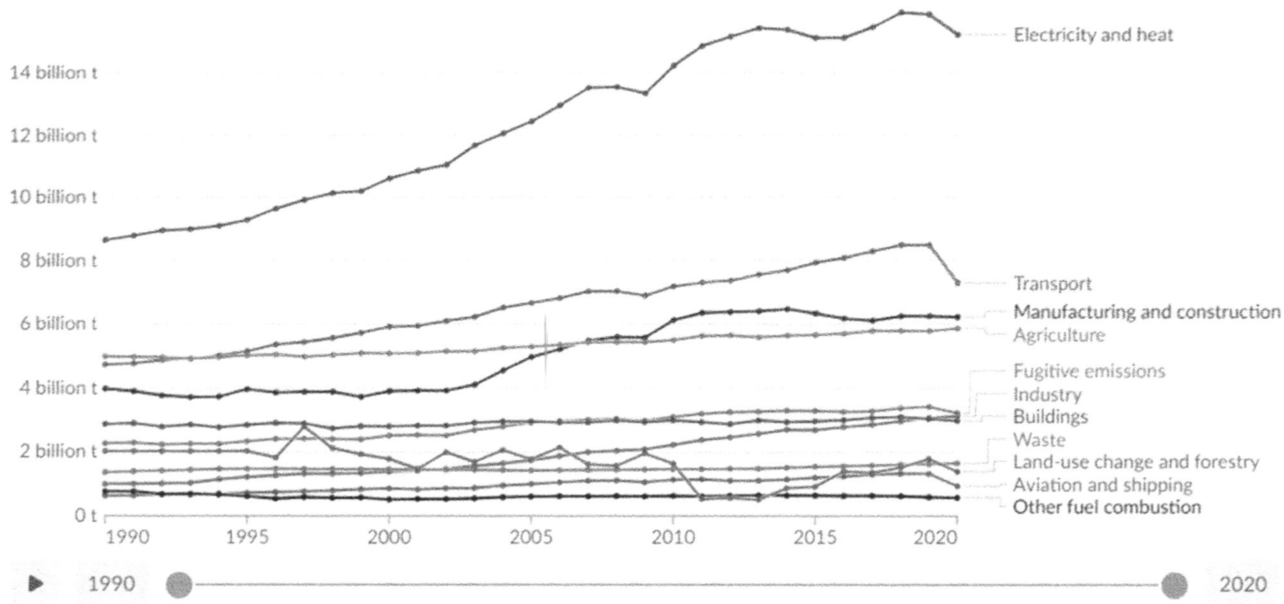

Fig. 2. Greenhouse Gas Emissions by Sector. *Source:* Climate Watch (2024). *Note:* The above chart indicates the breakdown of the sum of greenhouse gases measured in tons of CO_2 equivalents by global sectors.

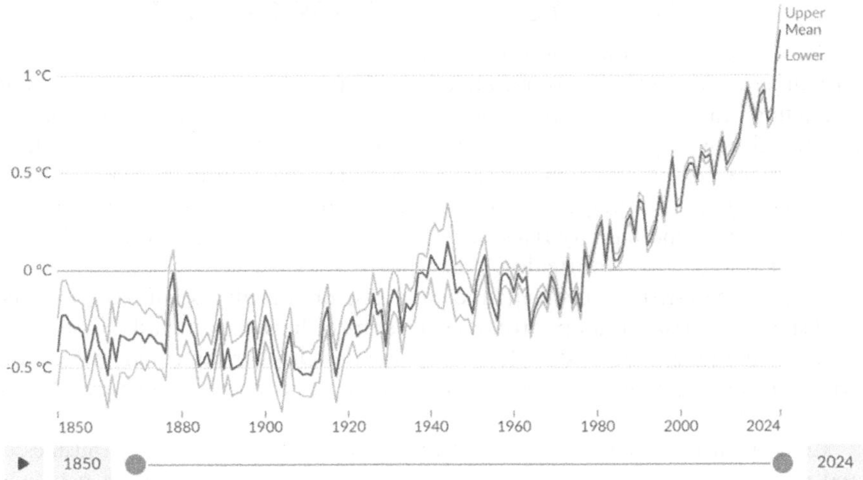

Fig. 3. Average Temperature Anomaly. *Source:* Met Office Hadley Centre (2024). https://ourworldindata.org/grapher/temperature-anomaly *Note:* The above chart shows the global average temperature relative to a baseline between 1961 and 1990, with the grey lines representing the upper and lower bounds of the 95% confidence interval.

The emissions of CO_2 and other related greenhouse gases by human activities are the major contributors to the rise in global temperatures (see Fig. 3). The analysis was made based on the CO_2 global emission history. Average temperatures have risen above 0.8°C since those periods. Also, the temperatures in 1850 were around 0.4°C cooler than the baseline, giving us a total temperature rise of about 1.2°C compared to the pre-industrial era. The periods marked the beginning of global warming to the present although this could vary across the globe between the northern hemisphere and southern hemisphere.

6. DEFINITION OF RISK AND ASSURANCE REPORTING

This is the process of providing validation and assurance to stakeholders that the information disclosed about the organization's actions on climate change risks is transparent, reliable and accurate (Braasch & Velte, 2023). This can include actions on climate risks and opportunities in financial and non-financial reports, such as sustainability and annual reports. Assurance and reporting practices may also include third-party independent verification of climate-related data and information, processes, and controls to show credibility and trust in what was disclosed (Braasch & Velte, 2023). Usually, independent actors like auditors and climate-risk assurance providers are the parties mainly employed to verify and provide adequate assurance on the reliability, relevance, accuracy and completeness of data and information disclosures and performance metrics.

7. CONCEPTUAL OVERVIEW OF CRRPA

CRRPA encompasses a wide range of climate-related risk disclosures, particularly in terms of potential adverse impacts and opportunities. CRRPA focuses on evaluating, analyzing and providing assurance on potential impacts and opportunities relating to physical risks, such as extreme weather events, rises in sea level and extreme temperature changes. This includes the transition risks, such as policy changes, technological advancements and market dynamics in response to climate change, and liability risks, such as legal actions and reputational damage (Borghei et al., 2023; Katirtzidou et al., 2023).

After climate-risk assessment and analysis, organizations must report and publish climate risks and opportunities in terms of how they identify, assess and manage climate-related risks. Managing climate-related risks could include the decarbonization process and the transition to clean or renewable energy (Bedi & Singh, 2024).

Consequently, risk reporting practices are the standards used by businesses and organizations to disclose information about exposure to climate risks and methods for managing these risks. That is a transparent way of communicating climate-related risks, opportunities and efforts taken to manage those risks or capitalize on opportunities arising from climate change. Assurance, on the other hand, is the measure of the accuracy and reliability of disclosed climate information for verification and validation (Pizzi et al., 2024).

8. THE BENEFITS OF CRRPA

CRRPA enables businesses to plan the long-term sustainability impacts of climate change on supply chains, business operations, market forecasts, financial performance and stakeholders' interests (Daddi et al., 2018). This will promote sustainable organizational practices and boost resilience to climate threats. It promotes transparency in climate-related risk disclosure so that communities, customers, employees and investors understand and have trust in how businesses are responding to climate change risks, including its impact on their business operations. Specific benefits of CRRPA are highlighted below:

- *CRRPA enhances investors' confidence* when making investment decisions. Transparent reporting is clearly emphasized in the CRRPA, and it can reflect investors' confidence in managing climate change-related risk and investment and capitalize on opportunities derived from climate change events.
- *CRRPA promotes an understanding of climate-risk management* by assessing, identifying, analyzing and reporting climate-related risks and integrating them into policies and corporate strategic objectives.
- *CRRPA provides a competitive market advantage.* Organizations that transparently disclose how they manage climate-related risks may gain good market competition by attracting customers and investors who value sustainability as well as are conscious of climate change.

- *CRRPA improves climate change regulation and compliance.* Recently, many countries have established regulatory frameworks for climate-risk reporting, including actions employed to mitigate the risks (Braasch & Velte, 2023). Hence, regulatory compliance may enhance business reputation and prevent penalties for legal sanction.

Overall, the importance of CRRPA is that it provides credibility for the information disclosed in climate-risk reporting, which enhances investors' or stakeholders' confidence. This is due to the standards framework, independent verification of data, methodologies and processes that were built on assurance and trustworthiness.

9. STRATEGIES THAT UNDERPIN CRRPA

In practice, organizations and businesses implement some common climate-risk and assurance strategies as follows:

- *Engagement With Stakeholders:* Organizations engage communities, customers, employees, investors, regulators and environmental management activists to work together on expectations and concerns related to climate change risks in return for feedback that enhances decision-making in terms of highlighting and disclosing climate risks that are comprehensive, credible, transparent which address concerns of diverse stakeholders. This stakeholder engagement also ensures valuable insights on how businesses can better manage and mitigate climate risks.
- *Risk Assessment and Scenario Analysis:* This involves assessing the potential impacts of climate change risk on the organization's business operations, financial status, supply chain network and reputation. It often includes analyzing or modelling different aspects of potential climate change risks and opportunities for future understanding and prediction.
- *Continuous Monitoring and Review:* This involves constant review and monitoring of climate-related actions and performance to ensure that the measuring metrics are aligned with changes in climate-risk regulations, market development, scientific measures and stakeholder interests.
- *Internal Controls and Governance:* This is a critical step in managing and overseeing climate change risks efficiently. Hence, internal controls and governance include establishing board oversight on climate concerns and implementing climate-risk management frameworks and metrics into performance management objectives.
- *Capacity Building and Training:* This is an aspect of the climate-risk and assurance programme involving the training of expertise to improve organization capacity on awareness and understanding of climate-related risks and opportunities.

- *Disclosure and Reporting:* This is the method used in publishing or disclosing climate-related risks and opportunities in terms of financial and non-financial information. This could be an organization's annual financial reports, stand-alone sustainability reports, sustainability reports, or regulatory proceedings. In recent times, the TCFD has become a famous convention that provides a reporting framework and standards for good climate-related disclosures (Ehalaiye et al., 2025).
- *Third-Party Assurance and Verification:* This is the process of engaging independent third parties like auditors or independent climate-risk assurance providers, to verify and provide satisfactory opinions on the reliability, relevance, accuracy and completeness of climate change risk disclosures and performance metrics. Additionally, third-party assurance and verification involves the services of assurance providers like auditors and specialized sustainability consultants (Pizzi et al., 2024).

10. CRRPA-RELATED STANDARDS

The ISSB's effort to consolidate the disclosure framework and develop a global baseline standard is expected to prompt significant changes in this field as well as provide opportunities for future research. Given the sheer amount of risk management information disclosed via the CRRPA offers a promising tool to examine disclosure practices with scale (Heenetigala et al., 2016).

Currently, organizations are making efforts to appear green and comply with the new norms of the environmental accountability initiative. This has led to a series of standards on sustainability reporting, ESG disclosure, corporate social responsibility (CSR) disclosure and the recent CRRPA. Those standards are set to promote climate-related disclosures (O'Dwyer & Owen, 2005). Specifically, CRRPA is a standard set to provide detailed information on the assurance practice of carbon emission reporting. That is, organizations are required to assess and analyze risks and opportunities related to their impacts on climate change. The global TCFD requires industries to disclose financial information about significant sustainability risks and opportunities to provide stakeholders with a complete set of sustainability-related financial disclosures. The International Auditing and Assurance Standards Board (IAASB), on the other hand, issued an audit practice on 1 October 2020, highlighting auditors' responsibility for climate change risks and assurance under International Auditing Standards. The aim is to promote CRRPA (Braasch & Velte, 2023).

In recent times, countries have been formulating and implementing policies on CRRPA. There is also a recent trend towards mandatory CRRPA around the world. For example, New Zealand and the United Kingdom have become pioneers in requiring their largest listed companies to disclose climate-related financial information from 2022 to 2023, respectively (Ehalaiye et al., 2025). New Zealand enacted a new law that requires around 200 large financial institutions under the Financial Markets Conduct (FMC) Act to publish climate-related disclosures from financial years commencing on or after 1 January 2023.

Followed by the United States Securities and Exchange Commission (SEC), which issued a proposal mandating companies to disclose climate-related information in their annual reports to investors (Hsiao et al., 2022; Saunders et al., 2020).

Also, Australia was one of the top five countries (5.1%), with companies' carbon emissions standard assurance engagements following the United Kingdom (16.2%), the United States (14.6%), Japan (13.7%) and France (6.8%) (Acharyya et al., 2019; Zhou, 2022). Usually, risk and assurance on carbon emissions were commonly assured among sustainability-related data. It is demanded that information on carbon emission-related issues be published in stand-alone reports or integrated into the annual report. However, it was found that almost two-thirds of existing engagements provided limited assurance (Garg, 2023). Additionally, New Zealand has passed a review of current practice suggesting that the disclosure of climate-related disclosures is still at an early stage and that there is much to do before such disclosures become relevant and useful. However, as with other new forms of reporting, climate-related disclosure is taking part in a journey, and the pattern of disclosure may evolve quickly (Khosa et al., 2023).

Globally, Klynveld Peat Marwick Goerdeler (KPMG) reviewed corporate reporting by the world's 250 largest companies (G250) for climate risk and net-zero reporting. Its review includes annual financial or integrated reports, sustainability reports, stand-alone reports and company websites between 2019 and 2020. Reporting quality is assessed against 12 quality criteria for good climate risk and net-zero reporting developed by KPMG professionals, covering four areas: governance of climate-related risks; identifying climate-related risks; impacts of climate-related risks and reporting and net-zero transition. The KPMG research suggests that the G250 companies are still far away from demonstrating good practice in reporting on climate risk and the net-zero transition. However, there are notable variations in reporting quality between companies in different geographies and operating in different sectors. Japan, France and Germany lead in most areas of reporting (Ghosh, 2024; Millar & Slack, 2024; Mrema, 2024).

11. THEORETICAL PRINCIPLES RELATED TO CRRPA

Theory and practice go together in both scientific and social science research. For example, the operations of organizations have a significant impact on society and can play a key role in managing climate-related risks by disclosing their impacts, mitigating risks and highlighting opportunities (Dutta & Dutta, 2021). This leads to the importance of theoretical frameworks in CRRPA. Prior studies have employed a series of theories explaining the concept of CRRPA, such as the principles of institutional norms and legitimized institutionalized structures and practices that promote disclosure, transparency and accountability as legitimate to stakeholders' interests. Among the existing theories, the most commonly adopted theories include institutional theory (Comyns, 2018), agency theory, legitimacy theory (Daddi et al., 2018) and stakeholder theory (De Grosbois & Fennell, 2022). In addition, both institutional theory and legitimacy theory have prominent perspectives in organizational theories by offering insights into how organizations respond to external pressures and seek to maintain their legitimacy. Regarding mechanisms of legitimacy, institutional theory focuses on institutional norms through institutionalized structures and practices. Legitimacy theory, on the other hand, emphasizes legitimacy through stakeholders' interests and the role of disclosure in transparency and accountability (Park et al., 2023).

CRRPA is also explained by some theoretical concepts underpinned by corporate sustainability reporting, corporate governance and risk management guidelines. These principles and concepts are discussed further below:

- *Transparency Disclosure:* This promotes trust and accountability that boosts stakeholder-informed decisions, because of easy access to authentic, relevant and timely reports about business exposure to climate-related risks and actions for mitigating them. Transparency disclosure underpins the principle of legitimacy theory, in which stakeholders have legitimate power to hold businesses accountable for what should be disclosed and the accuracy of what is reported as climate-related information (Datt et al., 2022).
- *Stakeholders Interest:* Connecting with stakeholders on expectations, priorities and interests regarding climate-related risks and reporting will boost good perceptions and understanding of climate-related risk management in terms of threat and advantage. Hence, based on the principle of stakeholder theory, climate-risk reporting must address the concerns of various stakeholders. Stakeholders or parties to CRRPA include regulatory agencies, investors, employees, climate or environmental activists, customers and communities (Borghei et al., 2023).
- *Materiality:* This is a theoretical concept that recognizes the impact of the omission or misstatement of climate-related information on stakeholders' decision-making. The materiality of climate-risk disclosure should focus on what is of financial and strategic significance to business in terms of threats and opportunities as they may influence performance (Thai et al., 2022).
- *Regulatory Compliance:* This is related to legitimacy theory, which emphasizes regulatory requirements, sanctions and guidelines imposed on businesses by regulatory agencies, industry associations and standard-setting bodies to comply with climate-risk reporting. This also recognizes the concept of voluntary reporting and best practices.
- *Integrated Reporting:* This can be defined by institutional theory as a principle that measures performance in terms of ESG factors and financial factors. Climate-risk reporting should be integrated into broader institutional frameworks that will provide a complete picture of how climate-related risks and opportunities are managed, including how they can influence a better society for long-term sustainable wealth and well-being creation.

12. HYPOCRISY BEHIND CRRPA

The scientific research findings estimate that the world's emissions of CO_2 will exceed 40 billion tons in 2023, including nearly 37 billion tons from fossil fuels. Overall emissions are up 1.1% compared to 2022 and 1.5% compared to pre-pandemic levels (University of Exeter and Stanford Doerr School of Sustainability, 2023).

The impacts of climate risk can be seen in the increased frequency and magnitude of extreme weather conditions like winter storms, heatwaves, floods, droughts, hurricanes and wildfires. Recently, a sudden, sharp rise in global average temperature above the pre-industrial period was reported in a series of scientific and academic studies (University of Exeter and Stanford Doerr School of Sustainability, 2023).

To increase commitment to reduce global emissions, the ideas of CRRPA come into play. Today, almost all global business organizations are aware of and understand the concept of climate change, and they have been claiming to publish sustainability reports. Unfortunately, there are no viable physical actions or efforts to prove the difference between reporting and practical efforts to mitigate climate change (Sanusi & Johl, 2020). To date, big companies like Chevron, Shell and Exxon Mobil are still investing billions of dollars in offshore oil companies (Borghei et al., 2024). Not only that but some notable countries that were also the initiators of the 2015 Paris Agreement still found themselves massively immersed in unsustainable industrial and economic practices (Estrada & Botzen, 2021). The question remains, 'Who is deceiving who on the climate threat?' Against this background, this book chapter identifies the following:

The hypocrisy of *greenwashing*. Greenwashing is a current problem that creates a false impression of CRRPA about sustainability reporting, which represents insufficient efforts in climate-risk mitigation (Estrada & Botzen, 2021). Greenwashing masks misrepresentation and exaggeration of climate-related risk mitigation efforts by some organizations, which could affect the standard of accuracy and reliability in CRRPA. Greenwashing ranges from the disclosure of false data and an insufficient level of climate-risk information disclosure.

This is followed by the hypocrisy of *conflict of interest*, which could compromise the independence, materiality and impartiality of climate-related risk assessment, leading to inaccurate or biased CRRPA reporting. Conflict of interest occurs when independent verifiers/auditors or climate-risk assessment consultants hired to do the job, have economic ties or financial interest in the organizations they are evaluating. This could compromise the CRRPA process.

Unfair distortion of CRRPA findings: This is a situation where organizations only focus on or recognize positive data and information aspects of climate-risk assessment while overlooking or neglecting negative impacts or omitting areas where they fall short. This is otherwise known as selective disclosure or cherry-picking, which positions CRRPA in the best possible light. This can equally affect the accuracy and authenticity of CRRPA.

Another hypocrisy to be considered is *cosmetic or tokenism*, a situation where businesses are only interested in CRRPA to avoid legal sanction or appear sustainability conscious to meet stakeholders' demands rather than genuine climate accountability. *Cosmetic or tokenism in climate-risk reporting* are always misleading, and superficial, and do not address the greenhouse gas emission problem.

Lack of *transparency and accountability* is another hypocritical point considered. It occurs when there is no credibility and reliability in the CRRPA data and information disclosed to global audiences. In most cases, CRRPA of this nature lacks independent auditing and assurance. Thus, in the name of meeting sustainability regulatory requirements, some organizations may report self-assessed climate-risk mitigation practices, withhold key material sensitive data, lie about methodologies or fail to disclose likely conflicts of interest. This raises questions about the integrity of the CRRPA assessment process.

The last hypocrisy to be considered is the *ambiguous reporting practice. This* is the art of using terminology that is misleading or difficult to understand without clear standards or benchmarks. This could constitute difficulties in interpreting climate-related risk performance as well as evaluating accurate efforts in the CRRPA. This lack of clarity can undermine the credibility and reliability of reported data, leading to scepticism among stakeholders.

Addressing and limiting these hypocrisies will promote stakeholder engagement and foster greater trust and accountability in the CRRPA, as it will further enhance greater transparency, accountability, and integrity in CRRPA. This is critical because CRRPA is a standardized assurance mechanism that should provide robust oversight on climate-risk mitigation about environmental performance and commitments.

Nevertheless, there is a need to examine the potential road ahead or roadmap for advancing sustainable CRRPA as it continues to evolve. Since CRRPA is a process, there should be a commitment to *continuous improvement and refinement*. Especially in the areas of methodology, standards, and framework using the available regulatory requirements, technology and climate science in line with stakeholder expectations. This also includes regular reviews of assessment criteria to ensure they are up-to-date and suitable for identifying and mitigating climate-related risks.

13. SUSTAINABLE CRRPA: WHAT LIES AHEAD?

Integration with the existing reporting guidelines or standards: There should be connection and collaboration on CRRPA assessment with the existing guidelines and standardized frameworks, especially on CSR disclosures and sustainability reporting, to formulate best practices for reporting on climate-related risks and sustainability practices.

Another important road ahead in CRRPA is *collaboration and knowledge sharing* among industrial associations, climate-risk management experts, NGOs and researchers to establish best practices in CRRPA implementation and sustainable climate management.

The *need for award and recognition:* Parties and organizations that play a leading role in CRRPA and sustainable climate reporting practices should be recognized and rewarded for compliance and commitment. This could be through a climate resilience recognition programme, an award party, or certifications to incentivize and reward businesses with good records of CRRPA and sustainability activities. This will thus promote resilience and participation in climate-risk management.

Establishing *capacity building* in the form of training like seminars, workshops, conferences, symposiums, courses and online and physical lectures will benefit auditors, climate consultant specialists, sustainability experts and businesses on how to conduct CRRPA assessments. Such programs will provide guidance on suitable methods to be adopted in data collection, analysis and reporting to enhance accuracy and consistency.

Advocacy for policy support is another important initiative for the future to achieve the best CRRPA practice. This includes potential carbon pricing incentives and active policymaker involvement to promote climate-risk disclosure regulations, as well as other mechanisms that encourage accountability and transparency in CRRPA implementation.

Standardization and guidelines for achieving the best CRRPA cannot be overemphasized. This could be collaborating with relevant stakeholders, policymakers, and experts to establish standardized uniform guidelines for global best CRRPA implementation. In this case, there would be a single globally recognized methodology for reporting on climate-related risks and sustainability practices. Harmonizing different reporting frameworks for climate-risk reporting and assurance practice involves combining standards to create a consistent, comparable approach to climate-risk disclosure. If achieved, this will establish a unified reporting framework, promote local adaptation to meet specific regional climate-risk disclosure needs and provide a global baseline for sustainability disclosures. It will also promote ethical and assurance frameworks for reliable, internationally recognized standards. The merging of frameworks like ISSB and TCFD will enhance effective risk management. In summary, harmonization is a valuable effort to create a reliable and comparable system for climate-risk and assurance reporting practices, facilitating easier evaluation and comparability.

The last point to be considered is *stakeholder engagement*. This defines the extent of connecting with stakeholders on matters related to CRRPA and sustainability practices. This could indicate education, information, awareness and feedback on sustainability practices. Discussing and engaging stakeholders in CRRPA matters and incorporating their input into findings will improve understanding and commitment to climate-risk management practices.

The ability to achieve and follow these roadmaps will indicate successful integration between sustainable CRRPA and sustainability practices, contributing to further transparency and accountability in climate-related risk management.

14. SUMMARY

The global temperature rise since the Industrial Revolution, driven largely by fossil fuel, agricultural, industrial and domestic waste generations, has led to the consequences of global warming in recent decades. CRRPA could have a positive effect on reducing the rate of global warming. Since it allows organizations to assess and publish climate risks and opportunities in terms of climate action.

CRRPA is a continuous process that requires continuous improvement in response to climate change circumstances, stakeholder priorities and evolving best practices. Hence, some organizations lag in independent and regular reviews of climate-risk strategies and methodologies, making their reporting practices obsolete, irrelevant and less effective in addressing climate-related risks and opportunities. Reflecting on CRRPA can lead to some valuable conclusions like the possibility of achieving collaboration and collective action across different participants and stakeholders. This will eventually lead to innovative solutions, best practices and resource mobilization and sharing to address the interconnected challenges of sustainability effectively.

In conclusion, CRRPA can lead to several valuable performance objectives that include promoting transparency, credibility, improvement in business strategy, standardized frameworks and guidelines for climate-risk reporting that enhance consistency, an effective risk management plan, long-term sustainable performance and recognition of stakeholder contributions in risk reporting practices. This will contribute to more resilient and sustainable business models that foster greater accountability in addressing climate change.

NOTE

1. Businesses and other organizations are exposed to climate-related risks in terms of transition and physical risks. Transition risks arise as businesses are shifting towards a carbon-free society in relation to green energy and infrastructure. These include technological advancements (investment in green technology); regulatory changes that require effective modifications in business models, new laws and regulations that focus on reducing carbon emission and market shifts (i.e., the consumer interest in environmentally friendly products) (Thai et al., 2022). Physical risks on the other hand refer to the direct impacts of climate change on the people and environment, such as extreme weather events that can cause imminent damage to business infrastructures, stop production processes, increase the cost of production and disrupt supply chain (Nobanee & Nghiem, 2024; Thai et al., 2022). These can cause long-term losses to business operations. In summary, both risks can have negative impacts on business operations, including the competitive pressure of sustainable business practices. Therefore, understanding how to manage these risks is critical for long-term business sustainability in a changing climate world.

REFERENCES

Acharyya, M., Kakar, G., & Sturgess, E. (2019). Climate risk reporting practices by UK insurance companies and pension schemes. *British Actuarial Journal, 24*.

Andersen, I. (2024). *Inclusive multilateralism at UNEA-6 boosts environmental movement*. https://www.unep.org/news-and-stories/speech/inclusive-multilateralism-unea-6-boosts-environmental-movement

Bedi, A., & Singh, B. (2024). Climate governance and carbon emission disclosure. *Social Responsibility Journal, 20*.

Borghei, Z., Linnenluecke, M., & Bui, B. (2024). The disclosure of climate-related risks and opportunities in financial statements: The UK's FTSE 100. *Meditari Accountancy Research, 32*(3), 1031–1063.

Borghei, Z., Linnenluecke, M., & Bui, B. (2023). The disclosure of climate-related risks and opportunities in financial statements: The UK's FTSE 100. *Meditari Accountancy Research, 32*.

Braasch, A., & Velte, P. (2023). Climate reporting quality following the recommendations of the task force on climate-related financial disclosures: A focus on the German capital market. *Sustainable Development, 31*(2), 926–940.

Chai, Q., Fu, S., Xu, H., Li, W., & Zhong, Y. (2017). The gap report of global climate change mitigation, finance, and governance after the United States declared its withdrawal from the Paris Agreement. *Chinese Journal of Population Resources and Environment, 15*(3), 196–208.

Climate Watch. (2024). With major processing by our world in data "Agriculture" [Dataset]. Climate Watch, "Greenhouse gas emissions by sector". [Original data]. https://ourworldindata.org/emissions-by-sector

Cointe, B., & Guillemot, H. (2023). A history of the 1.5°C target. *Wiley Interdisciplinary Reviews: Climate Change, 14*(3), e824.

Comoli, M., Tettamanzi, P., & Murgolo, M. (2023). Accounting for 'ESG'under disruptions: A systematic literature network analysis. *Sustainability, 15*(8), 6633.

Comyns, B. (2018). Climate change reporting and multinational companies: Insights from institutional theory and international business. *Accounting Forum, 42*(1).

Daddi, T., Todaro, N. M., De Giacomo, M. R., & Frey, M. (2018). A systematic review of the use of organization and management theories in climate change studies. *Business Strategy and the Environment, 27*(4), 456-474.

Datt, R., Prasad, P., Vitale, C., & Prasad, K. (2022). International evidence of changing assurance practices for carbon emissions disclosures. *Meditari Accountancy Research, 30*(6), 1594–1628.

De Grosbois, D., & Fennell, D. A. (2022). Determinants of climate change disclosure practices of global hotel companies: Application of institutional and stakeholder theories. *Tourism Management, 88*, 104404.

Dutta, P., & Dutta, A. (2021). Impact of external assurance on corporate climate change disclosures: New evidence from Finland. *Journal of Applied Accounting Research, 22*(2), 252–285.

Ehalaiye, D., Moses, O., Laswad, F., & Botica Redmayne, N. (2025). Local government enterprises climate action: An exploration of New Zealand container seaports' climate-related disclosure practices. *Financial Accountability & Management, 41*(1), 60–88.

Estrada, F., & Botzen, W. W. (2021). Economic impacts and risks of climate change under failure and success of the Paris agreement. *Annals of the New York Academy of Sciences, 1504*(1), 95–115.

Fernandez, M. O., & Trasande, L. (2024). The global plastics treaty: An endocrinologist's assessment. *Journal of the Endocrine Society, 8*(1), bvad141.

Friedrich, T. J., Velte, P., & Wulf, I. (2023). Corporate climate reporting of European banks: Are these institutions compliant with climate issues? *Business Strategy and the Environment, 32*(6), 2817–2834.

Garg, M. (2023). *2.2 impact of climate-change financial disclosures on accounting numbers and assurance practices*. Deakin-AUASB Sustainability Assurance Research Workshop.

Garg, M., Campbell, J. L., Foerster, A., & Langer, L. (2023). *Impact of climate-change financial disclosures on accounting numbers and assurance practices*. Deakin-AUASB Sustainability Assurance Research Workshop.

Ghosh, P. (2024). The Asian development bank's environment program: Challenges and directions. In Quibria, M. G. & Akanda, A. (Eds.), *The Elgar companion to the Asian development bank* (pp. 199–212). Edward Elgar Publishing.

Giannarakis, G., Andronikidis, A., Zopounidis, C., Sariannidis, N., & Tsagarakis, K. P. (2023). Determinants of global reporting initiative report: A comparative study between USA and European companies. *Sustainable Production and Consumption, 35*, 376–387.

Hazemba, M. (2024). Integrated waste management and circular economy. In S. A. Bandh, F. A. Malla, S. A. Wani, & A. T. Hoang (Eds.), *Waste management in the circular economy* (pp. 153–170). Springer.

Heenetigala, K., De Silva Lokuwaduge, C., Armstrong, A., & Ediriweera, A. (2016). *Investigation of criteria used for assurance practices of sustainability reporting in Australian listed companies.* Victoria University.

Hsiao, P.-C. K., Scott, T., & Zang, Z. (2022). A snapshot of sustainability assurance market in New Zealand. *Pacific Accounting Review*, *34*(5), 669–686.

Ivanova, M. (2012). Institutional design and UNEP reform: Historical insights on form, function and financing. *International Affairs*, *88*(3), 565–584.

Karamaneas, A., Koasidis, K., Frilingou, N., Xexakis, G., Nikas, A., & Doukas, H. (2023). A stakeholder-informed modelling study of Greece's energy transition amidst an energy crisis: The role of natural gas and climate ambition. *Renewable and Sustainable Energy Transition*, *3*, 100049.

Katirtzidou, M., Skoulikaris, C., Makris, C., Baltikas, V., Latinopoulos, D., & Krestenitis, Y. (2023). Modeling stakeholders' perceptions in participatory multi-risk assessment on a deltaic environment under climate change conditions. *Environmental Modeling & Assessment*, *28*(3), 367–388.

Khosa, A., Pandey, R., & Wilkin, C. (2023). *Accounting curricula and climate crisis: Evidence from Australia and New Zealand.* Taylor & Francis Group.

Kryk, B., & Kożuch, M. (2024). EU regulations on reporting sustainable development as a determinant of limiting the environmental pressure of chemical enterprises in Poland. *Economics and Environment*, *88*(1), 695.

Malik, I. H., & Ford, J. D. (2024). Addressing the climate change adaptation gap: Key themes and future directions. *Climate*, *12*(2), 24.

Millar, J., & Slack, R. (2024). Global investor responses to the international sustainability standards board draft sustainability and climate-change standards: Sites of dissonance or consensus. *Sustainability Accounting, Management and Policy Journal*, *15*(3), 573–604.

Mrema, E. M. (2024). World environment day: Turning point in our race to restoration. https://www.unep.org/news-and-stories/speech/world-environment-day-turning-point-our-race-restoration#:~:text=We%20are%20the%20first%20generation,marshes%2C%20on%20reviving%20our%20soils

Nobanee, H., & Nghiem, X.-H. (2024). Climate catastrophe insurance for climate change: What do we know and what lies ahead? *Current Opinion in Environmental Sustainability*, *66*, 101395.

O'Dwyer, B., & Owen, D. L. (2005). Assurance statement practice in environmental, social and sustainability reporting: A critical evaluation. *The British Accounting Review*, *37*(2), 205–229.

Park, J. D., Nishitani, K., Kokubu, K., Freedman, M., & Weng, Y. (2023). Revisiting sustainability disclosure theories: Evidence from corporate climate change disclosure in the United States and Japan. *Journal of Cleaner Production*, *382*, 135203.

Pizzi, S., Venturelli, A., & Caputo, F. (2024). Restoring trust in sustainability reporting: The enabling role of the external assurance. *Current Opinion in Environmental Sustainability*, *68*, 101437.

Ruane, A. C., Phillips, M., Jägermeyr, J., & Müller, C. (2024). Non-linear climate change impacts on crop yields may mislead stakeholders. *Earth's Future*, *12*(4).

Sanusi, F. A., & Johl, S. K. (2020). A proposed framework for assessing the influence of internal corporate social responsibility belief on employee intention to job continuity. *Corporate Social Responsibility and Environmental Management*, *27*(6), 2437–2449.

Saunders, W. S., Kelly, S., Paisley, S., & Clarke, L. B. (2020). Progress toward implementing the Sendai framework, the Paris agreement, and the sustainable development goals: Policy from Aotearoa New Zealand. *International Journal of Disaster Risk Science*, *11*(2), 190–205.

Scartozzi, C. M. (2024). Conflict sensitive climate finance: Lessons from the green climate fund. *Climate Policy*, *24*(3), 297–313.

Scott, D., Hall, C. M., Rushton, B., & Gössling, S. (2023). A review of the IPCC sixth assessment and implications for tourism development and sectoral climate action. *Journal of Sustainable Tourism*, 1–18.

Sebos, I., Nydrioti, I., Katsiardi, P., & Assimacopoulos, D. (2023). Stakeholder perceptions on climate change impacts and adaptation actions in Greece. *Euro-Mediterranean Journal for Environmental Integration*, *8*(4), 777–793.

Susilowati, I., Sholeh, M., Yunus, N. R., & Ainaya, D. A. (2024). The role of the United Nations Environment Program (UNEP) in overcoming deforestation in central Kalimantan 2017-2020. In *IOP Conference Series: Earth and Environmental Science*. IOP (Institute of Physics) Publishing Ltd.

Thai, K., Xu, Y., & Herbohn, K. (2022). Reporting and assurance of material climate risks: Evidence from Australia. https://papers.ssrn.com/sol3/papers.cfm?abstract_id=4307685

Turzo, T., Marzi, G., Favino, C., & Terzani, S. (2022). Non-financial reporting research and practice: Lessons from the last decade. *Journal of Cleaner Production*, *345*, 131154.

University of Exeter and Stanford Doerr School of Sustainability. (2023). *Global carbon emissions from fossil fuels reached record high in 2023*. University of Exeter and Stanford Doerr School of Sustainability.

World Health Organization. (2022). *Annual report 2021: WHO Asia-Pacific centre for environment and health in the Western Pacific Region*. World Health Organization.

Wright, S. J., Sietsma, A., Korswagen, S., Athanasiadis, I. N., & Biesbroek, R. (2023). How do countries frame climate change? A global comparison of adaptation and mitigation in UNFCCC National Communications. *Regional Environmental Change*, *23*(4), 129.

Zhou, S. (2022). Reporting and assurance of climate-related and other sustainability information: A review of research and practice. *Australian Accounting Review*, *32*(3), 315–333.

TOWARDS STAKEHOLDER INCLUSIVE ENVIRONMENTAL REPORTING PRACTICE

Lindie Grebe

Akademia, South Africa

ABSTRACT

Environmental reporting is high on the global agenda. The recent International Financial Reporting Standards (IFRS) release of Sustainability Standards provides useful guidance for preparing reports on environmental impacts and addresses much of the past criticism against such reporting. However, information on which *stakeholders are interested in* what *environmental information is scarce, as existing frameworks are primarily general environmental guidance. While current environmental reporting embodies organizational environmentalism, distinct stakeholders perceive environmental activities differently. Specific issues that matter to distinct stakeholder groups must be identified to fully understand their environmental reporting requirements. This suggests a contextualized, stakeholder-oriented, perspective on environmental reporting that presents real-life and relevant information as part of environmental reporting. This conceptual chapter aims to outline a research agenda and the practical implications for researchers and practitioners to meet the reporting requirements of key stakeholders. This encompasses identifying tangible stakeholders that impact decision-making in organizations or industries and how they can generate valuable environmental information. It is done from a contextualized stakeholder lens to address gaps in the inclusiveness of environmental reports. These contributions have significant implications for reporting on environmental impacts within a context.*

Keywords: Environmental reporting; sustainability; stakeholder inclusivity; contextualized reporting; reporting requirements

Climate Risks Reporting Practices and Assurance
Advances in Environmental Accounting & Management, Volume 13, 25–36

ISSN: 1479-3598/doi:10.1108/S1479-359820250000013005

1. INTRODUCTION

Environmental reporting can be conceived as a sub-area of sustainability reporting, which has received considerable attention in the last few years. Concerns over the environment have remained central to important discourses globally, and as such, organizations are pressured to report information about their activities affecting the environment. Sustainability reporting frameworks, particularly the recently introduced International Financial Reporting Standards (IFRS) S1 General Requirements for Disclosure of Sustainability-related Financial Information and IFRS S2 Climate-related Disclosures, have contributed to the understanding, standardizing and enhancing the quality of environmental reporting (IFRS Foundation, 2023a, 2023b). They are aimed at addressing the absence of systematic and coherent environmental reporting, which is generally voluntary, fragmented and often misleading.

However, existing practice and research do not address the question of *who* is interested in *which* kind of environmental information. Present-day practices mostly rely on conventional reporting frameworks and are not very sensitive to different classes of stakeholders' requirements. For example, Mitchell et al.'s (1997) well-known Stakeholder Salience Model prioritizes stakeholders based on the three key attributes of power (the ability to influence decisions, actions and outcomes), legitimacy (the appropriateness of stakeholder relationships) and urgency (the degree to which immediate attention is required). Whilst this model assists in prioritizing stakeholders to allocate resources and attention, it could be argued that the model does not sufficiently aid in determining what issues matter most to these stakeholders.

Other recent frameworks and models that guide reporting on environmental matters include the Global Reporting Initiative (GRI) Standards (GRI, 2023) with guidance on sustainability reporting, including environmental factors, the Carbon Disclosure Project (CDP) (CDP, 2023) with a focus on specific issues such as climate change as part of environmental reporting and the widely used Integrated Reporting Framework (IRF) (IRF, 2021). While these frameworks and models contribute towards good environmental reporting, the specific issues that matter to distinct stakeholder groups must be identified to fully understand their environmental reporting requirements.

This chapter seeks to fill this gap by presenting a contextualized and stakeholder-oriented approach to explore to whom organizations should report, as well as an approach to determine the extent to which organizational and stakeholder views converge in terms of environmental reporting. It aims to improve the value of environmental reports and decision-making by acknowledging the expectations of particular stakeholder groups across particular organizational settings.

2. ENVIRONMENTAL REPORTING

It is a well-established fact that environmental reporting provides crucial information that informs managerial decision-making primarily through risk management, resource allocation and strategy formulation (Eccles et al., 2014). Accurate environmental information enables management to respond to probable threats and opportunities and increase awareness of changes that need to be made to an organization's sustainable practices (Deloitte, 2022).

Moreover, environmental reporting helps in harmonizing the decision-making process of management with sustainability objectives, thus aiding organizations to enhance their long-term sustainability (Ioannou & Serafeim, 2019). A good environmental report achieves a dual effect of implementing environmental efficiency while at the same time building stakeholder confidence and organizational legitimacy (Adams, 2017).

As a result, environmental reporting has developed from what was once carried out in most organizations as a voluntary activity to what has now become a more or less regulated process. The GRI, developed in the late 1990s, was one of the first strategic initiatives designed to help organizations understand how they could report on sustainability issues, including environmental issues. Since then, other frameworks, such as the Sustainability Accounting Standards Board (SASB) and the Task Force on Climate-related Financial Disclosures (TCFD), have been developed to offer more guidance on environmental reporting (SASB, 2021; TCFD, 2022).

The Sustainability Standards, issued by the IFRS Foundation, are a new addition to the constantly growing list of frameworks. These are meant to harmonize the reporting of sustainability matters within industries and across countries. They offer a roadmap for the sustainability report through the environmental, social and governance (ESG) performance of organizations. Their ultimate aim is to ensure that sustainability reporting has the same quality as financial reporting, seeking to increase the credibility, comparability and harmonization of sustainability disclosures, including environmental issues, across the world (Deloitte, 2022; IFRS Foundation, 2023a, 2023b).

Thus, the existence of comprehensive reporting requirements guarantees that the stakeholders have an opportunity to use reliable information concerning the environmental performance of a given organization (Deloitte, 2022). They are also intended to enhance the relevance and consistency of environment-related financial information presented by organizations transacting in different industries. In this way, the standards mean that any disclosed environmental impacts and risks are clearly described and comparable so that investors and other stakeholders can judge the comparative performance of organizations. This is a major improvement over other frameworks that in various degrees opened the door for large variations in the extent and quality of disclosures (Eccles & Serafeim, 2011).

These features of the standards – their requirement and their incorporation into a wider system of corporate financial reporting – serve to push organizations to be held more responsible for environmental issues. The standards make sure environmental factors are not viewed as outside the common financial management considerations of an organization. Such an approach is important in combating the future problems of environmental depletion and climate change (Adams, 2017; Clark et al., 2015).

Consequently, as the previously listed regulations concerning the environment and sustainability remain in a constant state of development, the IFRS Sustainability Standards ensure clear compliance with environmental legislation at the organizational level. This is especially the case given the current global trends of increased envelopment policies and standards, as governments in various nations implement enhanced sustainable reporting requirements like the European Commission's Corporate Sustainability Reporting Directive (CSRD) (European Commission, 2021). Using the said standards, organizations can improve their chances of catering to the requirements of every regulation on reporting in order to avoid non-compliance.

The two IFRS Sustainability Standards published up to date are IFRS S1 General Requirements for Disclosure of Sustainability-related Financial Information and IFRS S2 Climate-related Disclosures. IFRS S1: General Requirements for Sustainability-related Financial Information (IFRS Foundation, 2023a, 2023b) gives guidance regarding standards to be adopted by organizations in reporting on sustainability risks and opportunities. This standard seeks to bridge the gap between financial performance and sustainability impacts by requiring organizations to explain how sustainability issues, such as the environment, pose a threat to the organization and its strategic outlook for the future. IFRS S1 outlines standard content and format requirements that are common to all sustainability disclosures and presents the fundamental principles that form the basis of ESG disclosure (IFRS Foundation, 2023a).

Some of the key features of IFRS S1 are as follows:

- *Comprehensive and Coherent Information:* The standard makes sure that organizations make adequate disclosures that are not inconsistent and can be easily compared with prior period disclosures. This has the effect of enabling stakeholders to identify the financial influence of such sustainability risks and opportunities (Adams, 2017; IFRS Foundation, 2023a).
- *Integration With Financial Reporting:* IFRS S1 underscores how sustainability-related information, like environmental aspects, could be reported together with the traditional financial accounts and balances. This involves associating sustainability risks, such as climate change, with associated performance implications. The IFRS S1, therefore, assists organizations and their stakeholders in understanding sustainability and financial performance by integrating it within the traditional financial reporting process (Deloitte, 2022).
- *Impact on Stakeholders:* To key stakeholders such as investors, regulators and customers, IFRS S1 incorporates a stable framework through which the sustainability performance of organizations can be evaluated. Financial managers, for instance, gain greater clarity on environmental risks and opportunities within the value chain that may extend or detract value to an organization. All of these make decision-making by stakeholders more informed as a result of improved transparency (Clark et al., 2015; Deloitte, 2022).
- *Materiality:* Two of the general recognitions in IFRS S1 are relevance and stakeholders, and one of the most important concepts is materiality. This means

that organizations have to disclose sustainability information that is material to their financial statements. The materiality analysis helps determine which materials concerning sustainability are more important for stakeholders and ought to be reported on (Deloitte, 2022; IFRS Foundation, 2023a). This serves to ensure that the information disclosed meets the interests of the various stakeholder groups and, in the process, enables the relevant stakeholders to make sound decisions. However, the standard still does not provide enough detailed information on what environmental information is to be reported to which stakeholder groups.

The two elements, concerning the impact on stakeholders and materiality, tie directly with the purpose of this chapter, namely, to identify who organizations are reporting to and how organizational and stakeholder perspectives converge contextually. This purpose aligns with a stakeholder-oriented perspective taken to address an inclusivity deficit in environmental reporting. This is further explained in Section 4 below.

While IFRS S1 provides general disclosure of sustainability-related financial information in general, IFRS S2 focuses on specifications for climate-related disclosures as part of environmental reporting (IFRS Foundation, 2023b). Arguably, one of the most significant questions facing organizations relates to the environment and climate change. IFRS S2 is particularly pertinent to the TCFD recommendations that have received unparalleled global acclaim for their efficiency in estimating climate change risks and opportunities (TCFD, 2022). Some of the key features of IFRS S2 are as follows:

- *Climate-Related Risks and Opportunities:* In IFRS S2, organizations are asked to explain what risks and opportunities related to the climate they consider, evaluate and mitigate. These are both physical environmental risks, such as storms, heat waves and rising sea levels, and transition risks, such as environmental regulatory shifts (IFRS Foundation, 2023b). Organizations need to show how these risks could impact their financial position and business in the short term as well as in the longer term.
- *Governance and Strategy:* The standard requires organizations to disclose their governance of environmental risks and opportunities. This pertains to where environmental risks are integrated into organizational strategy, risk management frameworks and decision-making at a management level. As was mentioned before, through stressing governance mechanisms, IFRS S2 is intended to promote the consideration and mitigation of environmental risks in the conceptually wider context of corporate governance (Deloitte, 2022; IFRS Foundation, 2023b).
- *Scenario Analysis:* One of the major features of IFRS S2 while preparing the financial report is the insistence on undertaking and reporting on scenarios. These analyses consider the risks of the changes in different environmental scenarios (IFRS Foundation, 2023b). Through a process of analysis of several scenarios of climate change, actors can determine how vulnerable an organization is in the face

of particular environmental futures and the opportunities that might result from this vulnerability.
- *Metrics and Targets:* IFRS S2 requires certain environmental reportable factors such as emissions, energy consumption and other related indicators. It mandates organizations to disclose material information, including progress to managing environmental risks and opportunities consistent with organizations' global environmental objectives (IFRS Foundation, 2023b). Such a breakdown of detailed, quantitative analysis grants stakeholders the exact status of an organization in terms of the effectiveness of managing environmental issues.
- *Impact on Stakeholders:* For the stakeholders, the IFRS S2 standard reveals extremely useful information as to how organizations are managing environmental risks and opportunities. Stakeholders require an understanding of how environment-related challenges might impact future earnings while, on the other hand, regulators need to ascertain whether organizations are aligned with emerging environmental legislation. The emphasis on the use of scenarios and quantitative factors that offer more accurate benchmarks for comparisons between organizations provides clearer evidence to stakeholders regarding those organizations that are ahead of others when it comes to environmental initiatives (Clark et al., 2015; Deloitte, 2022).

Once again, it should be noted that this focus of IFRS S2 aligns with a stakeholder-oriented perspective taken in this chapter. This is further explained in Section 4 below.

In combination, IFRS S1 and S2 are a giant step forward towards standardization and improvement of the quality of environmental reporting. These standards take a step towards addressing challenges associated with previous voluntary reporting frameworks such as GRI and the SASB. However, to date, there is still a dearth in the literature on determining which stakeholders will be interested in what information in environmental reporting. As mentioned, different interest groups perceive environmental activities and their effects, differently. Identifying the specific interests that different stakeholders have regarding environmental information in environmental reports deserves deeper understanding.

3. STAKEHOLDER INTEREST IN ENVIRONMENTAL REPORTING

Since the two IFRS Sustainability Standards represent a big step towards improving the quality of environmental reporting, many organizations now apply not only these standards to comply with regulatory requirements but also to create sustainable values through sustainable strategies as part of strategic management. From this, it can be seen that these sustainability standards are actively oriented towards the recognition of aspects of reporting on environmental information; environmental reporting should disclose information important to key stakeholders. For example, investors, regulators, customers, employees, local communities including non-governmental organizations (NGOs), policymakers and supply chain partners may hold different views and values of organizations' environmental practices. Appreciation of these different interests is important if organizations are to meet the needs of their stakeholders as they strive to produce reports that meet the necessary criteria.

As noted earlier, the challenge of navigating the myriads of possible environmental issues to report on is answered by IFRS S1 using the principle of materiality, in much the same way as it obliges organizations to carry out materiality assessments. Based on this, organizations should find out which environmental reporting issues concern which stakeholders most and rank their reports appropriately (Deloitte, 2022; IFRS Foundation, 2023a). This assures that the reported environmental information does meet the objective of the stakeholders in making decisions based on the reported information. However, there is not enough information available about how these assessments could be conducted in the context of particular organizations and from day-to-day organizational settings.

Implementing a one-size-fits-all environmental reporting practice simply doesn't meet the needs of all the stakeholders (Bebbington et al., 2020). There is a need to pay attention to who organizations are reporting to and how organizational and stakeholder views align from a contextually situated stakeholder point of view. Such knowledge will be useful in understanding the diverse and dynamic environmental issues which have to be communicated to meet the inclusiveness void in environmental reporting between organizations and their stakeholders.

The next sections will offer an approach to explore to whom organizations should report and how to determine the extent to which organizational and stakeholder views converge, through a contextualized stakeholder lens. These contributions have significant implications for both researchers and practitioners when it comes to reporting on environmental impacts.

4. A CONTEXTUALIZED STAKEHOLDER-ORIENTED APPROACH TO ENVIRONMENTAL REPORTING

An everyday-operation-based stakeholder-oriented approach can help to better address various stakeholder needs for environmental information. This entails, first, the identification of stakeholders within organizations or organizational contexts and, second, the identification of environmental information most relevant to each unique stakeholder group within the context of the organizations.

4.1 Stakeholder Identification and Understanding

Stakeholder theory enables organizations that operate in different environments to manage their stakeholders. According to Freeman (1984), stakeholders are those people who can influence or who are influenced by the operations of an organization in the achievement of its goals and objectives. Following Freeman (1984), Clarkson (1995) defines stakeholders as persons or groups that interact with organizations and further sub-divides stakeholders with matching interests into one group. Clarkson (1995) has also provided two classifications of stakeholders, namely primary and secondary stakeholders.

Stakeholder interests consist of diverse elements, and this can foster varying responses to issues and messages received from an organization. Contemporary organizations are often confronted with understanding how they should interact with and communicate to stakeholders. Stakeholder identification work enables organizations or industry sectors to identify the relevant and most important stakeholders. It establishes the inclusiveness and advocacy of a particular entity, individual or group as a stakeholder (Lee, 2015; Mitchell et al., 2017). As such, depending on the degree of control and concern for environmental issues, stakeholders can be classified according to salience, interest and other factors in terms of environmental reporting.

The value of identifying and knowing who the key stakeholders are in a certain organizational environment can lead to a more useful and timely flow of environmental information as part of environmental reporting. Furthermore, if an organization and other stakeholders communicate different messages to different stakeholder groups, then such groups can act differently towards the organization's decision-making.

When important stakeholders have been defined, understanding these unique stakeholders starts. This includes arranging activities to acquire information about what issues related to environmental reporting are of interest within specific parts of the organizational or industry constituencies (Lee, 2015). For example, today's shareholders and other stakeholders also want to know the effects that natural environments have on an organization's financial profitability and future stability. In turn, regulators might be more focused on whether organizations follow environmental law and legislation. Local communities may pay much attention to organizations' direct effects on the environment, like polluting or using up some resources. This is important to know when it comes to such disparity in the stakeholder community so that organizations can offer valuable reporting by targeting their efforts to the particular concerns of the community where it operates.

4.2 A Research Agenda and Implications for Researchers and Practitioners

In supporting the above argument, Grebe et al. (2023) posit that movement towards stakeholder engagement is useful in designing a reporting framework that will best suit the needs of stakeholders. In a study of the South African mining industry, Grebe et al. (2023) provided examples of how organizational reports are not necessarily aligned to issues that matter to individual stakeholder groups. Furthermore, these interests are organizational and industry-specific and can vary significantly (Grebe et al., 2023; Ioannou & Serafeim, 2019).

From the above, it appears that researchers and practitioners should investigate how organizations ought to better identify and ascertain what matters to their material stakeholders in environmental reporting processes. Technology presents new possibilities for improving environmental disclosures' responsibility, credibility and promptness (Eccles et al., 2015). These technologies may assist the organization in collecting and analyzing sustainability data for reporting activities to eliminate human interference, leading to more accurate reports. It could enable a shift towards creating high-level stakeholder mapping methodologies incorporating big data and Artificial Intelligence (AI) to enhance identifying and ranking stakeholders (Eccles et al., 2015). These technologies can identify new stakeholder groups or new issues that could not be identified by employing conventional organizational methods.

Since environmental issues are usually global, researchers and practitioners could use technology to explore new forms of communication that can improve interaction with multiple stakeholders across a global landscape. For example, social media is useful when it comes to engaging different stakeholders in real-time. Digital engagement can help organizations maintain steady communication with stakeholders, which can make reporting easier and responsive to dynamic environmental issues. An example of such responsiveness is looking at the state of community engagement and the engagement approaches most organizations utilize, particularly those operating in industries highly likely to have negative environmental effects in the communities in which they operate, effects that may include things like land degradation due to mining or use of large tracks of land for growing crops. Digital engagement could assess the applicability of the use of participatory methods between organizations and communities and so enhance the reporting process to incorporate the views of local communities (Grebe et al., 2023).

It could further also be possible to leverage AI and big data analytics to provide real-time environment reports to interested stakeholders. These technologies can help organizations monitor their progress on the environment more frequently and tweak the status of sustainability accordingly. At the same time, the Internet of Things (IoT) could be used to gather current environmental data from sensors installed in manufacturing facilities or any other structures as part of operations that affect the environment. Technology integration, for example, by conveying IoT into environmental reporting systems to give stable and updated statistics on crucial environmental indicators inclined to certain classes of stakeholders could be considered.

Further stakeholder engagement to ensure alignment between the organizational and stakeholder priorities include the use of double materiality assessments. Double materiality assessments, in this regard, assist organizations in determining which environmental issues are relevant to their stakeholders and ought to be reported on in environmental reports (Eccles & Serafeim, 2011; SASB, 2021). Thus, organizations can regulate environmental reporting by ensuring that the reporting focuses on issues that are relevant to the stakeholders to ensure the reports produced meet their expected use in enhancing decision-making (Bebbington et al., 2020; SASB, 2021).

The guidance given on financial materiality, as well as double materiality, by both the ASB and IASB, should be extended by researchers and practitioners. This should be done as part of the creation of models and tools that can be used to implement materiality assessments within organizational environments. These models have to incorporate both the financial and non-financial viewpoints showing organizations which way to turn to meet stakeholder expectations regarding environmental reporting (Boffo & Patalano, 2020; Eccles et al., 2014).

Consequently, research is required on how materiality assessments can be conducted based on the specific organization or industry, as environmental challenges vary with the sector. Industry sectors such as energy, mining and technology, among others, are different in their impact on the environment (SASB, 2021). Flexible materiality frameworks provide a way of ensuring that relevant sector-specific environmental issues are not overlooked or underreported.

Another important research question is whether and how the implementation of materiality as defined in IFRS S1 in environmental reporting impacts business strategy and decision-making. More research should be conducted on how organizations can leverage materiality to serve organizational and societal environmental interests, including climate change, as proposed in the European Commission Green Deal (European Commission, 2021). This is important since environmental issues could be significantly different from one country to another due to differences in laws, societal concerns and environmental conditions. A deeper understanding of the role of geographical factors on the naturality of environmental concerns and the extent to which reporting methodologies may vary across regions is justified (Clark et al., 2015).

Finally, as environmental considerations become increasingly important, there is a need for researchers and practitioners to investigate potential ways in which organizations could enhance the compatibility of their environment reporting with social and governance information to enrich stakeholders' understanding of their sustainability in terms of the environment (Ioannou & Serafeim, 2019). It could be useful for researchers and practitioners to further study how sustainability reporting standards, including GRI, SASB or IFRS, can be combined to present more extensive information on environmental issues (Deloitte, 2022).

It is, therefore, possible and important for researchers and practitioners to identify material stakeholders, get to know their concerns and then offer them organization and context-relevant information through environmental reporting. Thus, adjusting the content of environmental reports in a contextualized stakeholder-oriented way makes them more valuable and useful (Bebbington et al., 2020; Boffo & Patalano, 2020; Eccles et al., 2015; Grebe et al., 2023; Mitchell et al., 2017).

5. CONCLUSION

This chapter highlighted the need to apply a contextualized, stakeholder-oriented lens to address existing gaps in the inclusiveness of environmental reports. Information on *which* stakeholders are interested in *what* environmental issues are scarce, as existing frameworks are primarily general environmental disclosure guidance, as in the case of the Sustainability Standards. Based on IFRS S1 and S2, which suggest structured and informative environmental reporting, this chapter stresses that stakeholders and their specific interests in environmental information need to be identified and understood to improve environmental reporting. By identifying stakeholders and understanding the environmental issues that matter to each unique stakeholder group within an organizational or industry sector context, organizations can generate valuable environmental information for stakeholders.

This chapter offered an approach to explore to whom organizations should report and how to determine the extent to which organizational and stakeholder views converge. It reasons that precise recognition and understanding of stakeholders can only be done within definable organizational contexts. In other words, the chapter revealed the need for a more sophisticated approach to environmental reporting that is well-anchored in the expectations of the stakeholders as well as the goals of the organizations. Presenting a stakeholder theoretical framework appreciated by researchers and practitioners, this chapter offered a research agenda and implications for such an approach.

The approach offered in this chapter creates various practical implications as far as key stakeholders are concerned. For example, environmental information that aligns with material financial risks and rewards and is sufficient to utilize in environmental-financial metrics could enable investors and customers to facilitate informed sustainable financial decision-making and investment. Standardized and transparent environmental disclosure would provide clear signals to regulators in terms of adherence to environmental sustainability standards and compliance with legislative frameworks. This would further inform better sustainability decision-making for various key stakeholders interacting with certain organizations or industry sectors. In addition, quality environmental information and disclosures could inform the development and refinement of environmental regulations and public policies. Policymakers would benefit from detailed disclosures on industry-related practices, ensuring evidence-based policy development and implementation.

Complete and transparent environmental reporting would enable NGOs and communities to evaluate organizations' legitimacy and their social licences to operate. Context-specific information would equip NGOs and communities to monitor and advocate for better environmental practices that affect their immediate environments. Similarly, employees and supply-chain partners, such as contractors and service providers, should be provided with environmental information that is relevant to their operational environment, including mitigation and consequences. With such knowledge, these stakeholders would be able to negotiate measures that encourage accountability and involvement among internal and external organizational networks to ensure fair practices towards employees and supply chain partners.

In conclusion, this chapter sought to show that, through better identification and understanding of stakeholders and the environmental issues that matter to them, organizations can enhance environmental reporting structures and make sensible decisions for their long-term sustainability. This knowledge is particularly important at present, as many global environmental issues, including climate change, mean that organizations need to identify and report on the environmental issues for which they are responsible and which matter to stakeholders.

REFERENCES

Adams, C. A. (2017). Conceptualising the contemporary corporate value creation process. *Accounting, Auditing & Accountability Journal, 30*(4), 906–931.

Bebbington, J., Schneider, T., Stevenson, L., & Fox, A. (2020). Fossil fuel reserves and resources reporting and unburnable carbon: Investigating conflicting accounts. *Critical Perspectives on Accounting, 66*, 102083.

Boffo, R., & Patalano, R. (2020). *ESG investing: practices, progress and challenges*. Éditions OCDE.

Carbon Disclosure Project. (2023). *CDP Guidance and Standards*. https://www.cdp.net. Accessed on January 9, 2025.

Clark, G. L., Feiner, A., & Viehs, M. (2015). *From the stockholder to the stakeholder: How sustainability can drive financial outperformance*. Oxford University Press.

Clarkson, M. E. (1995). A stakeholder framework for analyzing and evaluating corporate social performance. *Academy of Management Review, 20*(1), 92–117.

Deloitte. (2022). *IFRS S1 and S2 standards: Transforming climate and sustainability reporting*. https://dart.deloitte.com/USDART/home/publications/deloitte/heads-up/2023/global-esg-disclosure-standard-coverage-issb-finalizes-ifrs-s1-s2. Accessed on October 22, 2024.

Eccles, R. G., Herron, J., & Serafeim, G. (2015). Reliable sustainability ratings: The influence of business models on information intermediaries. In T. Hebb, J. P. Hawley, A. G. Hoepner, A. L. Neher, & D. Wood (Eds.), *The Routledge handbook of responsible investment* (pp. 620–631). Routledge.

Eccles, R. G., Ioannou, I., & Serafeim, G. (2014). The impact of corporate sustainability on organizational processes and performance. *Management Science, 60*(11), 2835–2857.

Eccles, R. G., & Serafeim, G. (2011). *Accelerating the adoption of integrated reporting*. InnoVatio Publishing Ltd.

European Commission. (2021). *Corporate sustainability reporting directive*. https://finance.ec.europa.eu/regulation-and-supervision/financial-services-legislation/implementing-and-delegated-acts/corporate-sustainability-reporting-directive_en. Accessed on October 13, 2024.

Freeman, R. E. (1984). *Strategic management: A stakeholder approach*. Pitman.

Global Reporting Initiative (GRI). (2023). GRI standards. https://www.globalreporting.org. Accessed on January 9, 2025.

Grebe, L., Moloi, T., & Marx, B. (2023). A conceptual framework of corporate reputation constructs and items for the African mining sector. *African Journal of Business & Economic Research, 18*(3).

IFRS Foundation. (2023a). *IFRS S1: General requirements for disclosure of sustainability-related financial information*. https://www.ifrs.org/supporting-implementation/supporting-materials-for-ifrs-sustainability-disclosure-standards/ifrs-s1/an-in-depth-explainer-ifrs-s1/

IFRS Foundation. (2023b). *IFRS S2: Climate-related disclosures*. International Financial Reporting Standards Foundation. https://www.ifrs.org/supporting-implementation/supporting-materials-for-ifrs-sustainability-disclosure-standards/ifrs-s2/an-in-depth-explainer–ifrs-s2-climate-related-disclosures/

International Integrated Reporting Council. (2021). *The international <IR> framework*. https://www.integratedreporting.org. Accessed on January 9, 2025.

Ioannou, I., & Serafeim, G. (2019). *Corporate sustainability: A strategy?* Harvard Business School Accounting & Management Unit Working Paper (19-065). Harvard.

Lee, J. H. (2015). *Stakeholder work and value creation stakeholder engagement: An integrative framework*. Unpublished doctoral dissertation. Texas TechUniversity.

Mitchell, R., Agle, B., & Wood, D. (1997). Toward a theory of stakeholder identification and salience: Defining the principle of who and what really counts. *Academy of Management Review, 22*, 853–886.

Mitchell, R. K., Lee, J. H., & Agle, B. R. (2017). Stakeholder prioritization work: The role of stakeholder salience in stakeholder research. In *Stakeholder management* (pp. 123–157). Emerald Publishing Limited.

SASB. (2021). SASB materiality map. http://sasb.s3-website-us-east-1.amazonaws.com/. Accessed on 13 October 2024.

Task Force on Climate-related Financial Disclosures. (2022). *Task force on climate-related financial disclosures overview*. assets.bbhub.io/company/sites/60/2022/12/tcfd-2022-overview-booklet.pdf. Accessed on October 2, 2024.

CLIMATE-RELATED PERFORMANCE DISCLOSURE OF IFRS S2 EARLY ADOPTERS IN NIGERIA

Innocent Okwuosa

Pan Atlantic University, Nigeria

ABSTRACT

The study examines the quality of performance disclosures on climate related risks and opportunities of early adopters of International Financial Reporting Standards (IFRS) S2 Climate-Related Disclosures in Nigeria and the motivations for the early adoption of the standard. Data were collected from their 2023 sustainability reports and seven semi-structured interviews involving their sustainability officers, accountants and consultants. Based on the metrics and targets specified in IFRS S2, a non-weighted disclosure index was constructed and used to score the sustainability reports of the early adopters. The findings provide evidence of low-quality performance disclosures on climate-related risks and opportunities owing to the non-disclosure of certain items required by IFRS S2. Thematic analysis used in the analysis of the interview data revealed that the motivation to early adopt the standard is dominated by a desire to signal superior performance about climate-related disclosures as opposed to legitimation. Another dominant motivation is signalling this information to investors to attract capital. The study calls for support from both the standard setters and regulators so the IFRS's adoption in Nigeria succeeds.

Keywords: Disclosure; climate risks; signalling; quality; early adopters; legitimacy; sustainability; IFRS S2; opportunities

Climate Risks Reporting Practices and Assurance
Advances in Environmental Accounting & Management, Volume 13, 37–75

Published under exclusive licence by Emerald Publishing Limited
ISSN: 1479-3598/doi:10.1108/S1479-359820250000013007

1. INTRODUCTION

There has been a recent increase in global attention to climate-related disclosures as a result of climate change-related risks and opportunities (DiSalvio & Dorata, 2014; Downar et al., 2021; Friedrich et al., 2023; Tauringana & Moses, 2023). Climate-related risks and opportunities have become of much interest to academics, regulators and professional bodies (Jiang et al., 2021; Orazalin et al., 2024) as well as institutional investors (Blackrock, 2021; Ilhan et al., 2023). The growing demand for a more transparent and accurate reporting of climate-related risks and opportunities (Freedman & Jaggi, 2010) touches upon the wider call for harmonization of sustainability reporting standards (Adams & Abhayawansa, 2022; Abela, 2022) which will serve as a global baseline for climate-related disclosures. The latter has led to the emergence of International Financial Reporting Standards (IFRS) S2 which specifically deals with climate-related disclosures (Frendy et al., 2024).

Prior literature on climate-related disclosures has examined the importance or value relevance of such disclosures to institutional investors (see for example Bolton & Kacperczyk, 2021; Flammer et al., 2021; Griffin et al., 2017; Ilhan et al., 2023; Kundu & Ruenzi, 2021; Krueger et al., 2020). Although this stream of study may indirectly explain why a firm may choose to engage in voluntary climate-related disclosures, it does not directly address the quality of such disclosures under the new framework or why a firm may early adopt a climate-related disclosure framework.

Another stream of studies on the topic has examined market reaction to voluntary climate-related disclosure and the value relevance of such information (Choi & Luo, 2021; Clarkson et al., 2015; Jiang et al., 2021; Lee et al., 2015; Matsumura et al., 2014; Ziegler et al., 2011), the effect of such disclosure on cost of capital (Bui et al., 2020; Kim et al., 2015; Palea & Drogo, 2020) or the effect of such disclosure on financial performance (Gallego-Álvarez et al., 2014; Gallego-Alvarez et al., 2015). Again this stream of studies may indirectly address why a firm may choose to voluntarily disclose climate-related information, but it does not directly address the quality of such disclosures or why a firm may early adopt a climate-related disclosure framework.

Some studies have examined the quality of climate-related disclosures (Amran et al., 2014; Friedrich et al., 2023; Kouloukoui et al., 2018; Lombardi et al., 2022; Luo et al., 2023; Maji & Kalita, 2022). For example, Lombardi et al. (2022) examined Italian firms, while Kouloukoui et al. (2018) studied the world's largest 100 companies using the Global Reporting Initiative (GRI) and Carbon Disclosure Project (CDP). Luo et al. (2023) focused on the quality of the CDP scoring guidelines. Friedrich et al. (2023) examine the quality of climate reporting by European banks using the Task Force on Climate-Related Financial Disclosure (TCFD) recommendations. Maji and Kalita (2022) studied Indian energy firms also using TCFD. The majority of these studies concluded low-quality climate-related disclosures and non-disclosure of certain items.

One major shortcoming of the above studies is that where they touch upon climate-related disclosure quality, the majority of them use GRI indicators or

CDP questionnaires as a measure of quality. GRI indicators aim to satisfy stakeholders' information needs (Boiral, 2013) and the same goes for CDP questionnaires. The few studies that aim at investors have used the TCFD recommendations and not those of IFRS S2: now regarded as the global baseline for climate-related disclosure (Frendy et al., 2024). It means that we know little or nothing about the quality of disclosure of performance on climate-related risks and opportunities assessed based on the recently released IFRS S2 as countries are just beginning to adopt this standard. Similarly, while many may have indirectly addressed the motivation for disclosure of performance on climate-related risks and opportunities, they do not directly examine why a business entity may voluntarily early adopt an emerging climate-related disclosure framework when it has a choice to defer such adoption. This latter point is instructive in the context of emerging markets given their arguments about justice energy transition, responsibility, equity and the implementation of fair climate policies (Creti & Ftiti, 2024; Wang & Lo, 2021).

The introduction of IFRS S2 provides an opportunity for a uniform, comparable and high-quality disclosure of performance on climate-related risks and opportunities by listed companies across jurisdictions which will serve the needs of both institutional investors and the market. The measure of the quality of disclosure on climate-related risks and opportunities becomes more standardized and comparable since it is based on a framework considered a global baseline. There are four early adopters of IFRS S2 in Nigeria viz: Access Bank Plc, Fidelity Bank Plc, MTN Nigeria Plc and Seplat Energy Plc (Financial Reporting Council of Nigeria – FRC, 2024). Based on the foregoing, the objective of this chapter is to examine the quality of performance disclosures on climate-related risks and opportunities of early adopters of International Sustainability Standards Board's (ISSB's) IFRS S2 in Nigeria using the metrics and targets specified in the standard. As such, the research questions addressed in the paper are:

- How have early adopters of IFRS S2 in Nigeria complied with the performance disclosures on climate-related risks and opportunities and what is the quality of such disclosure?
- What are the dominant motivations to early adopt the standard by the early adopters of IFRS S2 in Nigeria?

Our measure of quality of performance disclosure on climate-related risks and opportunities is the extent to which an early adopter complies with the disclosures on metrics and targets specified in IFRS S2. We focus on the metrics and targets because they are the measure of an entity's performance on climate-related risks and opportunities. According to IFRS S2 (para 27), 'The objective of climate-related financial disclosures on metrics and targets is to enable users of general purpose financial reports to understand an entity's performance in relation to its climate-related risks and opportunities'. Focusing on the quality of disclosure in the study enables us to address the motivation to early adopt. This is because the measure of quality of disclosure achieved by an early adopter may be an indication of a motivation to signal something to the market or stakeholders. To the best of our knowledge, there is currently no study providing evidence of the quality of performance disclosure in relation to climate-related risks and opportunities using the IFRS S2 or the motivation to early adopt the standard. The only exception is Frendy et al. (2024) but this study focuses on the value relevance of climate-related disclosures for Japanese firms.

Nigeria is the first country in Africa to announce its adoption of ISSB's standards (ISSB, 2022). We argue that the announcement of the adoption of a global standard on climate-related disclosure by an emerging market is good but what is more important is the extent of actual implementation. Actual implementation determines the quality of disclosure. As such, evidence provided in this study will be of interest not only to academics and the standard setters but also to policymakers, regulators and professional accountants globally and in particular, Africa, where Nigeria now leads in the adoption and implementation of ISSB's standards.

The study adopts a qualitative research design in which data were collected from the sustainability reports of the early adopters using whole sampling and seven semi-structured interviews using snowball sampling (see Table 1 for details). Based on content analysis, we developed an unweighted disclosure index

Table 1. Details of Interviewees.

S/N	Month	Interviewee's Role	Type	Duration (min)	Code
1	October 2024	General Manager Sustainability	Group 1	38	[GMS]
2	October 2024	Sustainability Officer	Group 1	38	[SO-1]
3	October 2024	Accountant	Group 1	38	[Acct-1]
4	October 2024	Big-4 Manager, CCaSS	Individual	50	[MCaS]
5	October 2024	Big-4 Partner, Sustainability/ Assurance	Individual	37	[Big4-PS]
6	October 2024	AGM/Head of Sustainability	Group 2	107	[AGM-HoS]
7	October 2024	Sustainability Officer	Group 2	107	[SO-2]
8	October 2024	AGM, ESRM	Group 2	107	[AESRM]
9	October 2024	Manager, Sustainability	Group 2	107	[MoS]
10	October 2024	Accountant	Individual	26	[Acct-2]
11	October 2024	Investor Relations Manager	Individual	35	[IRM]
12	October 2024	Head of Risk/Sustainability	Individual	15	[HoRS]

Source(s): Author's own work.

Note: CCaSS, Climate Change and Sustainability Services; ESRM, Environmental and Social Risk Management.

using the metrics and targets specified in IFRS S2 (see Appendix 1, 2a, 2b and 2c) against which the disclosure of performance in relation to climate-related risks and opportunities was scored. Thematic analysis was employed in the analysis of the interview data.

On the first research question, the overall quality of disclosure of performance on climate-related risks and opportunities can be regarded as poor. For cross-industry metrics, one early adopter achieved a very good performance score of 76%, while the next company achieved an average performance, scoring 57%. The remaining two adopters achieved a very poor performance, scoring 23% each. For industry metrics, only one company achieved an average performance scoring 52% with the rest scoring poorly. For targets, only one company achieved a good performance, scoring 64%, with the remaining three companies performing poorly. This performance can be explained by a disposition of seeing the decision to early adopt as the beginning of a journey 'to learn the ropes', not necessarily because they availed themselves of the reliefs in the standards.

On the second research question, our analysis shows that the dominant motivation to early adopt IFRS S2 is a desire to signal superior performance on (climate-related) sustainability practices and disclosures, as industry leaders. In the words of one of the interviewees, to have *that pride of place as one of the first if not the first.* This motivation aligns with the second dominant motivation of attracting capital by providing investors and stakeholders with information to make informed decisions. Other motivations include supporting the early adoption agenda of FRC, the opportunity to learn and board dictates. One interesting finding in our study is that even poor-performing companies on sustainability practices disclosures could set out to signal superior performance because of the perception that their performance represents the industry best at that time.

The main contribution of this chapter is providing the first evidence of the quality of disclosure of performance in relation to climate-related risks and opportunities of early adopters of IFRS S2 in the first African country to adopt IFRS S2. The evidence of poor quality of disclosure of performance calls for more support on the part of ISSB and the local regulatory authority so that both the early and voluntary adoption phases will succeed. Nigeria being the first country in Africa to announce the adoption of ISSB's sustainability standards needs the greatest support as its success will mean much to the traction of the standards in Africa and globally. The study also contributes to the literature explaining the motivation to early adopt a climate-related disclosure standard, by providing evidence that even poor-performing companies could set out to signal superior performance because their performance represents the industry's best at that time.

The rest of this chapter is structured as follows: Section 2 discusses the literature showing the theoretical underpinning of the study. Section 3 outlines the research method, while Section 4 presents the findings. Finally, Section 5 is on conclusion, limitations and recommendations.

2. THEORETICAL UNDERPINNING

2.1 Voluntary Disclosure, Signalling and Legitimacy Theory

The incentives to voluntarily disclose information, hence disclosure of performance in relation to climate-related risks and opportunities may be explained within the signalling or legitimacy theory. Under signalling theory, such disclosure is aimed at addressing the problem of information asymmetry. The party possessing more information sends a signal to the other interested party with less information as a way of bridging the information gap (An et al., 2011). Such signal can be in the form of observable action, here, disclosure of performance in relation to climate-related risks and opportunities through early adoption of such disclosure framework, thereby communicating a message to the market. Akerlof (1970) conceptualizes the classic signalling model as occurring in the market setting between the seller and the buyer of goods. Here the seller is said to possess more information about the quality of the product than the buyer. The buyer who does not possess much information about the quality of the product will price it like any other product in the market (see Morris, 1987). The onus to volunteer more information on the quality of the product to distinguish it from less quality ones falls on the seller. This informs signalling in the form of voluntary disclosure to help the buyer appreciate the quality of the product thereby bridging the information gap between the seller and the buyer. Therefore, it is stated that high-quality product sellers have the incentive to signal their product quality to willing buyers to justify the higher prices of the products that are being sold. To be effective, that which constitutes the signal must be difficult to mimic by inferior quality product sellers (Clarkson et al., 2011). Voluntary disclosure may therefore be conceptualized as constituting the signal needed to communicate better quality.

Within the capital market setting, voluntary disclosure suggests that companies have incentives to disclose 'good news' to differentiate themselves from those with 'bad news' (Dye, 1985; Verrecchia, 1983). Such news is usually associated with signalling better financial and non-financial performance (Clarkson et al., 2011; Datt et al., 2018). This is motivated by the desire to avoid the adverse selection problem (Akerlof, 1970) discussed above as investors decide to invest in companies. Adverse selection arises as a result of the lemons problem (Akerlof, 1970; Healy & Palepu, 2001). Healy and Palepu (2001) suggest that the lemons problem is rooted in information asymmetry which arises because managers have more information about the true worth of a company compared to investors. Information asymmetry increases the risk perception of investors making them demand higher returns to compensate for this increased risk perception. Given this condition, managers signal to investors through voluntary disclosure of information above that mandatorily required, to reduce this information asymmetry.

While the above voluntary disclosure theory does not specifically address voluntary environmental disclosure, there have been prior studies that have examined environmental disclosures applying the theory (see, for example, Bewley & Li, 2000; Clarkson et al., 2011; Li et al., 1997). These authors suggest that companies with superior environmental performance have incentives to showcase this superior performance to the market by voluntarily disclosing more environmental information. Therefore, voluntary disclosure of performance in relation to climate-related risks and opportunities by early adopters of IFRS S2 may be explained using signalling theory. The theory will predict that early adopters have incentives to signal their superior performance about climate-related risks and opportunities to differentiate themselves from inferior-performing companies. Following Clarkson et al. (2011), we expect that early adopters' superior performance will translate to a high level of compliance with the metrics and targets specified in IFRS S2.

Legitimacy theory, on the other hand, is underpinned by an organizational desire to acquire a social licence to operate, which assumes that there is a social contract between the organization and the society at large (Lindblom, 1994; Magness, 2006), as opposed to just investors (Healy & Palepu, 2001). Corporations are therefore expected to conduct their operations within the expectations, values and norms of the society at large. Managers therefore employ voluntary climate-related disclosures to signal their conformance with societal values in order to acquire this social licence. Here, signalling through voluntary disclosure may fail to reveal objective and truthful disclosure (see Boiral, 2013). Some have argued that organizations can strategically choose what to include or omit in their voluntary sustainability disclosure as a strategy to communicate a desired message to stakeholders and society at large (Belal & Cooper, 2011; Guthrie & Abeysekera, 2006; Magness, 2006). In this situation, disclosure is deemed symbolic (Higgins et al., 2015; Michelon et al., 2015) as opposed to being factual and objective. Symbolic disclosure has been associated with legitimating strategy (Deegan, 2002; Lidblom, 1994). It offers a good explanation of why there may be decoupling (García-Sánchez et al., 2021), resulting in organizational climate-related sustainability practices being at variance with their external disclosures (Cho et al., 2015). It has been argued that the resultant outcome of symbolic voluntary disclosure is poor quality (Buhr et al., 2014; Higgins et al., 2015; Michelon et al., 2015).

Applied within the context of voluntary disclosure of performance in relation to climate-related risks and opportunities, signalling theory suggests that early adopters of IFRS S2 may have been motivated by a legitimation strategy to launder their public perception (Deegan, 2002; O'Donovan, 2002) and create an image of a better performance about climate-related risks and opportunities. They thereby deploy early adoption of IFRS S2 to mask their actual performance in this regard. In this situation, disclosure of performance about climate-related risks and opportunities by early adopters may be superficial, incomplete and fail to comply with the requirements of IFRS S2, hence low quality. The strategy is to use this to conceal poor performance and continue to create an image of a better performance. This explains why signalling to legitimate predicts poor compliance with the standard.

2.2 Literature: Climate-Related Risks Disclosure

There are many studies dealing with climate-related disclosures. One stream of such studies examines the importance or relevance of such disclosures to institutional investors (see for example Bolton & Kacperczyk, 2021; Dawkins & Fraas, 2011; Flammer et al., 2021; Griffin et al., 2017; Kundu & Ruenzi, 2021; Krueger et al., 2020). For example, Bolton and Kacperczyk (2021) examined whether investors care about climate risks as represented in carbon risk while Flammer et al. (2021) examined how shareholder activism influences or drives firms' voluntary disclosure of climate change risks. Krueger et al. (2020) and Griffin et al. (2017) are concerned with the relevance and importance of climate risks and greenhouse emissions to institutional investors, while Kundu and Ruenzi (2021)'s study is about institutional investors and carbon emission disclosure. Examining the importance or relevance of climate-risk information to institutional investors may be explained within the context of signalling and information asymmetry. These studies in one way or the other touch upon the motivation for a firm to voluntarily engage in voluntary climate-related disclosures. However, they do not focus specifically on the motivation to early adopt an emerging climate-related disclosure framework and the quality of such disclosure.

Another stream of studies has examined market reaction to voluntary climate-related disclosures (Clarkson et al., 2015; Lee et al., 2015; Matsumura et al., 2014; Ziegler et al., 2011) or the effect of such disclosure on cost of capital (Bui et al., 2020; Kim et al., 2015; Palea & Drogo, 2020) or financial performance (Gallego-Alvarez et al., 2015; García Sánchez et al., 2021). For example, Clarkson et al. (2015) show that firm valuation is not associated with carbon emission, but that greenhouse gas (GHG) emission reduction can be associated with a competitive advantage. Matsumura et al. (2014) and Lee et al. (2015) show that the market reacts negatively to disclosed carbon emissions leading to a valuation decrease but this decrease is worse for non-disclosing firms (see Chapple et al., 2013). Bui et al. (2020) find a positive association between GHG emission intensity disclosure and cost of capital while for financial performance, Gallego-Alvarez et al. (2015) show that carbon reduction is positively associated with financial performance. Maji and Kalita (2022) examine the association between climate-related disclosures and financial performance, using regression analysis. They provide evidence of a positive relationship between a firm's financial performance and climate-related financial disclosure. This suggests that better and increased climate-related financial disclosure leads to improved financial performance for a firm. Again this stream of studies does not specifically focus on the quality of disclosures and the motivation to early adopt an emerging climate-related disclosure framework.

There exists a stream of studies specifically focusing on the quality of climate-related disclosures (see Amran et al., 2014; Ben-Amar & McIlkenny, 2015; De Aguiar & Bebbington, 2014; Kouloukoui et al., 2018; Lombardi et al., 2022; Luo et al., 2023; Maji & Kalita, 2022). For example, Lombardi et al. (2022) examine the quality and quantity of climate-related disclosures by 34 large non-financial listed Italian public interest entities (PIEs) using their 2019 sustainability reports. This coincided with the period after the adoption of the European Union (EU) directive and its guidelines. Using content analysis, they identified 99 climate-related indicators based on the European Commission's guidelines against which the sustainability reports were scored for their climate-related disclosures. Their analysis provides evidence which shows that the sustainability reports failed to disclose many required climate-related information and where they do, there is no in-depth presentation of such information. They attributed the result of their findings to climate-related disclosure being at its early stage of compliance with EU directives.

Kouloukoui et al. (2018) investigate the level of climate-related disclosures of the world's largest 100 companies (as classified by the Bloomberg and Price Waterhouse Coopers, 2015) and the explanatory factors. Based on the GRI indicators and the 2015 CDP official questionnaires, they employed content analysis to construct a climate-related disclosure index which was used to score their sustainability reports. Their analysis showed that 14% of the companies did not disclose any climate-related risk information in the CDP questionnaire. Similarly, 9.9% of the GRI sustainability reporting companies failed to provide information about climate change risk mitigation strategies, policies and actions. Their overall conclusion in general is that of a low level of climate-related disclosure by these companies. Ben-Amar and McIlkenny (2015) examine the relationship between voluntary climate change disclosures and board of directors' effectiveness. The board of directors' effectiveness is measured as the quality of climate change-related risk disclosures based on the CDP questionnaire on carbon and the strategies to mitigate them. They show that there is a positive relationship between carbon disclosure quality and the board's effectiveness. It underscores the importance of the board's buy-in as an attribute that ensures the quality of climate-related risk disclosures.

Using content analysis to construct weighted and unweighted disclosure indices, Amran et al. (2014) examine the climate-related disclosures of a sample of firms in Asia Pacific's developed and emerging markets. They examine the quality and the determinants of climate change disclosures and their relationship to climate change reporting strategy. They provide evidence showing that climate change disclosure levels are low in some Asia Pacific emerging countries, suggesting how this can be improved. The study by Luo et al. (2023) examined the link between the quality of carbon disclosure and assurance. Quality of disclosure was measured using the CDP scoring guidelines based on the firm's responses to its questionnaires. They find that carbon assurance is associated with better carbon disclosure quality than where the carbon disclosure information is not assured.

Thus, majority of studies examining quality have relied on GRI metrics or CDP questionnaires both of which aim at information for stakeholders. There is a stream of study that has employed the recent TCFD recommendations focusing on investors to measure quality. For example, Maji and Kalita (2022) analyze the extent of disclosure compliance with the TCFD by Indian listed companies. They construct a disclosure index based on the four content elements required by TCFD against which the annual reports and/or sustainability reports of the companies covering the period 2018–2020 were scored. Their analysis provides evidence of a moderate level of disclosure of the requirements of TCFD by the Indian energy firms. Similarly, the studies by Demaria and Rigot (2020) and Moreno and Caminero (2022) also used TCFD recommendations to measure the quality of disclosure of climate-related risks and both reported evidence of poor quality. Demaria and Rigot (2020) specifically pointed out the low quality in the disclosure of quantified emission limitation targets over different time horizons while Moreno and Caminero (2022) identified gaps in the disclosure of targets and performance to achieve among financial institutions.

Friedrich et al. (2023) examine the quality of climate reporting by European banks during the 2017–2020 period, using the four major content elements of the TCFD recommendations. These included Governance, Strategy, Risks and Metrics and Targets. Although their analysis provides evidence of a significant increase in average climate reporting quality over the period using these measures, they identified some reporting gaps. Specifically, significant weaknesses in climate reporting quality were identified in the Strategy and Metrics and Targets categories. The analysis shows that the banks found it difficult to set targets and report their actual performance against the set targets.

Thus, existing literature that specifically focuses on the quality of climate-related disclosures has relied on either the TCFD, GRI frameworks or CDP questionnaires to measure disclosure quality with few relying on companies involved in Emission Trading Scheme (ETS). The global effort at standardizing climate-related risk saw the emergence of the ISSB framework (Abela, 2022). None of the above studies employed the new framework in their examination of climate-related disclosures. The only exception is Frendy et al. (2024) which focuses on the value relevance of disclosure of performance in relation to climate-related risks based on IFRS S2 metrics and targets for Japanese firms. The problem with this study is measuring conformance to IFRS S2 using 2014–2022 firm-year observation data to construct environmental disclosure performance, an indication of data from non-adopters. Secondly, the studies appear to concentrate on developed economies. Thirdly, they do not directly address specifically the motivation to early adopt an emerging climate-related disclosure framework. This study fills these gaps by using data from early adopters from the first country in Africa to adopt the new ISSB's sustainability framework.

2.3 Contextual Background About Nigeria and Climate-Related Risk Disclosure

With a population of about 236.7 million, Nigeria remains the most populous country and the largest African market economy as of 2023 (CIA, 2025). Its commitment to climate action is evidenced in some steps taken so far. The country has committed to net zero emissions by the year 2060 (Climate Action Tracker, 2023; Ogbonna et al., 2023). It has updated its Nationally Determined Contribution (NDC) pledging to reduce conditionally by 47%, economy-wide emissions, end gas flaring by 2030 and 2031 reduce oil and gas operation fugitive methane emission by 60% (Climate Action Tracker, 2023; IEA, 2022). The country has also signed into law the Climate Change Act and set up the National

Council for Climate Change (NCCC) to actualize the ambitious plan (Climate Action Tracker, 2023).

In the private sector, climate-related disclosure has been through voluntary sustainability reporting (Okwuosa, 2022). Sustainability reporting in Nigeria has evolved from different initiatives such as the FRC's Corporate Governance Code, which specifically requires the board to pay attention to sustainability in their board decision. Apart from this Code, the emergence of Sustainable Banking Principles (SBP) (Okwuosa, 2022) enjoined banks to consider their footprint and social and environmental risks in their lending. The Nigerian Exchange (NGX) formerly the Nigerian Stock Exchange specifically requires the eight premium board companies to publish their sustainability report (Okwuosa, 2022), although not mandatory. It can be stated that these, cumulatively provide a level of awareness in the private sector about disclosure of performance in relation to climate-related risks and opportunities. The few sustainability reports claim compliance with GRI, UN Global Compact and TCFD among others (see for example Seplat, 2024). Increased awareness about climate-related risks and opportunities arose when the President signed the Climate Change Act and established the NCCC, although most companies await directives from the NCCC.

In November 2022, at COP 27, Nigeria through the FRC announced its intention to adopt the IFRS Sustainability Standards when they were issued, thereby becoming the first country in Africa and among the few globally, to do so (ISSB, 2022). In June 2023, ahead of the release of the standard, FRC set up an Adoption Readiness Working Group (ARWG) to midwife the roadmap for the adoption and implementation of ISSB's sustainability standards. The ARWG submitted its roadmap which was launched by the ISSB Chair Emmanuel Faber in March 2024 (IFRS Foundation, 2024). Under the roadmap, early adopters are for the financial year ending on or before 31 December 2023, while voluntary adopters are for the financial year beginning 1 January 2024 to 31 December 2027 after which the mandatory period will be for the financial year beginning on or before January 2028.

Thus, a company can opt for the implementation of IFRS S1 and S2 subsequently as either a voluntary or mandatory adopter, without necessarily being an early adopter. We can therefore assume that the decision to early or voluntarily adopt must be motivated by a desire to signal something, otherwise, these adopters can wait for the mandatory period that commences in 2028. Whether it is signalling to showcase superior performance, bridge information asymmetry or to legitimate is not clear, hence this study.

Nigeria is known for poor environmental performance as a result of the operation of oil and gas companies in the Niger Delta (Denedo et al., 2017; Egbon & Mgbame, 2020) and the inability to decarbonize its cement manufacturing industry regarded as the largest in Africa (Roche, 2023). The oil and gas companies continue to flare gas giving rise to huge carbon emissions and so are the production activities of cement companies. The banks continue to finance these other high pollutant sectors giving rise to rarely reported emissions costs. Even though prior accounting studies on environmental concerns in

Nigeria have focused on environmental degradation and citizens' rights (Denedo et al., 2017; Egbon & Mgbame, 2020), not much has been done to interrogate the quality of disclosure of performance in relation to climate-related risks and its motivations. Thus, the emergence of IFRS S2 presents an opportunity to do so, hence this study.

3. METHOD

The objective of the study is to examine the quality of disclosure of performance about climate-related risks and opportunities of four early adopters of IFRS S2 in Nigeria and their motivations to early adopt IFRS S2. The study adopts a qualitative research design in which data were collected from (a) the sustainability reports of the early adopters using the whole sampling technique and (b) seven semi-structured interviews using snowball sampling (five individual and two group interviews) involving their sustainability officers, accountants and consultants details of which are as earlier shown in Table 1.

The interviews which lasted between 26 and 107 minutes were tape-recorded or zoom-recorded and later transcribed.

The study focuses on early adopters because prior studies that have examined climate-related disclosures using the Task Force on Climate-Related Financial Disclosures (TFCD) framework relied on actual adopters as opposed to intending adopters (see for example Maji & Kalita, 2022). The 2023 stand-alone sustainability reports of the four companies published in 2024 were downloaded from their website. One of them is yet to publish its sustainability report on its website but has a copy still marked first draft, and so far is the only 2023 sustainability report published and reported to FRC at the time of submitting this paper. Table 2 shows the list of the four early adopters, their sectors and their ranking among the top 50 most capitalized companies on the Exchange.

Table 2. Details of Early Adopters and the Reports Used.

S/N	Corporation	Sector	Mcap (₦billion)	NGX Top 50 Position Dec'23	Report
1	Access Bank Plc	Banking (Vol. 15)	823	14th	2023 SR
2	Fidelity Bank Plc	Banking (Vol. 15)	347	21st	2023 SR
3	MTN Plc	Telecommunication (Vol. 59)	5,543	2nd	2023 SR
4	Seplat Plc	Oil and gas (Vol. 159)	1,359	6th	2023 SR

Source: Author's own work.

Note: Mcap, Market capitalization; NGX Top 50, Top 50 most Capitalized stocks in Nigerian Exchange (NGX); SR, Sustainability Report.

Specifically, content analysis was employed to extract disclosed information from the sustainability reports. It has been suggested that qualitative research design using content analysis is suitable where researchers are interested in what is disclosed and how the information is disclosed (Beretta & Bozzolan, 2004; Boiral, 2013; Guthrie & Abeysekera, 2006; Tsalavoutas & Smith, 2010). Content analysis is common in accounting studies on voluntary disclosures of items in annual reports (see Guthrie & Abeysekera, 2006; Lombardi et al., 2022; Luo et al., 2023).

Prior studies examining disclosure quality using content analysis construct disclosure index (see for example Amran et al., 2014; De Aguiar & Bebbington, 2014; Lombardi et al., 2022), which may be weighted or unweighted index (Tsalavoutas & Smith, 2010). The disclosure index is then applied in scoring to measure the extent of compliance, hence the quality of disclosure. The major advantage attributable to the weighted index is that it attaches more importance to certain disclosures (Tsalavoutas & Smith, 2010), but the discretion in assigning weights has always been a challenge (Guthrie & Abeysekera, 2006). On the other hand, the unweighted scoring method awards 1 if an item is disclosed and 0 if not (Tsalavoutas & Smith, 2010) as it attaches equal importance to all items disclosed. Following the above, the study adopts an unweighted disclosure index as the study attaches equal importance to all the metrics and targets of IFRS S2 that are disclosed.

We identified all the metrics and targets that are expected to be disclosed by an entity adopting IFRS S2 for the first time subject to exemptions allowed by the reliefs. Incidentally, the early adopters did not avail themselves of those reliefs that would affect the number of disclosed items. For example, they did not avail themselves of the relief not to disclose scope 3 emission as they all disclosed this. Next, we then constructed an unweighted disclosure index using the metrics and targets of IFRS S2. We first identified 21 cross-industry metrics and 25 target items that all the companies are to disclose irrespective of their industry (see Appendix 1). Next, we identified the required specific industry metrics that each company ought to disclose because it operates in a specific industry. Three industries are applicable in our sample as follows: banking Vol. 16 (28 items); telecom Vol. 59 (18 items) and oil and gas Vol. 12 (51) (see Appendix 2a, 2b and 2c). The entire identified items were cross-checked with a sustainability consultant, a Big 4 Partner, a sustainability consultant and a staff of FRC to ensure they reflect the spirit of the standard. The consultant's feedback resulted in the elimination of certain items in the list leading to the final items in Appendix 1, 2a, 2b and 2c against which the scoring was done. For interpretation, we define the benchmark of quality of disclosure of performance based on scores as specified in Table 3.

On the second research question, we rely on the interview data to extract statements that reveal the motivation to early adopt. The analysis involved first transcribing the 7 interview data (comprising 12 interviewees), then reading to ensure the accuracy of transcription; re-reading to re-confirm and then extracting the first-level quotes as codes. The researcher then organized the codes making connections between them to form the themes that explain the motivations to

Table 3. The Benchmark for the Measure of Quality.

S/N	Score (%)	Quality Measure
1	<50	Poor
2	50–59	Average
3	60–69	Good
4	70–79	Very good
5	>80	Excellent

Source: Author's own work.

early adopt (Charmaz, 2006) as in a thematic analysis, noting instances of signalling and what is being signalled through what they say and how they say it. Doing this involved an iterative process moving between transcribed interview data and the emerging themes, linking them to the theoretical underpinning of the study (Gioia et al., 2013). For example, indicative phrases like 'this leadership position', 'pride of place', 'part of who we are' and 'leading and reputable brand' are the pointers to signalling superior performance and industry leadership, while phrases like 'investment decision' 'attract DFIs funding' 'access to capital' all point to investors information to unlock and attract capital. A further iteration reveals signalling superior performance in phrases like 'wanted that pride of place as one of the first', 'we want to be at the forefront' and 'leadership position that we place ourselves'. These phrases are then situated within our theoretical frame and the literature (see for example Gioia et al., 2013). The final emergent themes are discussed in the next section along with the disclosure quality.

4. FINDINGS

The findings are divided into two parts. The first part deals with the quality of disclosure of performance in relation to climate-related risks and opportunities, while the second part deals with the motivation behind the decision to early adopt IFRS S2.

4.1 Quality of Disclosure of Performance in Relation to Climate-Related Risks and Opportunities

According to IFRS S2 (para 27),

> . . .climate-related financial disclosures on metrics and targets enable users of general purpose financial reports to understand an entity's performance in relation to its climate-related risks and opportunities, including progress towards any climate-related targets it has set, and any targets it is required to meet by law or regulation.

An entity's performance is therefore measured in three dimensions using cross-industry metrics, industry metrics and then targets. Quality of disclosure is assessed by the percentage score of each company interpreted as poor, average, good, very good or excellent as defined by our quality benchmark under (1) Cross-industry metrics, (2) Industry-based metrics and (3) Targets, discussed in the next sub-sections.

4.1.1 Cross-Industry Metrics

For cross-industry metrics, the quality of disclosure as evidenced by the percentage scores of the companies is shown in Table 4.

From our defined quality benchmark, one of the early adopters did very well scoring 76% on this, while the next achieved an average performance, scoring 57%. The remaining two adopters achieved a very poor performance scoring 23% each. A further analysis shows that certain cross-industry metrics were not disclosed. For example, none of the adopters disclosed the price for each metric tonne of GHG emissions that it uses to assess the costs of its GHG emissions or disaggregated scope 1 and scope 2 carbon emissions between a consolidated accounting group and other investees. Similarly, except for one, they did not do well with disclosure of the amount and percentage of assets or business activities vulnerable to climate-related transition and physical risks as well as the percentage of executive remuneration recognized in the current period that is linked to climate-related considerations.

4.1.2 Industry-Based Metrics

Industry-based metrics are those associated with one or more particular business models, activities or other common features that characterize participation in an industry. They are therefore peculiar to that industry. The quality of disclosure as evidenced by the percentage scores of the companies is shown in Table 5.

Overall performance here is worse as none of the early adopters achieved what may be considered a good performance. All the companies scored poorly here,

Table 4. Cross-Industry Metrics.

1	Fidelity Bank	76%
2	MTN Nigeria	57%
3	Access Bank	23%
4	Seplat	23%

Source: Author's own work.

Table 5. Industry Metrics.

1	Fidelity Bank	46%
2	MTN Nigeria	44%
3	Seplat	31%
4	Access Bank	21%

Source: Author's own work.

with scores ranging between 21% and 46%. The banks struggled with clarity of disclosure around criteria used in assessing the quality of environmental, social and governance (ESG) incorporation, how they incorporate ESG factors when estimating credit losses and assessing credit worthiness of borrowers. The same goes for activity disclosures. Similarly, telecommunication struggled with disclosure around renewable electricity and energy as well as service disruptions, while disclosures around water, hydraulically fractured wells, estimated carbon dioxide emissions embedded in proved hydrocarbon reserves and the amount spent on renewable or alternative energy sources were not shown for the oil and gas sector.

4.1.3 Targets

This requires entities to disclose the quantitative and qualitative climate-related targets set to monitor progress towards achieving their strategic goals, and any targets required by law or regulation, including any GHG emissions targets. The quality of disclosure as evidenced by the percentage scores of the companies is shown in Table 6.

Here, only one of the early adopters achieved a good performance in the disclosure of targets used to measure performance and progress, scoring 64%. The remaining three performed poorly, scoring 48%, 40% and 20%, respectively. Again, some disclosures on targets were not made. For example, none of them disclosed how the latest international agreement on climate change, including how jurisdictional commitments have informed the target set, whether the target and the methodology for setting the target have been validated by a third party. Similarly, for greenhouse emission target, none of them disclosed whether and how achieving any net GHG emission target relies on the use of carbon credits; the type of carbon credit, including whether the underlying offset will be nature-based or based on technological carbon removals, which third-party scheme(s) will verify or certify the carbon credits. This lies at the core of climate-related targets and subsequent monitoring of performance, but all recorded poor performance.

In summary, the analysis provides evidence of overall poor quality of disclosure of performance in relation to climate-related risks and opportunities using the metrics and targets specified in IFRS S2. This is partly attributable to gaps or non-disclosure of certain items specifically required by IFRS S2 for cross-industry metrics, industry metrics and targets used in measuring performance. This is similar to evidence of the poor quality of climate-related disclosure

Table 6. Targets.

1	Access Bank	64%
2	Fidelity	48%
3	MTN Nigeria	40%
4	Seplat	20%

Source: Author's own work.

by prior studies that have measured the quality of disclosure using the GRI metrics or CDP questionnaire (Amran et al., 2014; Kouloukoui et al., 2018) or those based on TCFD recommendations (Demaria & Rigot, 2020; Friedrich et al., 2023; Maji & Kalita, 2022; Moreno & Caminero, 2022). For example, Friedrich et al. (2023) identified significant weaknesses in climate-related disclosures around metrics and targets. Similar to the evidence in this study, Lombardi et al. (2022) showed that Italian PIEs failed to disclose much required climate-related information. Explaining the poor quality within the context of the study's theory may suggest a legitimating strategy (Deegan, 2002) as it is generally agreed that the resultant outcome of symbolic voluntary disclosure is poor quality (Michelon et al., 2015). This explanation is further explored by examining the motivation behind early adoption by these companies and what is being signalled.

4.2 Motivation Behind Early Adoption

The analysis of our interview data provides evidence of two dominant motivations driving early adoption and three non-dominant motivations. These are discussed in the next sub-sections.

4.2.1 Signalling Superior Performance and Industry Leadership

One dominant motivation cited by all (100%) of the early adopters which influenced their decision to early adopt IFRS S2 is signalling superior performance and industry leadership in sustainability practices and by extension performance in relation to climate-related risks and opportunities. First, there is a recognition that sustainability is part of their current practice and strategy.

> ...we looked at where we were in line with our strategy, which is to embed sustainability practices in what we do, and disclosing and reporting on it ...because it is already part of who we are. **(IRM)**

Such sustainability practices include climate-related issues and for some early adopters may have been influenced by their western Development Finance Institutions (DFIs) making them take up membership in TCFD.

> So, we have been computing our climate induced emission and managing that for over 10 years and of course it is based on our relationship with the Western world, the DFIs, the stakeholders. You remember we have been a member of TCFD. **(AESRM)**

> Sustainability is at the core of our business and so we ensure we prioritize sustainability practices in all our business decisions. **(HoRS)**

> It is just who we are..., it feeds straight into our corporate objective, the core values of the corporation, we just want to be leading by example of a responsible banking, of a sustainable business and that is one of the things that stands us out.... **(MoS)**

Not only have early adopters been engaging in actual sustainability practices, but they have been engaging also in their reporting.

> ...because we have been reporting on our sustainability in terms of our practices, I think that was our 4th year. **(GMS)**

> ...we had already been reporting sustainability performance and initiatives since, and we have progressed over the years. **(IRM)**

Given the above, 100% of all the early adopters were unanimous on the motivation to signal superior performance and industry leadership in sustainability practices and by extension climate-related risks and opportunities. This is how one of the early adopters put it:

> ... as a leading and reputable brand in Nigeria, we also wanted to be at the forefront and show others how it should be done or what it could be..., we wanted that pride of place as one of the first if not the first, and we ended up being the first in the ... industry. **(GMS)**

Another early adopter put it in the following way:

> The other thing is this leadership position that we place ourselves in terms of disclosures and for our investors as well, and not just regulation-wise in Nigeria, but even in the UK, we saw an opportunity for us to actually lead the space.... **(IRM)**

Upscaling their sustainability reporting practices to international level through the early adoption of IFRS S2 then enables their report to compare with their international peers.

> ... we are trying to pitch ourselves or benchmark ourselves against other global organisations. So the standard for us represented that benchmark of comparability with other MNCs, so if you take **(our)** report and you take a Siemens report, or some European companies report, you will find some commonalities and you will be able to benchmark **(our)** performance. **(GMS)**

> ...so it is that our report will stand other international reports. That is the key element to us wanting to early adopt the standards. (SO-1)

The consultants supporting the early adopters share the same view on signalling leadership. This is how one of them puts it:

> So if you think about sectors, you have financial services, you have oil and gas and telecommunication where you have most of the early adopters coming in from, if an entity thinks of itself as occupying a strategic position, as a leader in the sector, they are trying to put their feet forward saying hey! if FRC reaches out to me, asking hey, are you going to early adopt, then for me if I consider myself a leader in that sector, then sure, I can go that way. **(MCaS)**

Explaining further, he sees this as the main motivation for early adopters.

> So I can understand why MTN can be an early adopter in the telecommunication industry, Seplat, oil and gas, and then Access within the financial services space. **(MCaS)**

Another Big4 partner sees signalling to their peers that they are ahead of the curve as one motivation to early adopt.

> I also saw something like they want to showcase their sustainability journey that already ...they are ahead of their colleagues. **(Big4-PS)**

Inherent in all these is a posture (signalling) that the standards will help to deepen their existing sustainability practices as this consultant puts it.

> One angle on motivation is leveraging leading practices that the standards present. ... They may see that the standards present them with the opportunity to deepen their sustainability practices. So whether it is on broader sustainability issues or climate-specific issues, so they take action by leveraging on the standards. For example, for a number of them, this is the first time they did a broader GHG emission assessment or the first time they took action to say we will have a climate strategy. **(MCaS)**

This view is confirmed by one of the early adopters.

> ...we saw the standard as something that will pitch us at the global scale and help us to translate our activities, our actions, our goals, and targets and bring them to the international level. **(GMS)**

Thus, it could be concluded that the main dominant motivation behind early adoption decision by these firms is to signal superior performance in actual sustainability practices about climate-related risks and opportunities enabling them to showcase industry or sectorial leadership. This supports evidence in prior studies which show that firms with superior environmental performance engage in voluntary disclosure to signal this superior performance (see for example Clarkson et al., 2011; Li et al., 1997). To showcase industry leadership in a practice is to show superior performance because a leader in an industry practice (here disclosure of performance about climate-related risk) impliedly should have superior performance when compared to peers. For example, being first in Nigerian Sustainable Banking Principles (NSBP), Equator Principles, and TCFD, are clear evidence of leadership. Being a Nigerian company that is cross-listed in the United Kingdom or South Africa and is the first to implement IFRS S2 for both Nigeria and UK operations is genuine evidence of leadership in superior performance among peers. We argue that this is evidence of a motivation to genuinely engage in superior sustainability practices that will change business behaviour and they should be supported to actualize this. This signalling of superior performance became clearer when they spoke in terms of deepening their sustainability practices and benchmarking international peers.

4.2.2 Investors Information to Unlock and Attract Capital

Another dominant motivation cited by all (100%) of the early adopters that influenced their decision to early adopt is providing investors with information to attract capital. This is pervasive among early adopters in financial institutions. First, there is an understanding that:

> On the other hand, for those that use the standard to disclose would have increased access to capital. **(AGM-HoS)**

There is therefore an understanding that investors are demanding sustainability information to make informed investment decisions.

> I guess our investors as well have started to ask us a lot. So they do send us questionnaires asking us to improve on our disclosures and for our rating agencies as well. So whenever we are issuing bonds and stuffs, the rating agencies do rate us on ESG performance, whether what we have disclosed aligns with the global standards and the way we saw it is that the ISSB standards were looking to consolidate that space. So it just makes sense to be in alignment early. **(IRM)**

> Apart from investors who are increasingly prioritizing sustainability as a major criterion for investment decisions, we believe that our stakeholders deserve information to enable them to make informed investment decisions regarding our company. **(HoRS)**

There is evidence of a natural pressure or expectation from investors that when it comes to IFRS S2, one of the early adopters must be at the forefront in its sector as this information is tied to certain streams of funding.

> . . .they (DFI's) understand the level of commitment that we have on sustainability or . . . what it is, is that they expect us to always be ahead of the sustainability curve as a sustainability top leader, the expectation is that when there is any significant global initiative, as this, naturally they expect that we should be involved, so it is a natural outcome, it is not, if you don't do S1, S2, you won't get funding from us. **(AGM-HoS)**

Even where there is no direct pressure from investors for a company to early adopt, there is evidence of these adopters positioning themselves proactively for investors. This is how one of the early adopters put it:

> But what we are doing is taking a proactive stance to be where, should any investor require it (sustainability information) from us and because we don't see our investors as only in Nigeria or only in Africa, we are getting ourselves ready to be compared with any other investment in the world. **(GMS)**

The early adopters who primarily have the motivation to attract capital through engaging in sustainability are already doing that and doing well.

> . . .we are seeing ourselves attract DFIs funding as a result of our sustainability strategy. . . . **(AESRM)**

The consultants also share the same view on attracting capital:

> But if you see that the FRC thought about the whole idea of Nigeria attracting direct foreign investment (through ISSB's standards), that is one of the key motivations for Nigeria's early adoption, I can always feel that many entities who are early adopters possibly have this at the back of their minds. **(MCaS)**

He provides more insight:

> Having worked in a bank, I understand how these things work between banks and IFC. If you know the bank and how IFC finances the private sector, many banks are positioned to access some kind of concession from them through sustainability. **(MCaS)**

What is clear from the above is that most of the early adopters have international investors that are not strictly restricted to Nigeria given cross-listing and are aware of global attention to climate-related disclosures (Bolton & Kacperczyk, 2021). As one of them put it:

> We have businesses not just across Africa, but also in the Western world and we have …investors across the world that are interested in our sustainability commitment and journey. **(AGM-HoS)**

Thus, it could be concluded that signalling sustainability information, hence disclosure on performance about climate-related risks and opportunities to investors to unlock and attract capital is one dominant motivation to early adopt. It therefore supports evidence in prior studies which suggest that investors care about climate-related disclosures (Bolton & Kacperczyk, 2021; Kundu & Ruenzi, 2021; Krueger et al., 2020). For example, Krueger et al. (2020) suggest that institutional investors care about disclosures on climate-related risks, while Bolton and Kacperczyk (2021) suggest that institutional investors care much about their exposure to carbon emission risk. Therefore, signalling of superior performance earlier discussed is directed at investors to unlock and attract capital and may be an indication of hoping to bridge information asymmetry. They show awareness that climate-related risks are of much interest to institutional investors (Blackrock, 2021; Freedman & Jaggi, 2010; Ilhan et al., 2023).

4.2.3 Other Motivations

Finally, there are other motivations cited by the early adopters which were not dominant but varied from one company to another. For example, two of the early adopters cited learning by becoming an early adopter. This is how one of them captured it:

> …the quality of what early adopters will put out there will be much, much better, improved than what others will be able to put out if they are not early adopters because this first one allows you to learn the ropes. **(AGM-HoS)**

Also, three referred to supporting FRC to achieve its objective of announcing Nigeria's early adoption of the standard. We interpret this as regulatory consciousness even though they speak in terms of support.

> One it showcases that as an organisation, we are aligned with what Nigeria is aligned with. Our origin is Nigeria, we are headquartered in Nigeria and Nigeria is an earlier adopter and so it is natural that right, we support Nigeria in being an early adopter. **(AGM-HoS)**

> We believe in collaborating with stakeholders as we journey in our strides for a more sustainable environment; hence our determination to ensure that the commitment to early adopt, made by the Financial Reporting Council (FRC) on behalf of the Federal Government of Nigeria at COP27 was actualized. **(HoRS)**

> …and so, when FRC came to say, these standards are out, we want some companies to step up and adopt. (IRM)

One early adopter referred to additional motivation arising from the promise made by their chairman of the board that the company would early adopt.

> …our chairman Dr …was actually in the room and sent a goodwill message. In that goodwill message, he conveyed … early adoption of the standards so, it wasn't whether we should early adopt or not, he made it clear that we will early adopt. **(GMS)**

So apart from the two dominant motivations, learning, regulatory pro-activeness and Board dictates were the other ancillary motivations supporting early adoption. One phrase that was echoed by many of the interviewees was 'sustainability is a journey', and by this, they mean a learning journey. Regulatory pro-activeness was de-emphasized, but we suspect this may be more pervasive than expressed.

5. CONCLUSION, LIMITATIONS AND RECOMMENDATIONS

The objective of the study is to examine the quality of the performance disclosures on climate-related risks and opportunities of early adopters of IFRS S2 using the metrics and targets specified in the standard as well as the motivation behind the decision to early adopt the standard. Previous studies on the topic have examined quality based on GRI, CDP or TCFD, and as such we do not know much about quality as defined by IFRS S2. We argue that the motivation to early adopt IFRS S2 may influence the actual implementation, hence the quality of performance disclosure and so unlike previous studies we explore the motivation behind early adoption. It employed a qualitative research design in which data were collected from the sustainability reports of the early adopters and 7 semi-structured interviews (comprising 5 individuals and 2 groups) involving 12 interviewees. The quality of performance disclosures on climate-related risks and opportunities was based on an unweighted disclosures index constructed using the metrics and targets specified in IFRS S2. Disclosed information from the sustainability reports of the companies was extracted using content analysis and scored against our self-constructed unweighted disclosure index.

Scoring the sustainability reports of the early adopters returned scores that are indicative of the quality of performance disclosures on climate-related risks and opportunities which ranged from poor to excellent performance. On the first research question, the overall score indicates poor quality of performance disclosures on climate-related risks and opportunities of the early adopters of IFRS 2. For example, on the cross-industry metrics used to measure performance, one of the early adopters achieved a very good disclosure quality scoring 76% with the next company achieving an average quality, scoring 57%, and the remaining two recording poor performance. On industry metrics, none of the companies achieved a good performance as they all scored poorly. Finally, on the targets, only one of the early adopters achieved a good quality scoring 64% with the rest scoring poorly. The poor performance can be attributable to the non-disclosure of certain cross-industry and industry metrics and targets.

On the second research question, our analysis shows that the dominant motivation to early adopt IFRS S2 is a desire to signal superior performance on (climate-related) sustainability practices and disclosure among peers, as sectorial or industry leaders. In the words of one of the interviewees, *to have that pride of place as one of the first if not the first*. This aligns with the second dominant motivation, which shows that the signalling is directed at investors. Here, climate-related sustainability disclosures are provided to attract capital. Most of the early adopters have international investors that are not strictly restricted to Nigeria whom they claim are aware of and demand such information. Other motivations include supporting the early adoption agenda of FRC, which we interpret as proactive regulatory consciousness; opportunity to learn and board dictates.

The overall quality of performance disclosure is poor whereas signalling through voluntary disclosure predicts superior performance. One thing is to desire to signal superior performance, another thing is for the firm to have the superior performance. In the absence of a firm having a superior performance to signal, it may be interpreted that early adoption was employed to signal a legitimation of an image of superior performance and industry leadership. However, one can argue that even though the quality of performance disclosure on climate-related risks and opportunities by the early adopters may be poor, that represents superior performance among peers meaning there is genuine motivation to signal superior performance among peers as opposed to legitimation. The main issue to focus on from this evidence is that early adopters care about their sustainability practices. In this lies the opportunity to leverage IFRS S2 to drive a change in business behaviour by promoting better sustainability practices. Secondly, the study provides evidence which suggests that climate-related disclosures are of importance to investors in emerging markets and are capable of unlocking and attracting capital. Herein lies a pathway that standard setters and regulators in emerging markets can focus on to engage in the arguments about just energy transition, responsibility, equity and the implementation of fair climate policies.

The main contribution of this chapter is providing the first evidence of the quality of performance disclosure on climate-related risks and opportunities of early adopters of IFRS S2 in the first African country to adopt IFRS S2. The evidence of poor quality of performance disclosure calls for more support on the part of ISSB and the local regulatory authority so that both the early and voluntary adoption phases will succeed. Nigeria being the first country in Africa to announce the adoption of ISSB's sustainability standards, needs the greatest support as its success will mean much to the traction of the standards in Africa and globally. The study also contributes to the literature explaining the motivation to early adopt a climate-related risks and opportunities disclosure standard, by providing evidence that even poor-performing companies could set out to signal superior performance because the poor performance represents the industry's best at that time.

Given the evidence in the study, it is recommended that the ISSB should prioritize capacity building and collaborate with the FRC to deepen sectoral implementation capacity. Similarly, the accounting profession through the Pan African Federation of Accountants (PAFA) and national Professional Accountancy Organisations (PAOs) in Africa and Nigeria should get on board.

The limitation of the study draws from its small sample of early adopters of IFRS S2 in a qualitative research design that focuses on the quality of performance disclosure and motivation to adopt a new climate-related risks and opportunities disclosure standard in an emerging market.

As there is evidence of a desire to signal superior performance and sectorial leadership in climate-related sustainability practices, we argue that actual superior performance is evidenced by how the adoption of IFRS S2 leads to a change in business behaviour. As such, future studies should examine how leveraging IFRS S2 to deepen current sustainability practice leads to a change in business behaviour. Similarly, there is evidence of framing climate-related disclosures as decision-useful investment information that helps to unlock and attract capital. Future studies should explore how the adoption of IFRS S2 leads to the attraction of quantifiable capital in emerging markets. Evidence of non-disclosure of certain items may be an indication of challenges of implementation of IFRS S2 not addressed by this study. Future studies can explore in-depth the challenges of the adoption of IFRS S2.

ACKNOWLEDGEMENT

This research project has been supported by the Nigerian Integrated Reporting Committee (NIRC).

REFERENCES

Abela, M. (2022). A new direction? The "mainstreaming" of sustainability reporting. *Sustainability Accounting, Management and Policy Journal*, *13*(6), 1261–1283. https://doi.org/10.1108/SAMPJ-06-2021-0201

Adams, C. A., & Abhayawansa, S. (2022). Connecting the COVID-19 pandemic, environmental, social and governance (ESG) investing and calls for 'harmonisation' of sustainability reporting. *Critical Perspectives on Accounting*, *82*. https://doi.org/10.1016/j.cpa.2021.102309

Akerlof, G. (1970). The market for 'lemons': Quality uncertainty and the market mechanism. *Quarterly Journal of Economics*, *90*, 629–650.

Amran, A., Periasamy, V., & Zulkafli, A. H. (2014). Determinants of climate change disclosure by developed and emerging countries in Asia Pacific. *Sustainable Development*, *22*(3), 188–204. https://doi.org/10.1002/sd.539

An, Y., Davey, H., & Eggleton, I. R. C. (2011). Towards a comprehensive theoretical framework for voluntary IC disclosure. *Journal of Intellectual Capital*, *12*(4), 571–585. https://doi.org/10.1108/14691931111181733

Belal, A. R., & Cooper, S. (2011). The absence of corporate social responsibility reporting in Bangladesh. *Critical Perspectives on Accounting*, *22*(7), 654–667. https://doi.org/10.1016/j.cpa.2010.06.020

Ben-Amar, W., & McIlkenny, P. (2015). Board effectiveness and the voluntary disclosure of climate change information. *Business Strategy and Environment*, *24*(8), 704–719. https://doi.org/10.1002/bse.1840

Beretta, S., & Bozzolan, S. (2004). A framework for the analysis of firm risk communication. *The International Journal of Accounting*, *39*, 265–288. https://doi.org/10.1016/j.intacc.2004.06.006

Bewley, K., & Li, Y. (2000). Disclosure of environmental information by Canadian manufacturing companies: A voluntary disclosure perspective. *Advances in Environmental Accounting & Management*, *1*, 201–226. https://doi.org/10.1016/S1479-3598(00)01011-6

Blackrock. (2021). Larry Fink's 2021 letter to CEOs. https://www.blackrock.com/corporate/investor-relations/2021-larry-fink-ceo-letter. Accessed on October 20, 2024.

Boiral, O. (2013). Sustainability reports as simulacra? A counter account of A and A? GRI reports. *Accounting, Auditing & Accountability Journal*, *26*(7), 1036–1071. https://doi.org/10.1108/AAAJ-04-2012-00998

Bolton, P., & Kacperczyk, M. (2021). Do investors care about carbon risk? *Journal of Financial Economics*, *142*(2), 517–549. https://doi.org/10.1016/j.jfineco.2021.05.008

Buhr, N., Gray, R., & Milne, M. J. (2014). Histories, rationales, voluntary standards and future prospects for sustainability reporting. In J. Unerman, B. O'Dwyer, & J. Bebbington (Eds.), *Sustainability accounting and accountability* (pp. 51–71). Routledge.

Bui, B., Moses, O., & Houqe, M. N. (2020). Carbon disclosure, emission intensity and cost of equity capital: Multi-country evidence. *Accounting and Finance*, *60*(1), 47–71. https://doi.org/10.1111/acfi.12492

Central Intelligence Agency (CIA). (2025). *The world fact book – Nigeria*. https://www.cia.gov/the-world-factbook/countries/nigeria/. Accessed on January 02, 2025

Chapple, L., Clarkson, P. M., & Gold, D. L. (2013). The cost of carbon: Capital market effects of the proposed Emission Trading Scheme (ETS). *Abacus*, *49*(1), 1–33. https://doi.org/10.1111/abac.12006

Charmaz, K. (2006). *Constructing grounded theory: A practical guide through qualitative analysis*. Sage.

Cho, C. H., Laine, M., Roberts, R. W., & Rodrigue, M. (2015). Organized hypocrite, organizational façades, and sustainability reporting. *Accounting, Organisation & Society*, *40*, 78–94. https://doi.org/10.1016/j.aos.2014.12.003

Choi, B., & Luo, L. (2021). Does the market value greenhouse gas emissions? Evidence from multi-country firm data. *British Accounting Review*, *53*(1). https://doi.org/10.1016/j.bar.2020.100909

Clarkson, P. M., Li, Y., Richardson, G. D., & Vasvari, F. P. (2011). Does it really pay to be green? Determinants and consequences of proactive environmental strategies. *Journal of Accounting and Public Policy*, *30*(2), 122–144. https://doi.org/10.1016/j.jaccpubpol.2010.09.013

Clarkson, P. M., Pinnuck, Y. L. M., & Richardson, G. D. (2015). The valuation relevance of greenhouse gas emissions under the European Union carbon emissions trading scheme. *European Accounting Review*, *24*, 551–580. https://doi.org/10.1080/09638180.2014.927782

Climate Action Tracker. (2023). *Nigeria's net zero targets*. Available at: https://climateactiontracker.org/countries/nigeria/net-zero-targets/

Creti, A., & Ftiti, Z. (2024, November). Energy, just transition, and sustainability: What's new? *Energy Economics*, *139*. https://doi.org/10.1016/j.eneco.2024.107872

Datt, R., Luo, L., Tang, Q., & Mallik, G. (2018). An international study of determinants of voluntary carbon assurance. *Journal of International Accounting Research*, *17*(3), 1–20. https://doi.org/10.2308/jiar-52221

Dawkins, C., & Fraas, J. W. (2011). Coming clean: The impact of environmental performance and visibility on corporate climate change disclosure. *Journal of Business Ethics*, *100*(2), 303–322. https://doi.org/10.1007/s10551-010-0681-0

De Aguiar, T. R. S., & Bebbington, J. (2014). Disclosure on climate change: Analyzing the UK ETS effects. *Accounting Forum*, *38*(4), 227–240. https://doi.org/10.1016/j.accfor.2014.10.002

Deegan, C. (2002). The legitimising effect of social and environmental disclosures—A theoretical foundation. *Accounting, Auditing & Accountability Journal*, *15*(3), 282–311.

Demaria, S., & Rigot, S. (2020). Corporate environmental reporting: Are French firms compliant with the task force on climate financial disclosures' recommendation? *Business Strategy and the Environment*, *30*(1), 721–738. https://doi.org/10.1002/bse.2651

Denedo, M., Thomson, I., & Yonekura, A. (2017). International advocacy NGOs, counter accounting, accountability and engagement. *Accounting, Auditing & Accountability Journal*, *30*(6), 1309–1343. https://doi.org/10.1108/AAAJ-03-2016-2468

DiSalvio, J., & Dorata, N. T. (2014). SEC guidance on climate change risk disclosures: An assessment of firm and market responses. *Advances in Environmental Accounting and Management*, *5*, 115–130. https://doi.org/10.1108/S1479-359820140000005013

Downar, B., Ernstberger, J., Reichelstein, S., Schwenen, S., & Zaklan, A. (2021). The impact of carbon disclosure mandates on emissions and financial operating performance. *Review of Accounting Studies*, *26*, 1137–1175. https://doi.org/10.1007/s11142-021-09611-x

Dye, R. A. (1985). Disclosure of non-proprietary information. *Journal of Accounting Research*, *23*(1), 123–145. https://doi.org/10.2307/2490910

Egbon, O., & Mgbame, C. O. (2020). Examining the accounts of oil spills crises in Nigeria through sense giving and defensive behaviours. *Accounting, Auditing & Accountability Journal*, *33*(8), 2053–2076. https://doi.org/10.1108/AAAJ-12-2018-3794

Flammer, C., Toffel, M. W., & Viswanathan, K. (2021). Shareholder activism and firms' voluntary disclosure of climate change risks. *Strategic Management Journal*, *42*, 1850–1879. https://doi.org/10.1002/smj.3313

FRC. (2024). *Congratulations "Our Early Adopters" – Sustainability reporting IFRS S1 and S2*. https://frcnigeria.gov.ng/wp-content/uploads/2024/08/Congratulations-on-Leading-the-Way-in-Sustainability-Reporting-in-Nigeria-Notice.pdf

Freedman, M., & Jaggi, B. (2010). Global warming and corporate disclosures: A comparative analysis of companies from the European Union, Japan and Canada. *Advances in Environmental Accounting and Management*, *4*, 129–160. https://doi.org/10.1108/S1479-3598(2010)0000004009

Frendy, Oshika, T., & Saka, C. (2024). *Value relevance and determinants of Japanese firms conformance to the IFRS S2 climate-related disclosures*. https://ssrn.com/abstract=4880164

Friedrich, T. J., Velte, P., & Wulf, I. (2023). Corporate climate reporting of European banks: Are these institutions compliant with climate issues? *Business Strategy and the Environment*, *32*(6), 2817–2834. https://doi.org/10.1002/bse.3272

Gallego-Álvarez, I., García-Sánchez, I. M., & da Silva-Vieira, C. (2014). Climate change and financial performance in times of crisis. *Business Strategy and Environment*, *23*(6), 361–374. https://doi.org/10.1002/bse.1786

Gallego-Alvarez, I., Segura, L., & Martınez-Ferrero, J. (2015). Carbon emission reduction: The impact on the financial and operational performance of international companies. *Journal of Cleaner Production*, *103*, 149–159. https://doi.org/10.1016/j.jclepro.2014.08.047

García-Sánchez, I.-M., Hussain, N., Khan, S.-A., & Martínez-Ferrero, J. (2021). Do markets punish or reward corporate social responsibility decoupling? *Business & Society*, *60*(6), 1431–1467. https://doi.org/10.1177/0007650319898839

Gioia, D. A., Corley, K. G., & Hamilton, A. L. (2013). Seeking qualitative rigor in inductive research: Notes on the Gioia methodology. *Organizational Research Methods*, *16*(1), 15–31. https://doi.org/10.1177/1094428112452151

Griffin, P. A., Lont, D. H., & Sun, E. Y. (2017). The relevance to investors of greenhouse gas emission disclosures. *Contemporary Accounting Research*, *34*(2), 1265–1297. https://doi.org/10.1111/1911-3846.12298

Guthrie, J., & Abeysekera, I. (2006). Content analysis of social, environmental reporting: What is new? *Journal of Human Resource Costing and Accounting*, *10*(2), 114–126. https://doi.org/10.1108/14013380610703120

Healy, P. M., & Palepu, K. G. (2001). Information asymmetry, corporate disclosure, and the capital markets: A review of the empirical disclosure literature. *Journal of Accounting and Economics*, *31*(1–3), 405–440. https://doi.org/10.1016/S0165-4101(01)00018-0

Higgins, C., Milne, M. J., & Van Gramberg, B. (2015). The uptake of sustainability reporting in Australia. *Journal of Business Ethics*, *129*(2), 445–468. https://doi.org/10.1007/s10551-014-2171-2

IEA. (2022). *Nationally determined contribution (NDC) to the Paris agreement: Nigeria*. https://www.iea.org/policies/11784-nationally-determined-contribution-ndc-to-the-paris-agreement-nigeria. Accessed on October 15, 2024.

IFRS Foundation. (2024). ISSB Chair meets with leaders in Kenya, Nigeria and South Africa. https://www.ifrs.org/news-and-events/news/2024/03/issb-chair-meets-with-leaders-in-kenya-nigeria-and-south-africa/

Ilhan, E., Krueger, P., Sautner, Z., & Starks, L. T. (2023). Climate risk disclosure and institutional investors. *The Review of Financial Studies*, *36*(7), 2617–2650. https://doi.org/10.1093/rfs/hhad002

ISSB. (2022). Financial Reporting Council of Nigeria to adopt IFRS sustainability disclosure standards. https://www.ifrs.org/news-and-events/news/2022/11/issb-at-cop27-frc-of-nigeria-to-adopt-ifrs-sustainability-disclosure-standards/. Accessed on December 10, 2024.

Jiang, Y., Luo, L., Xu, J., & Shao, X. (2021). The value relevance of corporate voluntary carbon disclosure: Evidence from the United States and BRIC countries. *Journal of Contemporary Accounting & Economics*, *17*(3). https://doi.org/10.1016/j.jcae.2021.100279

Kim, Y. B., An, H. T., & Kim, J. D. (2015). The effect of carbon risk on the cost of equity capital. *Journal of Cleaner Production*, *93*, 279–287. https://doi.org/10.1016/j.jclepro.2015.01.006

Kouloukoui, D., Gomes, S. M., Marinho, M. M., Torres, E. A., Kiperstok, A., & de Jong, P. (2018). Disclosure of climate risk information by the world's largest companies. *Mitigation and Adaptation Strategies for Global Change*, *23*(8), 1251–1279. https://doi.org/10.1007/s11027-018-9783-2

Krueger, P., Sautner, Z., & Starks, L. T. (2020). The importance of climate risks for institutional investors. *The Review of Financial Studies*, *33*(3), 1067–1111. https://doi.org/10.1093/rfs/hhz137

Kundu, S., & Ruenzi, S. (2021). *Institutional Investors and carbon emissions: Evidence from the US EPA's semi-scientific reporting mandate*. Working Paper. University of Mannheim. https://www.uibk.ac.at/congress/dgf2021/

Lee, S., Park, Y., & Klassen, R. D. (2015). Market responses to firms' voluntary climate change information disclosure and carbon communication. *Corporate Social Responsibility and Environmental Management*, *22*(1), 1–12. https://doi.org/10.1002/csr.1321

Li, Y., Richardson, G. D., & Thornton, D. B. (1997). Corporate disclosure of environmental liability information: Theory and evidence. *Contemporary Accounting Research*, *14*(3), 435–474. https://doi.org/10.1111/j.1911-3846.1997.tb00535.x

Lindblom, C. K. (1994). *The implications of organizational legitimacy for corporate social performance and disclosure. Paper presented at Critical Perspectives on Accounting Conference*, New York, NY.

Lombardi, R., Schimperna, F., Paoloni, P., & Galeotti, M. (2022). The climate-related information in the changing EU directive on non-financial reporting and disclosure: First evidence by Italian large companies. *Journal of Applied Accounting Research*, *23*(1), 250–273. https://doi.org/10.1108/JAAR-04-2021-0117

Luo, L., Tang, Q., Fan, H., & Ayers, J. (2023). Corporate carbon assurance and the quality of carbon disclosure. *Accounting and Finance*, *63*(1), 657–690. https://doi.org/10.1111/acfi.13060

Magness, V. (2006). Strategic posture, financial performance and environmental disclosure: An empirical test of legitimacy theory. *Accounting, Auditing and Accountability Journal*, *19*(4), 540–563. http://doi.org/10.1108/09513570610679128

Maji, S. G., & Kalita, N. (2022). Climate change financial disclosure and firm performance: Empirical evidence from Indian energy sector based on TCFD recommendations. *Society and Business Review*, *17*(4), 594–612. https://doi.org/10.1108/SBR-10-2021-0208

Matsumura, E. M., Prakash, R., & Vera-Muñoz, V. (2014). Firm-value effects of carbon emissions and carbon disclosures. *Accounting Review*, *89*(2), 695–724. https://doi.org/10.2308/accr-50629

Michelon, G., Pilonato, S., & Ricceri, F. (2015). CSR reporting practices and the quality of disclosure: An empirical analysis. *Critical Perspectives on Accounting*, *33*, 59–78. https://doi.org/10.1016/j.cpa.2014.10.003

Moreno, A. I., & Caminero, T. (2022). Application of text mining to the analysis of climate-related disclosures. *International Review of Financial Analysis*, *83*, 102307. https://doi.org/10.1016/j.irfa.2022.102307

Morris, R. D. (1987). Signalling, agency theory and accounting policy choice. *Accounting and Business Research*, *18*, 47–56. https://doi.org/10.1080/00014788.1987.9729347

O'Donovan, G. (2002). Environmental disclosures in the annual report: Extending the applicability and predictive power of legitimacy theory. *Accounting, Auditing & Accountability Journal*, *15*(3), 344–371. https://doi.org/10.1108/09513570210435870

Ogbonna, C. G., Nwachi, C. C., Okeoma, I. O., & Fagbami, O. A. (2023). Understanding Nigeria's transition pathway to carbon neutrality using the multilevel perspective. *Carbon Neutrality*, *2*(1), 1–21. https://doi.org/10.1007/s43979-023-00065-5

Okwuosa, I. I. (2022). Examining disclosure of contribution towards SDG-6 and its motivation among Nigeria's premium board companies. *Advances in Environmental Accounting & Management*, *10*, 135–157. https://doi.org/10.1108/S1479-359820220000010007

Orazalin, N. S., Ntim, C. G., & Malagila, J. K. (2024). Board sustainability committees, climate change initiatives, carbon performance, and market value. *British Journal of Management*, *35*(1), 295–320. https://doi.org/10.1111/1467-8551.12715

Palea, V., & Drogo, F. (2020). Carbon emissions and the cost of debt in the Eurozone: The role of public policies, climate-related disclosure and corporate governance. *Business Strategy and the Environment*, *29*(8), 2953–2972. https://doi.org/10.1002/bse.2550

Roche, M. Y. (2023). Built for net-zero: Analysis of long-term greenhouse gas emission pathways for the Nigerian cement sector. *Journal of Cleaner Production*, *383*. https://doi.org/10.1016/j.jclepro.2022.135446

Seplat. (2024). *Seplat energy Plc 2023 sustainability report*. https://www.seplatenergy.com/media/nqujey5g/seplat-energy_sustainability-report_2023_screen.pdf. Accessed on October 05, 2024.

Tauringana, V., & Moses, O. (2023). Greenhouse gas reporting and management in top emitting countries and companies. *Advances in Environmental Accounting and Management*, *11*, 1–9. https://doi.org/10.1108/S1479-359820230000011001

Tsalavoutas, I., & Smith, M. (2010). Comparison of two methods for measuring compliance with IFRS mandatory disclosure requirements. *Journal of Applied Accounting Research*, *11*(3), 213–228. https://doi.org/10.1108/09675421011088143

Verrecchia, R. (1983). Discretionary disclosure. *Journal of Accounting & Economics*, *5*, 179–194. https://doi.org/10.1016/0165-4101(83)90011-3

Wang, X., & Lo, K. (2021, December). Just transition: A conceptual review. *Energy Research & Social Science*, *82*. https://doi.org/10.1016/j.erss.2021.102291

Ziegler, A., Busch, T., & Hoffmann, V. H. (2011). Disclosed corporate responses to climate change and stock performance: An empirical analysis. *Energy Economics*, *33*(6), 1283–1294. https://doi.org/10.1016/j.eneco.2011.03.007

Appendix 1. Scoring – Dichotomous Scoring of Cross Industry Metrics and Targets.

	Disclosure Score	Total	Access	Fidelity	MTN	Seplat
a	*Cross Industry Metrics categories of Greenhouse gas emission*					
i	absolute gross greenhouse gas emissions generated during period expressed as metric tonnes of CO_2 equivalent	1	0	1	1	1
1	Scope 1 greenhouse gas emissions	1	0	1	1	1
2	Scope 2 greenhouse gas emissions	1	0	1	1	1
3	Scope 3 greenhouse gas emissions	1	0	1	1	1
ii	measure its greenhouse gas emissions in accordance with the Greenhouse Gas Corporate Accounting and Reporting Standard (2004) or jurisdictional requirement	1	1	1	1	1
iii	the approach it uses to measure its greenhouse gas emission					
1	the measurement approach, inputs and assumptions (I and A)	1	0	1	1	0
2	the reason why the entity has chosen the measurement approach I and A	1	0	1	1	0
3	any changes the entity made to the measurement approach (I and A)	1	0	1	0	0

Appendix 1. *(Continued)*

	Disclosure Score	Total	Access	Fidelity	MTN	Seplat
iv	for Scope 1 and Scope 2 greenhouse gas emissions disclosed, disaggregate b/w					
	the consolidated accounting group	1	0		0	0
	other investees such as associates, joint venture and unconsolidated subs	1	0		0	0
v	for Scope 2 greenhouse gas emissions; disclose its location and any contractual instruments to aid Scope 2 emission's understanding by users	1	0	1	0	0
vi	for Scope 3 greenhouse emission, disclose					
1	the categories included within the entity's measure of Scope 3 GHG emission in accordance with GHG Protocol Corporate Value Chain Standard (2011)	1	0	1	1	0
2	additional information about the entity's Category 15 GHG emission or those associated with its investments (financed emission)-(banks, asset mgt and insurance)	1	0	1	0	0
b	climate-related transition risks – the amount and percentage of assets or business activities vulnerable to climate-related transition risks	1	0	1	0	0
c	climate-related physical risks – the amount and percentage of assets or business activities vulnerable to climate-related physical risks	1	0	1	0	0
d	climate-related opportunities – the amount and percentage of assets or business activities aligned with climate-related opportunities	1	1	1	0	0
e	capital deployment – the amount of capital expenditure, financing or investment deployed towards climate-related risks and opportunities	1	1	1	1	0
f	internal carbon prices – the entity shall disclose					
i	an explanation of whether and how the entity is applying a carbon price in decision-making example, investment decision, transfer pricing, scenario analysis)	1	1	1	1	0
ii	the price for each metric tonne of greenhouse gas emissions the entity uses to assess the costs of its greenhouse gas emissions	1	0	0	0	0
g	remuneration – the entity shall disclose					
i	a description of whether and how climate-related considerations are factored into executive remuneration	1	1	0	1	0
ii	the percentage of executive management remuneration recognized in the current period that is linked to climate related considerations	1	0	0	1	0
		21	*5*	*16*	*12*	*5*

(Continued)

Appendix 1. *(Continued)*

	Disclosure Score	Total	Access	Fidelity	MTN	Seplat
Climate-related targets						
	An entity shall disclose the quantitative climate-related targets it has set to monitor progress towards achieving strategic goals	1	0	1	1	1
	An entity shall disclose the qualitative climate-related targets it has set to monitor progress towards achieving strategic goals. The entity shal disclose:					
a	the metric used to set the target	1	1	1	0	1
b	the objective of the target (for example, mitigation, adaptation or conformance				1	
	with science-based initiatives)	1	1	1	1	1
c	the part of the entity to which the target applies (for example, the enitity in its entirety or only a part of the entity)	1	1	1	0	1
d	the period over which the targets applies	1	1	1	1	1
e	the base period from which progress is measured	1	1	1	1	0
f	any milestones and interim targets	1		1	1	0
g	if the target is quantitative, whether it is an absolute target or an intensity target	1	1	1	1	0
h	how the latest international agreement on climate change, including jurisdictional commitments that arise from that agreement has informed the target	1	1	0	0	0
	information about its approach to setting and reviewing each target, and how it	1	1	0	0	0
	monitors progress against each target, including					0
a	whether the target and the methodology for setting the target has been validated by a third party	1	0	0	0	0
b	the entity's processes for reviewing the target	1	1	0	0	0
c	the metrics used to monitor progress towards reaching the target; and	1		0	1	0
d	any revisions to the target and an explanation for those revisions	1	1	0	0	0
	information about its performance against each climate-related target and an analysis of trends or changes in the entity's performance	1	0	0	0	0
	For each greenhouse gas emissions target disclosed in accordance with					
a	which greenhouse gases are covered by the target	1	1	1	1	0
b	whether Scope 1, Scope 2 or Scope 3 greenhouse gas emissions are covered by the target	1	1	1	0	0
c	whether the target is a gross greenhouse gas emissions target or net			1	1	0
	greenhouse gas emissions target. If the entity discloses a net	1	1	0	0	0
	greenhouse gas emissions target, the entity is also required to					
	separately disclose its associated gross greenhouse gas emissions target	1	1	1	0	0

Appendix 1. *(Continued)*

	Disclosure Score	Total	Access	Fidelity	MTN	Seplat
d	whether the target was derived using a sectoral decarbonization approach	1	1	0	0	0
	the entity's planned use of carbon credits to offset greenhouse gas emissions to achieve any net greenhouse gas emissions target. In explaining its planned use of carbon credits the entity shall disclose information including:	1	1	0	0	0
i	the extent to which, and how, achieving any net greenhouse gas emission target relies on the use of carbon credits	1	0	0	0	0
ii	which third-party scheme(s) will verify or certify the carbon credits	1	0	0	0	0
iii	the type of carbon credit, including whether the underlying offset will be nature-based or based on technological carbon removals, and whether the underlying offset is achieved through carbon reduction or removal, and	1	0	0	0	0
iv	any other factors necessary for users of GPFR to understand the credibility and integrity of the carbon credits the entity plans to use	1	0	0	0	0
		25	*16*	*12*	*10*	*5*

Summary of Cross Industry Metrics and Targets Dichotomous Disclosure Scoring

S/N	Cross Industry Metrics and Targets	Expect.	Actual							
			Access	%	Fidelity	%	MTN	%	Seplat	%
1	Cross industry metrics	21	5	23	16	76	12	57	5	23
2	Targets	25	16	64	12	48	10	40	5	20

Source: Author's own work.

Appendix 2a. Dichotomous Scoring Industry-Based Metrics (Banks Vol 16).

	Disclosure Items	Total	Access	Fidelity
1	its approach to the incorporation of ESG factors in credit analysis (CA)	1	0	1
2	separating between commercial and industrial lending as well as project finance	1	0	0
3	the policies that determine its approach to the incorporation of ESG factors in CA	1	0	1
4	how it incorporates ESG factors when estimating credit losses over the contractual term of the entity's financial assets	1	0	0
5	The entity shall describe its approach to implementation of the aspects of the entity's ESG incorporation practices including:	1	0	0
i	Parties responsible for the day-to-day incorporation of ESG factors	1	1	1
ii	Roles and responsibilities of employees involved	1	1	1
iii	Approach to ESG-related research	1	0	0

(Continued)

Appendix 2a. *(Continued)*

	Disclosure Items	Total	Access	Fidelity
iv	Approach to incorporating ESG factors into assessing credit worthiness of borrowers	1	0	0
6	Oversight and accountability approach to the incorporation of ESG factors including:			
i	Formal oversight individuals or bodies involved	1	1	1
ii	Roles and responsibilities of employees involved	1	1	1
iii	Criteria used in assessing the quality of ESG incorporation	1	0	0
7	whether it conducts scenario analysis or modelling in which the risk profile of future ESG trends are calculated at the portfolio level of commercial and industrial credit exp.	1	0	1
i	including climate change, natural resource constraints, human capital risks and opportunities, and cybersecurity risks	1	0	1
	ESG trends it considers apply broadly in terms of their effects on sectors and			
8	industries	1	0	0
	as well as the trends it deems as sector- or industry-specific	1	0	1
	The entity may further provide the discussion in the context of geographical			
i	Exposure of its commercial and industrial credit portfolio	1	0	0
	significant concentrations of credit exposure to ESG factors, which may include			
9	carbon-related assets, water-stressed regions and cybersecurity risks	1	0	1
10	how ESG factors are incorp. in the assessment of and influence the entity's view on			
i	Traditional macroeconomic factors such as the economic conditions, central bank monetary policy, industry trends, and geopolitical risks that affect creditworthiness of borrowers	1	0	0
	Traditional microeconomic factors such as supply and demand for products or			
ii	Services that affect financial conditions and operational results of borrowers as well as their creditworthiness	1	0	0
iii	Overall creditworthiness of a borrower	1	0	0
iv	Maturity or tenor of a loan	1	0	0
	Expected loss, including probability of default, expos. at default and loss given			
v	default	1	0	1
vi	Value of posted collateral	1	0	0
11	additional quantitative measures related to its approach to the incorporation of ESG			
	factors in credit analysis, such as			
	Number of commercial and industrial loans and project finance screened according			
i	to the equator principles (EP III) (or equivalent) by EP category			
	Number of loans for which a review of environmental or social risks was performed	1	1	1
ii	For example, by the entity's environmental and social risk management (ESMR) group	1	1	1
11	*Activity Metrics*			
i	Number and (2) value of checking and savings accounts by segment: (a) personal (b) small business	1	0	0
ii	Number and (2) value of loans by segment: (a) personal, (b) small business and (c) corporate	1	0	0
		28	*6*	*13*

Source: Author's own work.

Appendix 2b. Dichotomous Scoring Industry-Based Metrics (Telecomm Vol 59).

	Disclosure Items	Total	MTN
a	*Total energy consumed, (2) percentage grid electricity and (3) Percentage renewable* Total energy consumed, (2) percentage grid electricity and (3) percentage renewable		
1	The entity shall disclose (1) the total amount of energy it consumed as an aggregate figure, in gigajoules (GJ)	1	1
1.1	The scope of energy consumption includes energy from all sources including energy purchased from external sources and energy produced by the entity itself (self-generated), for example, direct fuel usage, purchased electricity, heating, cooling and steam energy are all included within the scope of energy consumption		
1.2	The scope of energy consumption includes only energy directly consumed by the entity during the reporting period		
1.3	In calculating energy consumption from fuels and biofuels, the entity shall use higher heating values (HHV), also known as gross calorific values GCV, which are measured directly or taken from the Intergovernmental Panel on Climate Change (IPCC)		
2	The entity shall disclose (2) the percentage of energy it consumed that was supplied from grid electricity.	1	1
2.1	The percentage shall be calculated as purchased grid electricity consumption divided by total energy consumption.		
3	The entity shall disclose (3) the percentage of energy it consumed that was renewable energy	1	1
3.1	Renewable energy is defined as energy from sources that are replenished at a rate greater than or equal to their rate of depletion, such as geothermal, wind, solar, hydro and biomass		
3.2	The percentage shall be calculated as renewable energy consumption divided by total energy consumption		
3.3	The scope of renewable energy includes renewable fuel the entity consumed, renewable energy the entity directly produced and renewable energy the entity purchased, if purchased through a renewable power purchase agreement (PPA) that explicitly includes renewable energy certificates (RECs) or Guarantees of Origin (GOs),		
	a Green-e Energy Certified utility or supplier programme, or other green power products that explicitly include RECs or GOs, or for which Green-e Energy Certified RECs are paired with grid electricity.	1	1
3.3.1	For any renewable electricity generated on site, any RECs and GOs shall be retained (not sold) and retired or cancelled on behalf of the entity for the entity to claim them as renewable energy	1	0
3.3.2	For renewable PPAs and green power products, the agreement shall explicitly include and convey that RECs and GOs be retained or replaced and retired or cancelled on behalf of the entity for the entity to claim them as renewable energy		
3.3.3	The renewable portion of the electricity grid mix outside the control or influence of the entity is excluded from the scope of renewable energy		
3.4	For the purposes of this disclosure, the scope of renewable energy from biomass sources is limited to materials certified to a third-party standard (for example, Forest Stewardship Council, Sustainable Forest Initiative, Programme for the Endorsement of Forest Certification or American Tree Farm System), materials considered eligible sources of supply according to the Green-e Framework for Renewable Energy Certification, Version 1.0 (2017) or Green-e regional standards, or materials eligible for an applicable jurisdictional renewable portfolio standard	1	0

(Continued)

Appendix 2b. *(Continued)*

	Disclosure Items	Total	MTN
4	The entity shall apply conversion factors consistently for all data reported under this disclosure, such as the use of HHVs for fuel usage (including biofuels) and conversion of kilowatt hours (kWh) to GJ (for energy data including electricity from solar or wind energy)		
5	The entity may disclose the trailing 12-month (TTM) weighted average power usage effectiveness (PUE) for its data centres	1	0
5.1	PUE is defined as the ratio of the total amount of power used by a computer data centre facility to the amount of power delivered to computing equipment		
5.2	If disclosing PUE, the entity shall follow the guidance and calculation methodology described in PUE™: A Comprehensive Examination of the Metric (2014), published by ASHRAE and The Green Grid Association		
b	*(1) System average interruption duration, (2) system average interruption frequency and (3) customer average interruption duration*		
1	The entity shall disclose its system average interruption duration in minutes	1	0
1.1	The system average interruption duration is defined as the total duration of service disruptions for the average customer during the reporting period		
1.2	A service disruption is defined as a significant degradation or interruption in the ability of a significant number of end users to establish and maintain a channel of communication in a particular service offered by the entity (voice, SMS, broadband, mobile data, etc.) because of failure or degradation in the performance of a communications provider's network.		
1.3	The entity shall calculate its system average interruption duration as the sum of the number of customers interrupted in each service disruption multiplied by the duration of each service disruption (restoration time), divided by the total number of customers served, written as Σ(ri × Ni)/NT		
2	The entity shall disclose its system average interruption frequency as a number of service disruptions per customer	1	0
2.1	The system average interruption frequency is defined as the average number of times a customer experienced a service disruption during the reporting period		
2.2	The entity shall calculate its system average interruption frequency as the total number of customers interrupted divided by the total number of customers served, written as Σ(Ni)/NT		
2.2.1	Σ = Summation function		
2.2.2	Ni = Number of customers interrupted in each service disruption		
2.2.3	NT = Average number of unique customer accounts with active service during the reporting period		
3	The entity shall disclose its customer average interruption duration in minutes	1	0
3.1	The customer average interruption duration is defined as the average amount of time required to restore service once a service disruption has occurred		
3.2	The entity shall calculate its customer average interruption duration as the sum of the number of customers interrupted in each incident multiplied by the duration of each service disruption (restoration time), divided by the total number of customers interrupted		
4	The scope of disclosure is restricted to:		
4.1	Wireline communications services		
4.2	Wireless communications services	1	0
4.3	Internet service provider (ISP) services	1	0
c	*Discussion of systems to provide unimpeded service during service disruption*		
1	The entity shall discuss business continuity risks associated with service disruptions affecting operations.	1	1

Appendix 2b. *(Continued)*

	Disclosure Items	Total	MTN
1.1	Examples of disruptions may include those caused by technical failures, programming errors, cyberattacks, weather events or natural disasters at hosting facilities		
2	The entity shall discuss how it manages business continuity risks, including an identification of critical business operations and redundancies or other measures implemented to enhance resilience of the system or to reduce impact, including insurance against loss	1	0
3	The entity may discuss the estimated amount of potential loss, probability of that loss and the associated time frame. These estimates may be based on insurance figures or other third-party or internal assessments of potential loss	1	0
	Activity		
	Number of wireless subscribers	1	1
	Number of broadband subscribers	1	1
	Network traffic	1	1
		18	8

Appendix 2c. Dichotomous Scoring Industry-Based Metrics (Oil and Gas Vol 11).

	Disclosure Items	Total	Seplat
	Gross global Scope 1 emissions, percentage methane, percentage covered under emissions-limiting regulations		
1	The entity shall disclose its gross global Scope 1 greenhouse gas (GHG) emissions to the atmosphere of the seven GHGs covered under the Kyoto Protocol – carbon dioxide (CO_2), methane (CH_4), nitrous oxide (N_2O), hydrofluorocarbons (HFCs), perfluorocarbons (PFCs), sulphur hexafluoride (SF6), and nitrogen trifluoride (NF3)	1	1
3	The entity shall disclose the percentage of gross global Scope 1 emissions from methane emissions	1	0
	the percentage of its gross global Scope 1 GHG emissions covered under an		
4	emission limiting regulation or programme intended to limit or reduce emissions directly, such as cap-and-trade schemes, carbon tax/fee systems and other emissions control (for example, command-and-control approach) and permit based mechanisms	1	0
5	The entity may discuss any change in its emissions from the previous reporting period including whether the change was because of emissions reductions, divestment, acquisition, mergers, changes in output or changes in calculation methodology	1	0
6	The entity may discuss the calculation methodology for its emissions disclosure, such as if data are from continuous emissions monitoring systems (CEMS), engineering calculations or mass balance calculations	1	0
	Amount of gross global Scope 1 emissions from: (1) flared hydrocarbons (2) other combustion, (3) process emissions, (4) other vented emissions and (5) fugitive emissions		

(Continued)

Appendix 2c. *(Continued)*

	Disclosure Items	Total	Seplat
1	Disclose the amount of direct greenhouse gas (GHG) emissions in CO_2-e from the following sources (1) flared hydrocarbons, (2) other combustion, (3) process emission, (4) other vented emissions and (5) fugitive emissions from operations	1	1
	Discussion of long- and short-term strategy or plan to manage Scope 1 emissions reduction targets, and an analysis of performance against those targets		
1	The entity shall discuss its long- and short-term strategy or plan to manage its Scope 1 greenhouse gas (GHG) emissions	1	1
2	The entity shall discuss its emission reduction target(s) and analyze its performance against the target(s), including, if relevant:	1	1
3	The entity shall discuss the activities and investments required to achieve the plans or targets, and any risks or limiting factors that might affect achievement of the plans or targets	1	1
4	The entity shall discuss the scope of its strategies, plans or reduction targets, such as whether they pertain differently to different business units, geographies or emission	1	1
4.1	Disclose categories of emissions sources to which this applies	1	1
4.1.1	Flared hydrocarbons, including all emissions emitted from flares and which are associated with the management and disposal of unrecoverable natural gas via	1	1
5	The entity shall discuss whether its strategies, plans, or reduction targets are related to, or associated with, emissions limiting or emissions reporting-based programmes or regulations (for example, the EU Emissions Trading Scheme, Quebec Cap-and-Trade System, California Cap-and-Trade Program), including regional, national, international or sectoral programmes	1	1
6	Disclosure of strategies, plans or reduction targets shall be limited to activities that were ongoing (active) or reached completion	1	1
	Total water withdrawn, (2) total water consumed; percentage of each in regions with High or Extremely High Baseline Water Stress		
1	The entity shall disclose the amount of water, in thousands of cubic metres, withdrawn from all sources	1	0
1.1	Break down the water sources: surface water (including water from wetlands, rivers, lakes and oceans), groundwater, rainwater collected directly and stored by the entity, and water and wastewater obtained from municipal water supplies, water utilities or other entities	1	0
2	The entity may disclose portions of its supply by source if, for example, significant portions of withdrawals are from non-freshwater sources	1	0
3	The entity shall disclose the amount of water, in thousands of cubic metres, consumed in its operations	1	0
4	The entity shall analyze all its operations for water risks and identify activities that withdraw and consume water in locations with High (40–80%) or Extremely High (>80%) Baseline Water Stress as classified by the World Resources Institute's (WRI) Water Risk Atlas tool, Aqueduct	1	0
5	The entity shall disclose water withdrawn in locations with High or Extremely High Baseline Water Stress as a percentage of the total water withdrawn	1	0
6	The entity shall disclose water consumed in locations with High or Extremely High Baseline Water Stress as a percentage of the total water consumed	1	0
	Volume of produced water and flowback generated; percentage (1) discharged, (2) injected, (3) recycled; hydrocarbon content in discharged water		
1	The entity shall disclose the volume, in thousands of cubic metres, of produced water and flowback fluid generated during its activities	1	0
4	The entity shall calculate the percentage of produced water and flowback fluid that was:		
4.1	Discharged directly to the environment or indirectly discharged through a third party, such as a local wastewater treatment plant	1	0

Appendix 2c. *(Continued)*

	Disclosure Items	Total	Seplat
4.2	Injected	1	1
4.3	Recycled for use in other wells, in fracturing fluids or in other drilling and production processes	1	1
5	The entity shall disclose the amount, in metric tons, of hydrocarbons water discharged to the environment	1	1
5.1	The scope of disclosure includes produced water, flowback, process water, storm water or other water discharged to the environment	1	1
	Percentage of hydraulically fractured wells for which there is public disclosure of all fracturing fluid chemicals used		
1	The entity shall disclose the percentage of hydraulically fractured wells for which there is public disclosure of all fracturing fluid chemicals used	1	0
1.2	The entity shall include in the percentage only those wells for which all fluid chemicals are publicly disclosed, including the chemicals that meet the definition of a trade secret		
	Percentage of hydraulic fracturing sites where ground or surface water quality deteriorated compared to a baseline	1	0
3	The entity shall determine whether water quality deteriorated against a baseline through monitoring of ground and surface water surrounding hydraulically fractured well sites, jurisdictional equivalent	1	0
3.2	The entity shall disclose the jurisdictional standard, guideline or regulation used for		
	for its calculation	1	0
8	The entity may disclose whether results of baseline groundwater quality tests and ongoing monitoring are communicated to applicable jurisdictional legal or regulatory authorities (where not required by local law) or residents and business owners in proximity to hydraulic fracturing sites	1	0
9	The entity shall describe its policies and practices related to its management of ground and surface water quality	1	1
	Reserves valuation and capital expenditures		
	Sensitivity of hydrocarbon reserve levels to future price projection scenarios that account for a price on carbon emissions		
1	The entity shall perform a sensitivity analysis of its reserves to determine how several future scenarios may affect the determination of whether the reserves are proved or probable	1	0
2	The entity shall analyze the sensitivity of its current proven and probable reserves using the price trajectories published by the International Energy Agency (IEA) in its World Energy Outlook (WEO) publication, including:	1	0
2.1	Current Policies Scenario, which assumes no changes in policies from the mid-point of the year of publication of the WEO		
2.2	New Policies Scenario, which assumes that broad policy commitments and plans that have been announced by countries (including national pledges to reduce greenhouse gas emissions and plans to phase out fossil-energy subsidies), occur even if the measures to implement these commitments have yet to be identified or announced. This broadly serves as the IEA baseline scenario		
3	The entity shall follow the applicable jurisdictional guidance for the following:		
3.1	Classifying reserves as proved and probable	1	0
3.2	Conducting a reserves sensitivity analysis and disclosing, in the aggregate, an estimate of reserves for each product type based on various price and cost criteria, such as a range of prices and costs that may reasonably be achieved, including standardized futures prices or management's own forecasts		

(Continued)

Appendix 2c. *(Continued)*

	Disclosure Items	Total	Seplat
3.2.1	The entity shall disclose the price and cost schedules and assumptions on which disclosed values are based	1	0
5	The entity may disclose the sensitivity of its reserve levels in other price and demand scenarios in addition to those described above, particularly if these scenarios vary depending on the type of hydrocarbon reserves, regulatory environment in the countries or regions where exploration occurs, end-use of the entity's products, or other factors	1	0
6	For additional sensitivity analyses, the entity should consider disclosing the following, per the Task Force on Climate- Related Financial Disclosures (TCFD) Recommendations Report Figure 8 as well as the Implementing the Recommendations of the TCFD Report, Section E:		
6.1	The alternative scenarios used, including other 2°C or lower scenarios	1	0
6.2	Critical input parameters, assumptions and analytical choices for the climate-related scenarios used, particularly as they relate to key areas such as policy assumptions, energy deployment pathways, technology pathways and related timing assumptions	1	0
6.3	Time frames used for scenarios, including short-, medium- and long-term milestones (for example, how organizations consider timing of potential future implications under the scenarios used)	1	0
	Estimated carbon dioxide emissions embedded in proved hydrocarbon reserves		
1	The entity shall calculate and disclose an estimate of the carbon dioxide emissions embedded in its proved hydrocarbon reserves	1	0
	Amount invested in renewable energy, revenue generated by renewable energy sales		
1	The entity shall disclose the total amount spent, including capital and research and development expenditures, on renewable or alternative energy sources	1	0
2	The entity shall disclose the sales generated from renewable energy sources		
2.1	Such disclosure generally corresponds to the renewable energy strategic development areas Section C4.5a of the CDP Climate Change Questionnaire	1	0
	Discussion of how price and demand for hydrocarbons or climate regulation influence the capital expenditure strategy for exploration, acquisition and development of assets		
1	The entity shall discuss how projections for price and demand for hydrocarbon products and the path of climate regulation influence the entity's capital expenditure (CAPEX) investment strategy	1	0
1.1	This discussion should include the entity's projections and assumptions about future hydrocarbon prices and the likelihood that various price and demand scenarios occur	1	0
2	The entity shall discuss the implications of how price and demand scenario planning (EM-EP-420a.1) may affect decisions to explore, acquire and develop new reserves	1	0
3	The entity may discuss factors that materially influence its CAPEX decision making		
3.1	How the scope of climate change regulation – such as which countries, regions or industries are likely to be affected – may influence the type of hydrocarbon on which the entity focuses its exploration and development	1	1
3.2	Its view of the alignment between the time horizon over which price and demand for hydrocarbons may be affected by climate regulation and time horizons for returns on capital expenditures on reserves	1	0
3.3	How the structure of climate regulation – a carbon tax versus cap-and trade – may differently affect price and demand, and thus the entity's capital expenditure decision-making	1	0

Appendix 2c. *(Continued)*

	Disclosure Items	Total	Seplat
4	The entity may discuss how these trends affect decision-making in the context of various types of reserve expenditures, including development of assets, acquisition of properties with proved reserves, acquisition of properties with unproved reserves, and exploration activities	1	0
4.1	The entity shall discuss capital expenditures, regardless of the accounting method it uses (full cost or successful efforts)	1	0
		52	16

Summary of Industry-Based Metrics Dichotomous Scoring Disclosure Scoring (see Appendix 2)

	Banking					Telecommunication			Oil and Gas		
	Expect.	Actual				Expect.	Actual		Expect.	Actual	
		Access	%	Fidelity	%		MTN	%		Seplat	%
Industry metrics	28	5	18	13	46	18	8	44	52	16	31

Source: Author's own work.

THE STATE OF PLAY OF CLIMATE-RELATED INFORMATION ASSURANCE IN NEW ZEALAND

Dimu Ehalaiye[a], Olayinka Moses[b] and Nives Botica Redmayne[a]

[a]*Massey University, New Zealand*
[b]*Victoria University of Wellington, New Zealand*

ABSTRACT

This study examines the state of New Zealand (NZ)'s climate-related information assurance standards setting, its effectiveness in developing appropriate assurance mechanisms for Climate Reporting Entities (CREs), and offers reflective insights into how regulatory expectations, particularly in relation to the current climate-related disclosures regime, may be successfully realized within NZ's regulatory and professional landscape. The authors found that the NZ External Reporting Board (XRB) responsible for developing the necessary assurance standards employs a strategic approach, which prioritizes broad stakeholder consultation (particularly with preparers and assurance providers though comparatively less emphasis is on users), substantial guidance and extended timelines to allow the sustainability assurance market in NZ to mature, develop consistency and build expertise. In reflecting on these issues, the authors highlighted concerns relating to the implications of timing delays and organizational readiness for standards implementation, the assurance market capability and consistency to deliver high-quality audits and associated cost implications. The authors also reflected on the need for further stakeholder engagement especially with users of assured reports to better meet stakeholders' expectations.

Keywords: Climate risks; External Reporting Board (XRB); New Zealand; sustainability assurance; Climate Reporting Entities

Climate Risks Reporting Practices and Assurance
Advances in Environmental Accounting & Management, Volume 13, 77–94

Published under exclusive licence by Emerald Publishing Limited
ISSN: 1479-3598/doi:10.1108/S1479-359820250000013010

1. INTRODUCTION

The growing sustainability reporting and regulatory advancements across jurisdictions have significantly raised the expectations of investors, regulators and other key stakeholders for reliable climate-related information that truly reflects reporting entities' performance (Ehalaiye et al., 2025; Tsang et al., 2023; Zhou, 2022). This shift has intensified the demand for climate information assurance via robust verified climate and sustainability reports, ideally produced by qualified experts, to reduce information asymmetry and mitigate the risk of greenwashing (Datt et al., 2022; Zhou, 2022).[1] Zhou (2022, p. 315) observes that recent 'global developments [are driving] demand for assurance engagements to enhance users' confidence in sustainability/ESG/non-financial reporting.' This trend reflects mounting expectations for reliable and verifiable sustainability reports that enhance accountability (Boiral, Heras-Saizarbitoria, & Brotherton, 2019; Bouten & Hoozée, 2024; Moses et al., 2024). However, despite these expectations, the assurance of climate-related information remains emerging, globally and particularly in New Zealand (NZ), where previously sustainability reporting was voluntary but now mandated for Climate Reporting Entities (CREs) (Ehalaiye et al., 2025). Since adopting the International Standards on Auditing (ISA) in 2010, NZ has aligned its auditing practices with global standards, later extending this alignment to include standards for reviews and other assurance engagements (MBIE, 2022). Yet, like many jurisdictions, NZ faces ongoing challenges in establishing suitable assurance standards for non-financial reporting, particularly for sustainability and climate-related disclosures (Datt et al., 2020).

The need for rigorous assurance standards became more pressing with the enactment of the Financial Sector (Climate-related Disclosures and Other Matters) Amendment Act 2021 (CRD Act), which introduced a new climate-related disclosures regime in NZ (CRD Act, 2021).[2] Under this Act, large financial market participants must disclose information on climate-related risks and opportunities within their annual climate statements (Ehalaiye et al., 2025; Ministry for the Environment, 2023). Considerably, the CRD Act mandates that greenhouse gas (GHG) emission data, which forms a critical part of climate-related disclosures, must be independently assured from the second year of reporting. This Act (CRD Act, 2021) amends the Financial Markets Conduct Act 2013 (FMC Act), where Section 461ZH (1) stipulates that 'Every climate reporting entity must ensure that the climate statements or the group climate statements that are required to be prepared under any of the sections 461Z to 461ZC are, to the extent that those statements are required to disclose GHG emissions, the subject of an assurance engagement.'

Additionally, Section 461ZJ of the FMC Act 2013 requires that each CRE's annual report includes a copy of the climate statement or a link to the website where it is accessible. As a result, auditors of these CREs are required to consider the climate statement as pertinent to their audit of the financial statements. If a CRE opts to use an exemption from including the climate statement in its annual report, auditors must disclose this information in their audit report, following ISA (NZ) 720, paragraph NZ22.1(b) (ii). When the assurance provider for GHG disclosures is different from the financial statement auditor, the classification of the climate statement within the annual report affects how it is treated for assurance purposes under NZ SAE 1. If the climate statement is presented separately from the annual report but linked to it, it is classified as 'other information' for GHG assurance purposes (CRD Act, 2021). This distinction plays a critical role in how GHG emissions assurance is integrated with financial and non-financial disclosures, reflecting the evolving standards and expectations around climate-related reporting and assurance in NZ.

This study seeks to critically explore NZ's journey towards establishing comprehensive assurance guidance for CREs. Our primary objective is to examine the current state of assurance practices and to offer insights into how regulatory expectations, particularly in relation to the CRD regime, may be successfully realized within NZ's regulatory and professional landscape. To achieve these objectives, our research is guided by two central research questions:

RQ1. How has New Zealand's climate reporting regime progressed towards establishing robust assurance standards, and to what extent has the regulatory process effectively developed appropriate assurance mechanisms for CREs?

RQ2. What reflective insights can New Zealand's regulatory bodies learn in their journey to developing of a comprehensive assurance mechanism for CREs?

In addressing these questions, this study aims to provide insights into the current development and implementation of assurance standards within NZ's climate reporting regime. Through this exercise, we intend to contribute meaningfully to the discourse on advancing credible assurance practices, particularly in areas where regulatory expectations align with the evolution of professional standards for non-financial disclosures. Central to our study is the recognition that the CRD Act and the incoming assurance standards anticipated to accompany it are ultimately designed to mitigate the adverse effects of climate change (Ehalaiye et al., 2025; Moses et al., 2022). The CRD Act and NZ's climate-related disclosures framework were introduced to ensure that climate change impacts are consistently integrated into business decision-making, enabling CREs to more effectively demonstrate responsibility and proactive management of climate-related risks. Additionally, this framework is intended to foster a more efficient allocation of capital, supporting NZ's broader objective of transitioning to a sustainable, low-emissions economy (Bui & De Villiers, 2017; Bui et al., 2020; Ehalaiye et al., 2025; XRB, 2022b). Our insights thus seek to support these goals, contributing to the creation of a resilient assurance framework that aligns with NZ's climate objectives.

2. CONTEXTUALIZING THE JOURNEY TOWARDS SUSTAINABILITY ASSURANCE IN NZ

2.1 How Has NZ's Climate Reporting Regime Progressed Towards Establishing Robust Assurance Standards?

The CRD Act empowered the XRB to develop NZ's climate-related disclosure framework, formalized through three Aotearoa NZ Climate Standards: Climate-related Disclosures (NZ CS 1); First-time Adoption of Aotearoa NZ Climate

Standards (NZ CS 2) and General Requirements for Climate-related Disclosures (NZ CS 3). These standards ensure alignment with international climate disclosure expectations, notably those set by the Task Force on Climate-related Financial Disclosures (TCFD) (Ehalaiye et al., 2025; Ministry for the Environment, 2021).

The *Climate-related Disclosures (NZ CS 1)* are modelled after the TCFD framework and require disclosures across four key areas: Governance, Strategy, Risk Management and Metrics and Targets (Ehalaiye et al., 2025). NZ CS 1 also outlines mandatory assurance requirements specific to GHG emissions disclosures under the Metrics and Targets section, specifying that these disclosures are subject to limited assurance for any accounting period ending on or after 27 October 2024 (XRB, 2022b). This date is linked to the passage of the CRD Act on 27 October 2021. The *First-time Adoption of Aotearoa New Zealand Climate Standards (NZ CS 2)* is conceived in consideration of diverse levels of experience and capability among CREs. Here, NZ CS 2 provides guidance for first-year adoption of climate reporting. To support a phased transition, it offers temporary exemptions in complex reporting areas, granting entities a one-year exemption for financial impacts and transition plans within the Strategy disclosure, as well as a one-year exemption for Scope 3 GHG emissions disclosure under Metrics and Targets (XRB, 2022c). These exemptions are intended to facilitate compliance, responding to concerns from entities preparing for the new reporting regime. Finally, *General Requirements for Climate-related Disclosures (NZ CS 3)* establishes both disclosure principles and general requirements for climate reporting (XRB, 2022d). Under NZ CS 3, CREs may defer compliance for 1–2 years concerning comparative information and trend analysis disclosures, recognizing the rationale for a gradual introduction to these requirements. These climate standards, as secondary legislation, apply to CREs as defined by law. NZ CS 1 specifies mandatory limited assurance over GHG emissions disclosures, establishing a baseline assurance level aimed at enhancing the trustworthiness of the reported information (XRB, 2022b).

The assurance mandate over CRDs addresses the need to build user trust and confidence in the reported information, which enhances the utility and reliability of disclosures for capital allocation decisions (XRB, 2022b). This is consistent with international research that suggests that sustainability assurance results in higher sustainability investment efficiency, reduced capital constraints and lower cost of debt (Carey et al., 2021; Steinmeier & Stich, 2019). As currently required, independent assurance applies solely to GHG emissions disclosures in climate statements. Other areas of the climate statements may be assured voluntarily; however, there are presently no prescribed standards for their assurance within NZ (XRB, 2022b). Unlike traditional audits and reviews, which primarily provide assurance over historical financial information, the assurance of CRDs involves both historical and forward-looking information (XRB, 2023a). This broader scope allows assurance engagements to address not only compliance with disclosure standards but also the processes and controls that underpin the disclosures. Accordingly, assurance engagements may offer insights into the design and operational effectiveness of an entity's climate-related controls and methodologies, extending beyond mere disclosure accuracy to encompass the reliability of the entity's underlying climate governance and risk management practices (XRB, 2023a).

There are varying levels of assurance applicable to climate-related statements, particularly for GHG emissions disclosures, and are classified as either *reasonable* or *limited* assurance (MBIE, 2022). Under the current requirements set out in NZ CS 1, GHG emissions disclosures are subject to limited assurance, i.e. review (XRB, 2022b), which entails a less extensive set of procedures by the assurance provider and a resulting opinion phrased in a negative form. This limited level of assurance requires less work than reasonable assurance (i.e. audit), which involves a more thorough examination and typically concludes with a positive opinion (XRB, 2023a). To facilitate assurance work on GHG emissions disclosures, the XRB introduced the New Zealand Standard on Assurance Engagements 1: Assurance Engagements Over GHG Emissions Disclosure (NZ SAE 1) in August 2023. This standard outlines the responsibilities of assurance providers in conducting assurance engagements over GHG emissions disclosures within climate-related statements, as required by the Financial Markets Authority (FMA) Act (XRB, 2023b). NZ SAE 1 permits assurance practitioners to follow either ISO 14064-3: 2019 GHGs (a component of the ISO 14064 suite, which addresses GHG quantification, monitoring, and reporting) or ISAE (NZ) 3410 Assurance Engagements on GHG Statements. Allowing the use of ISO 14064-3: 2019 accommodates practitioners who are already proficient with its specifications, fostering accessibility and adaptability in the assurance market. The rationale for offering compliance with both ISAE (NZ) 3410 and ISO 14064-3: 2019 is grounded in the XRB's aim to expand the market for GHG assurance services, thereby raising quality and capacity in this specialized domain (XRB, 2023b). By enabling both standards, XRB seeks to attract a broader range of skilled assurance providers, enhancing the overall quality and credibility of GHG assurance (XRB, 2023a).

In its Basis for Conclusions document on NZ SAE 1 (XRB, 2023a), the XRB explains the rationale behind this dual-standard approach as follows: 'NZ SAE 1 has been developed to allow for all competent, independent assurance practitioners to provide assurance as the GHG assurance regime begins. This is intended to build capacity in this specialised field. Allowing competent practitioners from financial and non-financial assurance backgrounds, and using two international GHG assurance standards, is intended to encourage learnings between practitioners and enhance the quality of assurance over GHG emissions.'

Perhaps, by supporting a diverse range of skilled assurance providers, the XRB aims to build a robust, competent pool of practitioners capable of delivering high-quality assurance in GHG emissions disclosures, fostering trust and credibility as the assurance field for climate-related disclosures matures. A potential counterargument could be that the options open to CREs might lead to variation and inconsistency over time due to the use of dual standards or differing levels of expertise in the assurance process. Hsiao et al. (2022) found for the voluntary sustainable assurance market in NZ that the presence of different forms of assurance and certification processes and a mixture of assurance levels for sustainable assurance, potentially contribute to an audit expectation gap. Zaman et al. (2021) examined the sustainability assurance statements published by the top 100 listed companies in Australia and NZ from 2017 to 2019 for sustainability assurance quality and noted that while sustainability reporting has risen, assurance rates remained significantly low, with accountants dominating the sustainability assurance market, and companies preferring to use their own auditors for sustainability assurance work. Farooq and de Villiers (2019) studied the competition between accounting sustainability assurance providers (ASAPs) and non-accounting sustainability assurance providers (NASAPs) in NZ and found that ASAPs prefer to use recognized professional international standards like Assurance Engagements 3000 (ISAE3000), which mirror their financial audit methodologies, thus making the case for a single reference point for financial audits and sustainability assurance. On the other hand, Farooq and de Villiers (2019) also found that NASAPs preferred the sustainability assurance standard, AA1000 Assurance Standard (AA1000AS), promoting it as a specialist standard to managers, by emphasizing the standard's sustainability enhancing qualities and its flexibility while discrediting ASAPs and ISAE3000 as out of touch with sustainability objectives. Farooq and de Villiers (2020) investigated how sustainability assurance providers' (SAPs) promotion of sustainability assurance influences the scope of engagements in NZ and its implications for professional and managerial capture. They found a tendency for managers to narrow the scope of sustainability assurance engagements, leading to client pressure (managerial capture) along with practitioners' desires to grow assurance income (professional capture) that could influence SAPs' independence and the quality of their assurance work.

The importance of having sustainable assurance reports that are credible cannot be over-emphasized (Boiral, Heras-Saizarbitoria, & Brotherton, 2019). The NZ SAE 1 does not mandate compliance with Professional and Ethical Standards (PESs): PES 1, PES 3, and PES 4.[3] However, the standard requires adherence to fundamental principles and independence requirements as specified within the standard, as well as management and reviewer requirements (XRB, 2023b). This approach acknowledges that some assurance providers may be more familiar with other ethics and quality management requirements in ISO standards rather than XRB's PES standards. The XRB considers it onerous for some GHG assurance providers to re-develop their business processes to comply with PES standards, and mandating such compliance could create barriers to entry in the assurance market, potentially excluding competent, independent practitioners in the early stages of the GHG assurance regime in NZ (XRB, 2023a).

Assurance providers accredited under ISO standards are expected to continue applying relevant ethical and quality requirements set by ISO standards and their respective accreditation programs to maintain their accreditation. This could include ISO 9001:2015, ISO 14065:2020, ISO 14066:2019, ISO 17029:2019 and ISO 19011:2018 (XRB, 2023a). The XRB has not mandated compliance with these specific ISO standards, recognizing that some specialized carbon professionals might not be part of an accredited programme or a professional body (XRB, 2023a). However, the intention is to allow experienced practitioners to perform services under a mandatory regime without being excluded (XRB, 2023a). Prior research has shown some key ethical issues involved in sustainability assurance are commercialism underlying sustainability assurance, the symbolic nature of the verification process, interdependency between auditing and consulting activities, and familiarity of the assurance provider with the audited companies (Boiral et al., 2019, 2020).

The NZ SAE 1, unlike other assurance standards, has very specific ethical requirements, independence requirements (including prohibitions) and competence requirements specified within the standard itself (XRB, 2023b). The standard also addresses the use of others, management bias, fraud, comparative information, written representations and independent assurance reports (XRB, 2023b). Interestingly, the permitted use of ISAE (NZ) 3410 and ISO 14064-3: 2019 could result in different outcomes for limited assurance on GHG assurance: under ISAE (NZ) 3410, one limited assurance report covers both future and current emissions while under ISO 14064-3:2019, two separate limited assurance reports are issued, one for current emissions and another for future emissions (XRB, 2023a).

The XRB has accompanied NZ SAE 1 with Staff Guidance and Illustrative Assurance Reports, issued in September 2023 (XRB, 2024b) to provide further explanations regarding the scope and requirements of this assurance of GHG emissions standard. NZ SAE 1 was purposefully developed by the XRB as a temporary, narrowly scoped standard addressing assurance required by legislation due to the transition period in climate-related reporting (XRB, 2023a, 2024b). For entities that voluntarily seek assurance over other parts of or their entire climate statement, ISAE (NZ) 3000 (Revised) is an existing XRB assurance standard that is perceived as helpful for voluntary assurance engagements over other parts of the climate statement (XRB, 2023a). In 2021, the XRB published the IAASB's comprehensive Guidance to Support Application ISAE 3000 (Revised) to Extended External Reporting (EER) Assurance Engagements with a navigation tool to help users find relevant chapters and illustrative examples. Furthermore, the XRB is noted as actively and closely monitoring international standards developments on sustainability reporting to further develop appropriate standards in NZ (Bradbury, 2020; Ehalaiye et al., 2020; Hay et al., 2023).

2.2 To What Extent Has the XRB's Regulatory Process Effectively Developed Appropriate Assurance Mechanisms for CREs?

Returning to the second half of our first research question on the extent to which the XRB's regulatory process has effectively developed appropriate assurance mechanisms for CREs in NZ, we draw insights from very recent developments in this space and the consolidating effort of enacting appropriate CRD assurance standards. In a recent consultation in October 2024, the XRB proposed and consulted on amendments to Climate and Assurance Standards and published a consultation document on those proposals.[4] The proposed amendments respond to CREs' challenges with obtaining reliable data for their disclosures, the high cost of reporting and the need for more comprehensive guidance on specific topics

(Ehalaiye et al., 2025; XRB, 2024a). Additionally, there have been reported difficulties in obtaining assurance over Scope 3 GHG emission disclosures due to challenges in acquiring sufficient reliable data from upstream (sourcing and production materials) and downstream (product distribution, usage and disposal) entities (XRB, 2024a). Ryan and Tiller (2022) found that the majority (51%) of a subsample of large NZ entities that had some form of voluntary GHG emission reporting do not receive assurance for their GHG emissions reports. Moreover, empirical evidence suggests that NZ local government-owned seaports made more substantial disclosures about governance and strategy compared to risk management, metrics and emission reduction targets, with a significant lack of information on GHG emission reduction targets and performance indicators, suggesting that these CREs faced challenges related to meeting climate commitments and appropriately reporting on Scope 3 emissions (Ehalaiye et al., 2025).

The amendments proposed by the XRB (XRB, 2024a) in this consultation document were to delay mandatory Scope 3 GHG emissions disclosure from one to two reporting periods (Proposal 1) and delay mandatory Scope 3 GHG emissions assurance from one to two-year periods (Proposal 2). Also, it was proposed that the availability of *Adoption Provision 2: Anticipated financial impacts in NZ CS 2* be delayed from one accounting period to two accounting periods (Proposal 3). Lastly, a proposal for an extension to the availability of *Adoption Provision 3: Transition Planning in NZ CS 2* from one accounting period to two accounting periods (Proposal 4) was stated. After the consultation round, the XRB approved three of the four proposed amendments, specifically Proposals 1, 2 and 3 to provide relief by amending NZ CS 2 and NZ SAE 1 (XRB, 2024c). Proposals 1 and 2 would lead to the assurance of the CRE's Scope 3 GHG emissions disclosures about accounting periods ending on or after 31 December 2025.[5] The rationale by XRB to offer these one-year delays is to enable the systems to mature in addressing the current challenges of obtaining sufficient reliable data supporting the GHG disclosures that are subject to assurance (XRB, 2024a). Early research evidence shows the non-maturation of GHG disclosures and its assurance in NZ. In this regard, Ryan and Tiller (2022) found that about 31% of their sample of 237 large NZ entities had some form of voluntary GHG emission reporting; however, a majority of these entities do not receive assurance for their GHG emissions. Similarly, Hsiao et al. (2022), in a study of voluntary sustainability assurance in NZ, found that approximately 20% of the 118 NZ-listed companies in 2020 that disclosed sustainability information provided a sustainability assurance report, indicating low levels of assurance compared to international practices.

Additionally, the one-year delay is also seen by the XRB as a period in which further consistency could be achieved in assurance reporting across the assurance market, anticipating that the need for emphasis of matter paragraphs or modified assurance conclusions in reports might persist for some years (XRB, 2024a). Prior research reveals that sustainability assurance is driven by a firm's need to reduce information asymmetry, inform stakeholders, commit to risk management and build a corporate reputation (Cuadrado-Ballesteros et al., 2017; Datt et al., 2022;

Fuhrmann et al., 2017; Simnett et al., 2009). Also, companies located in stakeholder-oriented countries and the use of sustainability assurance as a strategy for legitimacy have been identified as factors that increase assurance practices (Matsumura et al., 2014; Datt et al., 2018; Zhou et al., 2016). These factors seem to be present within the NZ setting, as the XRB consultation processes, overall government engagement and firms' stakeholder involvement in climate assurance issues, suggest that the stakeholders and the requirements for a developed assurance market and regime for GHG emissions are on the horizon.

3. REFLECTIONS OF NZ SUSTAINABILITY ASSURANCE JOURNEY: CONSOLIDATING THE KNOWNS AND UNKNOWNS

NZ's approach to sustainability assurance undoubtedly reflects its commitment to enhancing transparency, accountability and credibility in sustainability reporting. Developing a framework that aligns with international best practices while incorporating local context to address the unique climate-related risks faced by NZ appears to be a driving motivation in this journey (Ehalaiye et al., 2025). The XRB is also perceived to be committed to ensuring that a credible and reliable sustainability assurance mechanism is available to stakeholders in NZ in the near future. However, the primary challenge lies not in the intent but in the availability of resources, capacity and the timeliness of achieving this ambition.

While the journey towards a mature assurance regime is commendable, the challenges inherent in an incomplete and inconsistent assurance reporting framework for climate-risk disclosures remain a significant concern. As discussed, prior empirical evidence shows substantial variability in sustainability assurance mechanisms in the absence of strong commonalities. This variability creates opportunities for opacity in auditing procedures, including vagueness in audit methods, scope and materiality (Farooq & de Villiers, 2020; Hickman & Cote, 2019; Michelon et al., 2015; Michelon et al., 2019). This often results in audits that lack depth and quality. It is not difficult to foresee the consequences of poor sustainability assurance regulatory practices, especially given prior knowledge of audit practices and procedures. Uncertainties about the quality of verified data in reports are reflected in the prevalence of audit results that offer only limited levels of assurance. These results frequently fall short of stakeholders' expectations, particularly in relation to climate-risk assurance (Boiral, Heras-Saizarbitoria, Brotherton, et al., 2019; Gürtürk & Hahn, 2016; Mock et al., 2013). That said, in the case of NZ, how these issues evolve may be more a matter of time than an immediate concern.

In reflecting on the state of sustainability assurance in NZ, our overarching goal is to advance thinking considering prevailing circumstances that could offer practical pathways towards meeting the required sustainability standards. Our reflections are structured under three broad themes: (i) implications of timing and organizational readiness, (ii) assurance market capability and consistency and (iii) stakeholders' expectations.

3.1 Timing Implication: 'Kicking the Can Down the Road'?

> The optional delay in assurance of scope 3 GHG emissions disclosures by one year recognises current data challenges. During the consultation, we heard that systems are rapidly improving, with improvements from data providers expected within the year. (XRB, 2024a)[6]

We begin our reflections on the implications of timing thereby interrogating more deeply whether the XRB has merely 'kicked the can down the road'. A critical concern with the current delay in assurance is its potential impact on the quality of climate-related disclosures. Prior research findings on NZ readiness for climate-related disclosures (Ehalaiye et al., 2025) show that organizations disclose more comprehensive information about their carbon emissions and climate mitigation strategies, if they are motivated by external assurance requirements of their sustainability outcomes (Dutta & Dutta, 2021). This is likely because external assurance provides stakeholders with increased confidence in the accuracy and reliability of the reported information, thereby reducing concerns about greenwashing.

One certainty is that companies are most likely to comply with climate reporting obligations when guided by robust reporting guardrails. As Dutta and Dutta (2021, p. 257) note, 'the outcomes of the studies examining the impact of external assurance on the disclosure of nonfinancial information have converged, confirming that external assurance positively affects the level of nonfinancial disclosure.' Therefore, while the additional time before full assurance requirements take effect may allow for further maturation in climate-related reporting, it risks undermining prior gains in climate reporting compliance. Delaying implementation could result in a loss of momentum and diminishing levels of reporting quality, with the unintended consequence of *kicking the can down the road.*

We acknowledge the current difficulties faced by organizations in establishing the necessary reporting infrastructure to ensure assurance over Scope 3 GHG emissions, given the expressed challenges in acquiring reliable data (Ehalaiye et al., 2025; XRB, 2024a). These challenges are evident in the findings of Ehalaiye et al. (2025) regarding the readiness of NZ seaports for climate-related reporting. Their study reveals very low levels of alignment with TCFD guidelines in the 'Metrics and Targets' segment, with alignment levels as low as 15%. As suggested by Ehalaiye et al. (2025), this low alignment likely stems from the relatively new nature of these reporting requirements, with entities still in the early stages of understanding how to collect and report this specialized type of information (p. 12). Be that as it may, there seems to be a clear sense of willingness from reporting entities to continue in their journey of improving on their climate reporting practices in compliance with regulatory guidelines.

An alternative perspective might argue that accounting and reporting entities improve their performance with practice over time. However, we suggest that allowing additional time may not necessarily lead to the development of the required skills in advance. Instead, it may naturally risk merely deferring the problem and delaying necessary progress. Reporting entities tend to take up new challenges calculatedly, even when it involves concessions such as complying with regulations to maintain legitimacy or avoid sanctions. In the absence of clear requirements, however, there is little incentive for organizations to prioritize the necessary investment in climate-related reporting, potentially encouraging behaviour contrary to long-term corporate responsibility. Indeed, as highlighted in the findings of Ehalaiye et al. (2025), entities expressed readiness to make the necessary trade-offs to facilitate comparable climate-related reporting practices across their sector so long as their regulators demand for it. Our reflective summation here is that while the delay in implementing full assurance may offer short-term breathing space for organizations to adapt, it also poses the risk of eroding existing progress in climate reporting and delaying the development of the critical infrastructure and capabilities needed for robust climate-related disclosures.

3.2 The Assurance Market Capability and Consistency

Although preparers remain a critical consideration for the XRB in its decision to extend assurance requirements, this approach appears sensible and practical for assurance providers as well – many of whom are still grappling with assurance procedures for reporting entities that have made progress and have access to Scope 3 emissions data. However, providing reliable evidence to substantiate such information remains a significant challenge. A practical case to consider is how assurance providers can accurately validate disclosures from entities that are unable to collect their Scope 3 data due to complexities in their value chains and instead source this information from third-party data providers. What guarantees can these data providers offer regarding the accuracy of their data? How will assurers validate the adequacy of controls, audit trails and documentation across such complex reporting structures? These are genuine concerns, and it is understandable why the XRB has taken a cautious approach here.

That said, assurance providers eager to operate in this space are expected to have significantly invested in upskilling their professional expertise. Studies have criticized auditors for their 'catch-up approach' which results in inadequate education and the tendency to transpose known (old) traditional accounting procedures onto emerging (new) sustainability assurance ecosystem (Boiral et al., 2020; Krasodomska et al., 2021; Martínez-Ferrero et al., 2018; Ruiz-Barbadillo & Martínez-Ferrero, 2022). This lack of expertise in a continuing and emerging space as climate disclosure opens the door for discrepancies in sustainability assurance quality and scope (Larrinaga et al., 2020; Perego, 2009). While preparation is needed across the board, assurance providers should be expected to demonstrate leadership and innovation in this field. It is less a question of a lack of innovativeness among assurance providers and more an issue of systemic challenges. The additional time provided by the XRB's extension may give assurance providers and reporting entities alike an opportunity to refine their approaches.

Some entities, despite the XRB's extension, may choose to proceed with seeking assurance for their climate-related disclosures. However, the cost implications of such efforts cannot be ignored. Given the scarcity of talent and expertise, the cost of both obtaining and assuring high-quality GHG emissions information is significant, particularly at this early stage. This could create incentives for corporate opportunism. Prior research has highlighted managerial capture of assurance processes, business pressures inherent in the assurance market and potential auditor conflicts of interest (Farooq & de Villiers, 2020; Michelon et al., 2019; Smith et al., 2011). These factors can lead to assurance practices that prioritize corporate interests over stakeholder needs (Boiral, Heras-Saizarbitoria, Brotherton, et al., 2019; Jamali, 2010; Perego & Kolk, 2012).

Our position is that entities moving early to adopt assurance may serve as exemplars for others, but this space warrants careful monitoring by the XRB. We advocate for the XRB to examine the practical issues in this field during the interim period to ensure that, when full assurance requirements are implemented, all entities are on an equal footing. Specific focus points might include:

- The effectiveness of external assurance in preventing greenwashing, especially among CREs seeking assurance.
- The vagueness surrounding verification practices and the quality of expertise available for assurance in this specialized and complex field.
- The costs of the assurance process, particularly for smaller entities.
- The reliability of data used for assurance, especially when sourced from third-party providers.

These challenges stemming from an immature and inconsistent climate-risk assurance regime pose significant risks that the XRB must address with vigilance. By doing so, the XRB can foster a robust assurance ecosystem that balances the needs of stakeholders, preparers, and assurance providers.

3.3 Stakeholders' Expectations

Sustainability assurance practices must align more closely with stakeholder expectations as investors, regulators and broader societal stakeholders increasingly demand comprehensive, transparent reporting on climate risks (Bui et al., 2020; Ehalaiye et al., 2025; Moses et al., 2024). Assurance providers need to address these demands by delivering reports that not only validate the reliability of disclosed data but also provide insights into the robustness of organizations' sustainability strategies. Achieving this alignment requires clear communication, active stakeholder engagement and a commitment to continuous improvement in assurance practices – an area where the XRB has demonstrated foresight. However, the current trajectory of compliance timelines and upcoming assurance requirements seems to have marginalized users' interests.

To date, the need for sustainability assurance has primarily been framed within a regulator-preparer dynamic, overlooking the core intent of assurance: to meet the needs of users. Unfortunately, limited insight can be drawn from publicly available information regarding the extent to which user needs have been prioritized in the XRB's processes. While the assurance of Scope 3 emissions has garnered much attention, the completeness of Scopes 1 and 2 disclosures and users' broader expectations for sustainability information remain underexplored. In our view, discussions around assurance must be broadened beyond current priorities to foster robust accountability across the sustainability reporting ecosystem (Moses et al., 2024).

The complexity of balancing accountability and transparency can exacerbate information asymmetry over time. As Hsiao et al. (2022) note, the gap between user expectations and actual reporting widens when inconsistent assurance frameworks and mixed levels of assurance for sustainability reporting are adopted. Such gaps undermine trust and dilute the intended purpose of assurance, leaving stakeholders with insufficient clarity and confidence in the information presented. Moreover, frequent changes within the assurance landscape risk creating more uncertainty than clarity for users, who may struggle to understand what they can reliably expect from sustainability disclosures. Here, the XRB is expected to take a proactive role in providing users with adequate feedback, ensuring their concerns and expectations are integrated into assurance frameworks.

Addressing organizational readiness, market capability and stakeholder alignment is crucial but only to the extent that it serves the primary goal of aiding users' decision-making processes. We expect that the XRB will adopt a proactive, collaborative approach, actively engaging users in the development and refinement of assurance guidelines and their ensuing processes. Without such engagement, the resulting assurance mechanisms risk falling short of stakeholder expectations and undermining their potential to meaningfully contribute to NZ's broader climate-related and sustainability outcomes.

4. CONCLUDING REMARKS: NZ'S JOURNEY TOWARDS CLIMATE-RISK ASSURANCE STANDARDS

The question of how NZ's journey towards climate-risk assurance standards has unfolded yields different perspectives depending on whom it is posed to. Our assessment of the process is intentionally reflective rather than conclusive, acknowledging the complexity of this evolving space. One evident aspect is the XRB's strategic approach, which prioritizes broad stakeholder consultation (though with comparatively less emphasis on users), substantial guidance and extended timelines to allow the sustainability assurance market in NZ to mature, develop consistency and build expertise. While the rationale behind this approach is evident, whether it proves to be a winning strategy remains an open question. On the one hand, the XRB's incremental advocacy for a capacity-building approach aligns with the market's current readiness, reflecting the necessity for gradual adaptation (Ehalaiye et al., 2025). On the other hand, critics may view this as a missed opportunity or an unnecessary delay in establishing robust assurance mechanisms. Striking a balance between preparedness and urgency is critical, as delays could risk stalling progress in aligning sustainability disclosures with stakeholder expectations.

Looking ahead, the XRB has outlined two key focus areas for staff guidance publications in 2025 concerning climate statement assurance: *Guidance for Users and Preparers*: This initiative aims to help stakeholders interpret assurance reports, focusing on the scope, level and outcomes of GHG assurance engagements. While NZ SAE 1 includes tools for enhancing communication in assurance reports, the planned guidance will highlight essential elements for users to understand, ensuring greater clarity and accessibility of information (XRB, 2024a). *Guidance on Scope 3 GHG Emissions*: This guidance is tailored to assist CREs and assurance practitioners in navigating the complexities of preparing and assuring Scope 3 GHG emissions disclosures. Given the inherent challenges in collecting reliable data across value chains, this guidance is both timely and critical (XRB, 2024a).

While these initiatives are commendable, the task of creating an effective assurance framework for climate-risk disclosures remains formidable. The process appears to be progressing in the right direction, yet there is a risk that reporting entities may misinterpret extended timelines as a justification for postponing meaningful improvements. Evidence strongly suggests that assurance can act as a catalyst for increased transparency and actionable climate-related disclosures (Dutta & Dutta, 2021). Regulatory oversight and specific guidelines, combined with timely implementation, are necessary to maintain momentum and ensure comprehensive disclosures of carbon emissions, climate risks and mitigation strategies.

In terms of the extant assurance approaches and consistency – this is yet a critical consideration area for the XRB in light with the approach taken by assurance providers. Farooq and de Villiers (2019) highlight competition between ASAPs and NASAPs in NZ. Suggesting that ASAPs often favour recognized professional standards such as Assurance Engagements 3000 (ISAE 3000), which align with financial audit methodologies. Thus, highlighting the current departure in practice between providers in the market. Consequently, the XRB's openness to a broader class of assurance providers may introduce potential inconsistencies in this sense. For instance, some providers may rely on ISO standards, which emphasize ethics and quality management, rather than XRB's PES standards. This inclusivity is intended to accommodate diverse practitioners, especially during the nascent stages of NZ's GHG assurance regime (XRB, 2023a). Nonetheless, this approach could inadvertently create inconsistencies in assurance quality and practices, which necessitates vigilant oversight and regular reviews to maintain high standards and stakeholder trust.

In sum, NZ's progress towards establishing a credible sustainability assurance framework is commendable, but significant challenges persist. The XRB must strike a delicate balance between fostering market readiness and avoiding delays that could hinder progress. Maintaining consistency in assurance practices, ensuring clear guidance, and addressing stakeholder concerns will be pivotal to realizing the broader objectives of transparency, accountability and measurable action in climate-related disclosures. Only through proactive oversight and collaborative engagement with all stakeholders, especially users, can the XRB ensure that the assurance framework delivers on its promise to support NZ's sustainability goals effectively.

NOTES

1. The term assurance is a wider term, and it refers to expressions of opinions by a qualified assurance provider that is intended to increase users' confidence in the assured subject matter (MBIE, 2022).

2. The CRD Act in NZ traces its origins to the September 2020 announcement by the NZ Government, outlining the intention to implement mandatory climate-risk reporting (Ministry for the Environment, 2021). The government assigned the NZ XRB the responsibility of developing the necessary reporting standards to support this new framework. Initially, the announcement specified that the regime would operate on a 'comply or explain' basis and would align with the TCFD framework (Ministry for the Environment, 2021). It was further indicated that these disclosures would be required by 2023 (Ministry for the Environment, 2021). In response, the XRB developed the NZ Climate Standards, which were finalized in December 2022. These standards became effective for reporting periods commencing on or after 1 January 2023, with the expectation that the first climate-related statements would be produced beginning in early 2024 (XRB, 2022a; Ehalaiye et al., 2025).

3. Professional and Ethical Standard (PES) 1 refers to the international code of ethics for assurance practitioners (including international Independence Standards) in NZ. PES 3 is a standard that deals with quality management for firms that perform audits or reviews of financial statements or other assurance or related service engagements. PES 4 is a standard for engagement quality reviews.

4. Consultation on these proposed amendments was open until the end of October 2024, and amendments to the standards were expected to be made and published by December 2024 to apply to financial years commencing on or after 1 January 2024. The XRB announced in November 2024, the approved amendments.

5. A summary of the amendments to NZ CS 2 and NZ SAE 1 as approved by the XRB is provided in Appendix 1.

6. https://www.xrb.govt.nz/news/latest-news/

REFERENCES

Boiral, O., Heras-Saizarbitoria, I., & Brotherton, M. C. (2019). Assessing and improving the quality of sustainability reports: The auditors' perspective. *Journal of Business Ethics*, *155*, 703–721.

Boiral, O., Heras-Saizarbitoria, I., & Brotherton, M. C. (2020). Professionalizing the assurance of sustainability reports: The auditors' perspective. *Accounting, Auditing & Accountability Journal*, *33*(2), 309–334.

Boiral, O., Heras-Saizarbitoria, I., Brotherton, M. C., & Bernard, J. (2019). Ethical issues in the assurance of sustainability reports: Perspectives from assurance providers. *Journal of Business Ethics*, *159*, 1111–1125.

Bouten, L., & Hoozée, S. (2024). How sustainability assurance work gets done: Assurors' sensemaking, socialization and interactions with clients. *Accounting, Auditing & Accountability Journal*, *38*.

Bradbury, M. E. (2020). How the XRB uses research in setting accounting and assurance standards. *Australian Accounting Review*, *30*(4), 249–256.

Bui, B., Chapple, L., & Truong, T. P. (2020). Drivers of tight carbon control in the context of climate change regulation. *Accounting & Finance*, *60*(1), 183–226.

Bui, B., & De Villiers, C. (2017). Business strategies and management accounting in response to climate change risk exposure and regulatory uncertainty. *The British Accounting Review*, *49*(1), 4–24.

Carey, P., Khan, A., Mihret, D. G., & Muttakin, M. B. (2021). Voluntary sustainability assurance, capital constraint and cost of debt: International evidence. *International Journal of Auditing, 25*(2), 351–372.

CRD Act [Financial Sector (Climate-related Disclosures and Other Matters) Amendment Act]. (2021). https://www.legislation.govt.nz/act/public/2021/0039/latest/LMS479633.html

Cuadrado-Ballesteros, B., Martínez-Ferrero, J., & García-Sánchez, I. M. (2017). Mitigating information asymmetry through sustainability assurance: The role of accountants and levels of assurance. *International Business Review, 26*(6), 1141–1156.

Datt, R., Luo, L., & Tang, Q. (2020). Corporate choice of providers of voluntary carbon assurance. *International Journal of Auditing, 24*(1), 145–162.

Datt, R., Luo, L., Tang, Q., & Mallik, G. (2018). An international study of determinants of voluntary carbon assurance. *Journal of International Accounting Research, 17*(3), 1–20.

Datt, R., Prasad, P., Vitale, C., & Prasad, K. (2022). International evidence of changing assurance practices for carbon emissions disclosures. *Meditari Accountancy Research, 30*(6), 1594–1628.

Dutta, P., & Dutta, A. (2021). Impact of external assurance on corporate climate change disclosures: New evidence from Finland. *Journal of Applied Accounting Research, 22*(2), 252–285.

Ehalaiye, D., Laswad, F., Botica Redmayne, N., Stent, W., & Cai, L. (2020). Are financial reports useful? The views of New Zealand public versus private users. *Australian Accounting Review, 30*(1), 52–64.

Ehalaiye, D., Moses, O., Laswad, F., & Botica Redmayne, N. (2025). Local government enterprises climate action: An exploration of New Zealand container seaports' climate-related disclosure practices. *Financial Accountability & Management*. https://doi.org/10.1111/faam.12406

External Reporting Board [XRB]. (2022a). *Aotearoa New Zealand climate standards*. https://www.xrb.govt.nz/standards/climate-related-disclosures/aotearoa-new-zealand-climate-standards/

External Reporting Board [XRB]. (2022b). *Aotearoa New Zealand climate standard 1 climate-related disclosures (NZ CS 1)*. https://www.xrb.govt.nz/dmsdocument/4770/

External Reporting Board [XRB]. (2022c). *Aotearoa New Zealand climate standard 2 adoption of Aotearoa New Zealand climate standards (NZ CS 2)*. https://www.xrb.govt.nz/dmsdocument/5339/

External Reporting Board [XRB]. (2022d). *Aotearoa New Zealand climate standard 3 general requirements for climate-related disclosures (NZ CS 3)*. https://www.xrb.govt.nz/dmsdocument/4764/

External Reporting Board [XRB]. (2023a). *Basis for conclusions New Zealand standard on assurance engagements 1 (NZ SAE 1) assurance engagements over greenhouse gas emissions disclosures*. https://www.xrb.govt.nz/dmsdocument/4971/

External Reporting Board [XRB]. (2023b). *New Zealand standard on assurance engagements 1 assurance engagements over greenhouse gas emissions disclosures*. https://www.xrb.govt.nz/dmsdocument/4970/

External Reporting Board [XRB]. (2024a). *Proposed 2024 amendments to climate and assurance standards-consultation document*. https://www.xrb.govt.nz/dmsdocument/5188/

External Reporting Board [XRB]. (2024b). *Assurance of GHG emissions FAQs on NZ SAE 1: Assurance engagements over greenhouse gas emissions disclosures questions & answers*. https://www.xrb.govt.nz/dmsdocument/5068/

External Reporting Board [XRB]. (2024c). *2024 climate and assurance proposals announced*. https://mailchi.mp/xrb.govt.nz/pitopito-korero-14173096?e=67723be807

Farooq, M. B., & de Villiers, C. (2019). The shaping of sustainability assurance through the competition between accounting and non-accounting providers. *Accounting, Auditing & Accountability Journal, 32*(1), 307–336.

Farooq, M. B., & de Villiers, C. (2020). How sustainability assurance engagement scopes are determined, and its impact on capture and credibility enhancement. *Accounting, Auditing & Accountability Journal, 33*(2), 417–445.

Fuhrmann, S., Ott, C., Looks, E., & Guenther, T. W. (2017). The contents of assurance statements for sustainability reports and information asymmetry. *Accounting and Business Research, 47*(4), 369–400.

Gürtürk, A., & Hahn, R. (2016). An empirical assessment of assurance statements in sustainability reports: Smoke screens or enlightening information? *Journal of Cleaner Production*, *136*, 30–41.

Hay, D., Harding, N., Gan, C., Ge, I., Ho, L., Ranasinghe, D., Singh, H., Sultana, N., & Zhou, S. (2023). Comments of the AFAANZ auditing and assurance standards committee on the proposed standard on assurance engagements over GHG emissions disclosure. *Accounting and Finance*, *63*(4), 4813–4820.

Hickman, L. E., & Cote, J. (2019). CSR reporting and assurance legitimacy: A client–assuror dyad investigation. *Journal of Applied Accounting Research*, *20*(4), 372–393.

Hsiao, P. C. K., Scott, T., & Zang, Z. (2022). A snapshot of sustainability assurance market in New Zealand. *Pacific Accounting Review*, *34*(5), 669–686.

Jamali, D. (2010). MNCs and international accountability standards through an institutional lens: Evidence of symbolic conformity or decoupling. *Journal of Business Ethics*, *95*, 617–640.

Krasodomska, J., Simnett, R., & Street, D. L. (2021). Extended external reporting assurance: Current practices and challenges. *Journal of International Financial Management & Accounting*, *32*(1), 104–142.

Larrinaga, C., Rossi, A., Luque-Vilchez, M., & Núñez-Nickel, M. (2020). Institutionalization of the contents of sustainability assurance services: A comparison between Italy and United States. *Journal of Business Ethics*, *163*, 67–83.

Martínez-Ferrero, J., García-Sánchez, I. M., & Ruiz-Barbadillo, E. (2018). The quality of sustainability assurance reports: The expertise and experience of assurance providers as determinants. *Business Strategy and the Environment*, *27*(8), 1181–1196.

Matsumura, E. M., Prakash, R., & Vera-Muñoz, S. C. (2014). Firm-value effects of carbon emissions and carbon disclosures. *The Accounting Review*, *89*(2), 695–724.

Michelon, G., Patten, D. M., & Romi, A. M. (2019). Creating legitimacy for sustainability assurance practices: Evidence from sustainability restatements. *European Accounting Review*, *28*(2), 395–422.

Michelon, G., Pilonato, S., & Ricceri, F. (2015). CSR reporting practices and the quality of disclosure: An empirical analysis. *Critical Perspectives on Accounting*, *33*, 59–78.

Ministry for the Environment. (2021). Ministry for the Environment's climate-related disclosure. https://environment.govt.nz/assets/publications/climate-related-disclosure-2020.pdf

Ministry for the Environment. (2023). Mandatory climate-related disclosures. https://bly.to/BZVAdQr

Mock, T. J., Rao, S. S., & Srivastava, R. P. (2013). The development of worldwide sustainability reporting assurance. *Australian Accounting Review*, *23*(4), 280–294.

Moses, O., Ehalaiye, D., Sorola, M., & Lassou, P. (2024). Extractive sector governance: Does a nexus of accountability render local extractive industries transparency initiatives ineffective? *Meditari Accountancy Research*, *32*(1), 176–206.

Moses, O., Nnam, I. J., Olaniyan, J. O., & Tariquzzaman, A. (2022). Sustainable development goals (SDGS): Assessment of implementation progress in BRICS and MINT. *Advances in Environmental Accounting & Management*, *10*, 11–44.

Perego, P. (2009). Causes and consequences of choosing different assurance providers: An international study of sustainability reporting. *International Journal of Management*, *26*(3), 412–425.

Perego, P., & Kolk, A. (2012). Multinationals' accountability on sustainability: The evolution of third-party assurance of sustainability reports. *Journal of Business Ethics*, *110*, 173–190.

Ruiz-Barbadillo, E., & Martínez-Ferrero, J. (2022). The choice of incumbent financial auditors to provide sustainability assurance and audit services from a legitimacy perspective. *Sustainability Accounting, Management and Policy Journal*, *13*(2), 459–493.

Ryan, J., & Tiller, D. (2022). A recent survey of GHG emissions reporting and assurance. *Australian Accounting Review*, *32*(2), 181–187.

Simnett, R., Vanstraelen, A., & Chua, W. F. (2009). Assurance on sustainability reports: An international comparison. *The Accounting Review*, *84*(3), 937–967.

Smith, J., Haniffa, R., & Fairbrass, J. (2011). A conceptual framework for investigating 'capture'in corporate sustainability reporting assurance. *Journal of Business Ethics*, *99*, 425–439.

Steinmeier, M., & Stich, M. (2019). Does sustainability assurance improve managerial investment decisions? *European Accounting Review*, *28*(1), 177–209.

The Ministry of Business, Innovation and Employment [MBIE]. (2022). Assurance over climate-related disclosures: Occupational regulation and expanding the scope of assurance. https://www.mbie.govt.nz/dmsdocument/25652-assurance-over-climate-related-disclosures-occupational-regulation-and-expanding-the-scope-of-assurance

Tsang, A., Frost, T., & Cao, H. (2023). Environmental, social, and governance (ESG) disclosure: A literature review. *The British Accounting Review*, *55*(1), 101149.

Zaman, R., Farooq, M. B., Khalid, F., & Mahmood, Z. (2021). Examining the extent of and determinants for sustainability assurance quality: The role of audit committees. *Business Strategy and the Environment*, *30*(7), 2887–2906.

Zhou, S. (2022). Reporting and assurance of climate-related and other sustainability information: A review of research and practice. *Australian Accounting Review*, *32*(3), 315–333.

Zhou, S., Simnett, R., & Green, W. J. (2016). Assuring a new market: The interplay between country-level and company-level factors on the demand for greenhouse gas (GHG) information assurance and the choice of assurance provider. *Auditing: A Journal of Practice & Theory*, *35*(3), 141–168.

APPENDIX 1: SUMMARY OF AMENDMENTS TO NZ CS 2 AND NZ SAE 1 *AS AT NOVEMBER 2024*

Panel A: Amendments to NZ CS 2 *Adoption of Aotearoa New Zealand Climate Standards as at November 2024*

NZ CS 2 was amended as follows:

- Extend the adoption provisions for scope 3 GHG emissions for an additional year (and related extensions to the adoption provisions relating to comparatives for scope 3 GHG emissions and analysis of trends);
- Extend adoption provisions for anticipated financial impacts for an additional year; and
- Establish an adoption provision in relation to accounting periods ending before 31 December 2025 for the assurance of scope 3 GHG emissions disclosures, thus giving an additional year before the assurance over scope 3 GHG emissions disclosures is required. This means that the assurance of scope 3 GHG emission disclosures will apply in relation to accounting periods ending on or after 31 December 2025.

Panel B: Amendments to *NZ SAE 1 Assurance Engagements over GHG Emissions Disclosures as at November 2024*

New sections 7A and 7B were inserted in NZ SAE 1 as follows:

7A. In accordance with paragraph 24 of NZ CS 2, a climate reporting entity may use adoption provision 8 so that scope 3 GHG emissions disclosures are excluded from the scope of the assurance engagement in relation to accounting periods ending before 31 December 2025. This means that the assurance of scope 3 GHG emission disclosures will apply in relation to accounting periods ending on or after 31 December 2025.

7B. For the avoidance of doubt, if adoption provision 8 of NZ CS 2 is used, the scope 1 and scope 2 GHG emissions disclosures shall be the subject of an assurance engagement (see paragraphs 25, 26(a) (i) and (ii), 26(b) and 26(c) of NZ CS 1) in accordance with NZ SAE 1.

Source: Public announcements by External Reporting Board (XRB), Wellington, New Zealand. https://mailchi.mp/xrb.govt.nz/pitopito-korero-14173096?e=67723be807; https://www.xrb.govt.nz/dmsdocument/5337/

A SYSTEMATIC REVIEW OF PUBLIC SECTOR CLIMATE-RISK REPORTING AND ASSURANCE PRACTICES: A CONCEPTUAL FRAMEWORK TOWARDS RESPONSIBLE GOVERNANCE IN SUB-SAHARAN AFRICA

Joseph Tinarwo and Lourens Erasmus

University of South Africa, South Africa

ABSTRACT

Public sector institutions play an important role in advancing the achievement of global sustainable development goals. Tracking the milestones in achieving the sustainable development targets and informing diverse actors about progress towards achieving these goals through climate-risk reporting is vital in generating traction. Ensuring information integrity and independent and objective assessment through appropriate audit and assurance practices enhances transparency and accountability and builds credibility in reporting. This chapter systematically reviewed the literature on the sub-Saharan African perspective of climate-risk reporting and assurance practices, focusing on materiality and cost–benefit constraints. The review suggests that African public sector institutions face challenges in climate-risk reporting and assurance practices. These include a lack of statutory and policy landscape for mandatory disclosure, weak coordination and harmonization among stakeholders, lack of financial resources, weak human and institutional capacity and lack of education and awareness. Mitigating these challenges calls for measures that develop robust legal frameworks for climate-risk disclosure, establish human and institutional capacity-building programmes, ensure adequate

Climate Risks Reporting Practices and Assurance
Advances in Environmental Accounting & Management, Volume 13, 95–112

Published under exclusive licence by Emerald Publishing Limited
ISSN: 1479-3598/doi:10.1108/S1479-359820250000013012

funding, increase education and awareness and develop solid multistakeholder and multisectoral approaches.

Keywords: Climate-risk reporting; assurance practices; public sector; sub-Saharan Africa; capacity building

1. INTRODUCTION

Climate-risk reporting has become essential for diverse institutions across the private and public sectors to transparently report their environmental, social and governance (ESG) performance (Stolowy & Paugam, 2023). While private sector organizations have made significant efforts in adopting climate-risk reporting, there are increasing calls by diverse stakeholders for the public sector to reveal operational climate risks and impacts in financial statements (Uyar et al., 2022). The public sector remains vital in tackling global environmental challenges, as governmental entities and institutions have an essential role in the stewardship of public resources and service provision to their citizens (Marx & Van Dyk, 2011). Through implementing climate-risk reporting, the public sector can demonstrate its dedication to responsible governance, transparency and accountability (Assis et al., 2023). Specifically, climate-risk reporting would enable the public sector institutions to align their operational activities with the environmental statutory and policy frameworks at national, regional and global levels (Rezaee et al., 2023).

While sustainability reporting has recently become a 'buzz' word in sustainable development and accounting literature, little is known about climate-risk reporting and how it can be implemented in government or public sector institutions. Sustainability reporting characteristically focuses on a broader range of ESG performance, together with but not confined to climate risks. Conversely, climate-risk reporting entails assessing, managing and disclosing climate change-related risks and opportunities in the institution's strategy and operations. Although sustainability reporting focuses on providing a holistic assessment of an institution's general sustainability performance, climate-risk reporting narrows into the precise risks and financial implications related to climate change.

The development of climate-risk reporting standards currently being used by the private sector was predominantly influenced by developed countries with limited contributions from developing nations (Uyar et al., 2022). Further, implementing uniform and standardized climate-risk reporting standards for the public sector in poorer nations could be challenging given their different environments, such as resources and capacity constraints (Uyar et al., 2021). The International Public Sector Accounting Standards Board (IPSASB), in its strategic plan for 2024–2028, endeavours to investigate and set standards for climate-risk reporting in the public sector (IPSASB, 2024). It is thus imperative to consider the progress made by the developing countries concerning climate-risk reporting standards and assurance practices to minimize the resistance and failure in climate-risk reporting in the public sector. This chapter proposes a conceptual framework highlighting how sub-Saharan African countries can enhance public sector climate-risk reporting and assurance practices. The overall aim is to support the efforts of the IPSASB by providing a sub-Saharan African perspective on climate-risk reporting and assurance practices, focusing on materiality and cost–benefit constraints. In achieving this aim, the chapter seeks to attempt the subsequent research questions:

- What are the reasons for increased interest in climate-risk reporting and assurance practices in the public sector in recent years?
- In what ways are public sector climate-risk reporting and assurance practices in developed countries different from those of sub-Saharan African countries?
- How can sub-Saharan African countries enhance climate-risk reporting and assurance practices for the public sector?

2. BACKGROUND CONTEXT

While climate-risk reporting has been important in guiding institutions towards transparent and accountable sustainability practices, some common climate-risk reporting trends and frameworks have been used at local, regional and global levels. The Global Reporting Initiative (GRI) Standards are the most commonly used frameworks for sustainability reporting, and these standards provide the guidelines and principles institutions use for reporting on economic, environmental and social performance (Sethi et al., 2017). Characteristically, the GRI standards cover several sustainability topics, including governance, human rights, labour practices, biodiversity and emissions (Petera & Wagner, 2015). The Financial Stability Board developed the Task Force on Climate-related Financial Disclosures (TCFD) to support stakeholders by establishing recommendations for voluntary climate-related financial disclosures (Chua et al., 2022). The TCFD aims to help institutions disclose climate-related risks and opportunities that are material to the entity's financial performance, including governance, strategy, risk management and metrics (Braasch & Velte, 2023).

In Europe, big companies must disclose non-financial information, including environmental, social and employee-related matters, as enshrined in the European Union Non-Financial Reporting Directive (EU NFR) Directive (Muserra et al., 2020). In this context, several developed countries have significantly progressed in advancing climate-risk reporting in the public sector. In September 2024, the Australian government enacted the Treasury Laws Amendment Act to empower the Australian Accounting Standards Board (AASB) to adopt the Australian Sustainability Reporting Standards (ASRS) (Hossain, 2018). The ASRS resonate with the provisions of the International Financial Reporting Standards (IFRS) Sustainability Disclosure Standards. Fundamentally, the ASRS framework integrates with current worldwide sustainability standards, fostering a comparison of disclosures globally (Gamage & Sciulli, 2017). It includes key climate-risk reporting pillars like governance, strategy, risk management and metrics and targets. The ASRS is as follows: The AASB S1 is a voluntary Standard that covers sustainability-related financial disclosures and goes hand-in-hand with the provisions of IFRS S1 (Li & Lee, 2023). Similarly, AASB S2 is a compulsory standard incorporating the essential provisions outlined in IFRS S1, permitting it to operate and be recognized as a separate standard focusing on climate issues. These standards give public and private entities inclusive reporting on sustainability-related financial information, including climate risks, opportunities and greenhouse gas (GHG) emissions (Ho et al., 2023). Ensuring good governance pillars such as transparency and accountability ensures climate-risk reporting is vital to the institution's strategy and operations that according to Chua et al. (2022) supports emission reduction targets in Australia.

However, many developing countries, particularly in Africa, still face challenges regarding which key metrics to use in climate-risk reporting, especially in the public sector. For instance, the Accountant General of Mauritius is currently working with the Department of Climate Change and other technical teams to determine the metrics to use in public sector climate-risk reporting (World Bank, 2023). African governments are working with international financial institutions such as the International Monetary Fund (IMF), the World Bank and the African Development Bank to mobilize financial and technical resources to implement climate-risk reporting in the public sector (World Bank, 2023).

3. LITERATURE REVIEW

3.1 Theoretical Frameworks Underpinning Climate-Risk Reporting and Assurance Practices

This article draws on the legitimacy and stakeholder theory. While the legitimacy and stakeholder theory has been traditionally used in sustainability reporting, it can also be applied to climate-risk reporting. Public sector institutions significantly impact most countries' economies, societies and environments more than the private sector and other non-governmental organizations (Hughes, 2017). It is generally accepted that public sector institutions have a dual role as public service providers and regulators, with the mandate and ability to drive sustainable future development (An et al., 2017). Therefore, public sector institutions must be transparent and publicly accountable to various stakeholders, including policymakers, the public, academics and practitioners (Lyrio et al., 2018). In the context of the stakeholder theory, public sector institutions influence the external environments as their dual role affects the relevant stakeholders' conducive environment for their operation (Zharfpeykan & Askarany, 2023). A stakeholder is a person, group of people, institutions or concerned community with vested interests, entitlements and/or proprietorship in an institution and its activities (Dameri & Ferrando, 2022). Stakeholders usually have interests in the institution's activities and are affected by its actions (Pirozzi, 2019). These definitions imply that stakeholders contribute voluntarily or involuntarily to an institution's growth and success and are possible beneficiaries/recipients and risk bearers (Zharfpeykan & Askarany, 2023).

Additionally, the legitimacy theory stems from the notion of organizational legitimacy. It has long been applied to accounting and other research disciplines to understand the interest in sustainability integration and climate-risk reporting in the public sector (Moloi et al., 2020). According to He (2023, p. 241), legitimacy is generally conceptualized as 'a belief that the activities of an institution are deemed acceptable, suitable, or proper in the context of a socially and environmentally created system of customs, standards, principles, and definitions.' Climate-risk reporting is crucial to legitimate actions by an institution and conveys its accountability to stakeholders (Buallay, 2022). Combining the stakeholder and legitimacy theories deem fit for public sector institutions adopting climate-risk reporting and assurance practices to fulfil their social contract with the stakeholder communities (Ching & Gerab, 2017). Climate-risk reporting will enable them to establish and manage stakeholder expectations, bringing efficiency and effectiveness to public finance management and service delivery.

3.2 Conceptualizing Climate-Risk Reporting and Assurance Practices in the Public Sector

In recent years, there has been an increasing global interest in climate-risk reporting to demonstrate the importance of understanding and mitigating environmental impacts for a sustainable future. It has entered the policy domain of many governments and organizations to achieve ESG-set targets (Li & Lee, 2023). Climate-risk reporting denotes how institutions report to the public how they recognize, measure and manage climate-related physical and transition opportunities (US EPA, 2024). Abhayawansa and Adams (2021) provide a more refined definition of climate-risk reporting, stating that it is the practice of disclosing and conveying monetary and non-monetary information to stakeholders about climate change's short-term and long-term impacts on operations and investments or service delivery. For instance, institutions may use scenario analysis to measure the climate-related physical risks of an institution, such as potential damage to physical infrastructure and temperature and rainfall variations (Ens & Johnston, 2020). Similarly, an institution can assess the transition risks of climate change emanating from its operations, such as statutory and policy changes, consumer preferences and market dynamics and technological developments (Carattini et al., 2023).

In June 2023, the International Sustainability Standards Board (ISSB), established by the IFRS Foundation, issued its first two Sustainability Disclosure Standards, namely IFRS S1 General Requirements for Disclosure of Sustainability-related Financial Information and IFRS S2 Climate-related Disclosures (Habib et al., 2019; Laswad & Redmayne, 2015). IFRS S2 mandates an institution to reveal information about its physical and transition risks and opportunities from climate change to allow stakeholders of general-purpose financial reports to make informed choices about providing resources to the institution (Lin et al., 2019). Further, it mandates an institution to disclose financial and non-information that helps decision-makers of general-purpose financial reports to be informed of the governance processes, strategy, performance and processes involved in identifying, assessing and monitoring climate-related risks (Bodle et al., 2016).

On the other hand, climate-risk assurance refers to the objective analysis and validation of an institution's climate-related financial and non-information contained in its reports (Dutta & Dutta, 2021). The primary objective of this accounting practice in climate-risk reporting is to assure stakeholders such as investors that the information reported in the financial or non-financial statements is trustworthy, accurate and consistent with recognized standards and procedures (Bui et al., 2021). The International Auditing and Assurance Standards Board (IAASB), a worldwide autonomous standard-setting organization, established high-quality international standards assurance in climate-risk reporting and other related practices (Hegazy & Kamareldawla, 2021). Climate-risk assurance providers are entities that carry out independent and objective assessments or audits or assurance on an institution's financial statements and use the set standards by IAASB to gauge the accuracy, trustworthiness and comprehensiveness of an institution's sustainability reports or climate-risk disclosures (Alsahali & Malagueño, 2022).

3.3 Motivation of Climate-Risk Reporting and Assurance Practices in the Public Sector

Public sector climate-risk reporting stems from the realization that government institutions play a crucial role in enhancing national development and socio-economic transformation (Cappellieri et al., 2024). According to the IPSASB, public sector action boosts innovative changes needed to achieve sustainable development benefits (IPSASB, 2022). Since public spending significantly holds a large share of the global economy, public sector climate-risk reporting comprehensively influences the economic progress toward sustainable development (Bui et al., 2021). The origins of climate-risk reporting can be tracked from the realisation that there are a variety of risks (physical and transition) and opportunities posed on business operations caused by climate change (Tauringana, 2021). Further, by reporting climate risks and opportunities, public sector institutions are expected to be driven toward transparency and accountability to stakeholders in detecting, evaluating, and addressing climate-related risks and opportunities (Igwe et al., 2023). For instance, donor agencies have increasingly demanded comprehensive information from reports on climate risks and opportunities from governments (Songi & Dias, 2019). Even in the context of sovereign bonds, the public sector climate-risk reporting for capital markets resonates with the contents of the United Nations' Paris Agreement, which states that finance flows need to be in line with a trajectory to a low-carbon economy and climate-resilient development (UNFCCC, 2015). Therefore, climate-risk reports can help formulate policies and develop long-term adaptation and mitigation strategies to shift to a low-carbon economy (Tilt et al., 2021). Most importantly, they allow governments better decision-making in allocating resources and mainstreaming climate-risk considerations through green budgeting (Clayton et al., 2015; Girón et al., 2021).

As climate-risk reporting continues to evolve, independent external oversight is imperative to establish confidence and integrity in public sector institutions' financial and non-financial reports, necessitating effective internal and external audits and assurance of the climate-risk reports(Wambwa et al., 2024) to ensure that the policymakers are taking correct and appropriate actions in mitigating and adapting to climate risks (Erin & Ackers, 2024). Similarly, assurance of climate-risk reports informs stakeholders such as environmental regulators and the public about how climate change may impact an institution's operations and long-term sustainability (Chaka, 2018). Auditing climate-risk reports is essential to mitigate risks associated with greenwashing – reporting and giving stakeholders a false impression that an institution's products or services are environmentally friendly (Boiral et al., 2019). Therefore, Sustainability Assurance Initiatives (SAIs) have an important role in climate-risk assurance, which may include the assessment of the adequacy of the public sector institution's internal control arrangements for climate-risk reporting (Fernandez-Feijoo et al., 2018). The internal control assessment is crucial to establishing management controls over sustainability data and public sector institutions' regulatory and legislative frameworks (Wallage, 2000). However, the effective oversight of reported sustainability information hinges on the qualifications and experience of SAIs or internal audit functions in the public sector (Tumwebaze et al., 2022).

4. METHODOLOGY

The research methodology adopted in this chapter is a systematic review of current reporting standards for the private sector, global reports and academic literature on climate-risk reporting. The systematic literature review applied the Preferred Reporting Items for Systematic Reviews and Meta-Analyses (PRISMA) methodology to ensure that the latest and most relevant literature is covered. PRISMA methodology is essential because it provides a rigorous review of existing literature, identifies key themes and trends and offers insights into the issues around climate-risk reporting in the public sector, paying particular attention to the capacity and resource constraints facing developing countries (Page et al., 2021). This study primarily obtained articles from the Scopus database, Google Scholar and documents from credible institutions such as governments, development partners and donors. The researchers used the Boolean combinations of the following keywords: sustainability reporting, climate-risk reporting, assurance practices, public sector and Africa from 2015 to the present, as this was the year when there was an increased call for limiting global warming and climate-risk reporting (Brüggemann et al., 2022). The comma-separated value (CSV) file selected relevant articles using the inclusion and exclusion criteria based on abstract and full article screening.

5. FINDINGS

The Figure below shows the results obtained from the literature search and screening as illustrated in the PRISMA flow diagram.

The approach in a systematic literature review involves three main steps, informed by Tasdemir and Gazo (2018): identification, screening and eligibility (see Fig. 1). This initial step involved searching titles, abstracts and keywords. The search procedure was limited to research papers written in English, including those published online first. The search was conducted on 16 August 2024, resulting in over 968 articles. In the following step, research papers published before 2015 ($n = 244$) were excluded because stakeholders' attention to climate-risk reporting and assurance practices was limited before that date (Junior et al., 2014). It left the researchers with 724 articles after conducting the year-based filtering process. The abovementioned steps were repeated by undertaking the second identification process in September 2024. In the second step of the review process, 221 articles were included in the selection for analysis based on the original database searches. In the screening process, 968 research articles were analyzed to identify those focused on climate-risk reporting and assurance practices in the public sector. The screening process was started by screening article titles to eliminate papers that did not cover the keywords.

The next stage involved abstract screening, which yielded 532 articles. In determining the eligibility, the approach was to review the full texts of the articles to exclude articles covering topics other than climate-risk reporting and assurance practices. The remaining 206 articles were further scrutinized to include only articles covering Sub-Saharan African climate-risk reporting and assurance practices, yielding 26 articles.

5.1 Barriers to Climate-Risk Reporting and Assurance Practices in African Public Sector Institutions

While climate-risk reporting and assurance have become imperative worldwide, adopting such practices in the African public sector faces many challenges due to a lack of robust legal and policy frameworks and mandatory disclosures (He, 2022). Furthermore, most African countries lack clear strategies, standards and reporting guidelines that are profound in public sector institutions.

Additionally, the literature highlighted a lack of coordination and harmonization among government institutions and other stakeholders involved in Africa's climate-risk management and assurance practices (Igwe et al., 2023). There are diverse institutions that make climate-risk reporting and assurance practices successful, ranging from government agencies, civil societies, the private sector, development partners and research organizations. These actors require proper coordination to avoid duplication efforts and conflicts as they work together to ensure climate-risk reporting and assurance practice in the public sector (Songi & Dias, 2019).

Lack of adequate budgetary support is one of the significant challenges in effectively implementing climate-risk reporting and assurance practices in African public sector institutions (Tauringana, 2021). Most public sector institutions in

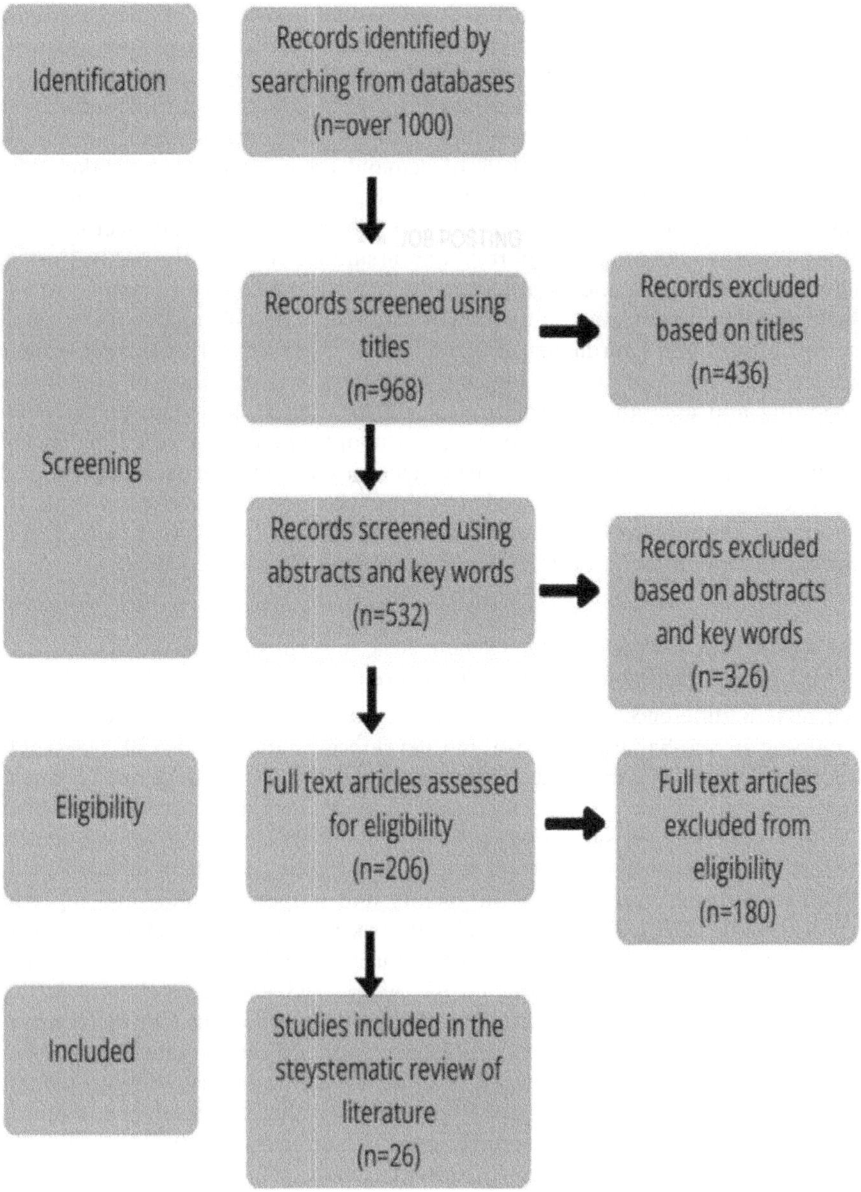

Fig. 1. PRISMA Flow Chart. *Source:* Authors' construction based on systematic literature review.

Africa and other low-income countries consider climate-risk reporting and assurance costly (Erin et al., 2022). This is mainly because implementing this process requires substantial investment in new technologies and specialized software. Moreover, implementing climate-risk reporting and assurance requires skilled and experienced personnel with substantial knowledge of climate science, risk analysis and assessment, environmental principles and guidelines, quantitative and qualitative methodologies, auditing and reporting frameworks.

Climate-risk reporting and assurance in African public sector institutions are constrained by competing priorities within government reporting entities (Kitsikopoulos et al., 2018), a lack of demand for information by stakeholders working on sustainable development and other sectors and a lack of human and institutional capacity building and training programmes in public sector institutions, covering climate-risk reporting and assurance (Erin et al., 2022). Further, climate-risk reporting and assurance in the African public sector is impacted by a lack of commitment and motivation towards climate-risk reporting by public sector institutions (Tauringana, 2021), a lack of champions from the government leaders and red tape, which impacts timeliness and accuracy of climate-risk reporting and assurance (Alshbili et al., 2020). Other challenges facing public sector institutions in African countries to adopt climate-risk reporting include voluntary disclosure (Erin et al., 2022), lack of data on climate change impacts (Igwe et al., 2023), lack of knowledge on the concept of climate-risk reporting and assurance and other information to disclose (Tilt et al., 2021) and lack of management commitment in public sector institutions (Erin et al., 2022).

5.2 Differences in Public Sector Climate-Risk Reporting and Assurance Practices in Developed and Sub-Saharan African Countries

There is a difference in the nature and context of public sector climate-risk reporting in sub-Saharan African and developed countries (He, 2022). Regulatory frameworks that mandate public sector organizations in developed countries to report on climate risk are relatively more mature and advanced (Buallay, 2020). Conversely, in sub-Saharan African countries, public sector climate-risk reporting has regulations that are usually less binding and lack detailed guidelines, resulting in variations in the quality and scope of climate-risk reporting (World Bank, 2023). Public sector climate-risk reporting in developed countries closely adheres to globally recognized reporting standards such as the International Integrated Reporting Framework or the GRI guidelines (Bhatia & Tuli, 2018), thus promoting reliability and credibility in reporting. On the contrary, sub-Saharan African countries do not have standardized climate-risk reporting frameworks for the public sector, leading to contradictory, fragmented and inconsistent reporting practices (Farisyi et al., 2022). Developed countries generally have adequate budgetary support and capacity to have adequate human and material resources to support climate-risk reporting in the public sector institutions, unlike sub-Saharan African countries (Buallay et al., 2021).

Public sector climate-risk reporting in sub-Saharan African countries primarily focuses on social performance while climate-risk reports from developed countries primarily focus on environmental performance (Bashtovaya, 2014; World Bank, 2023). More so, pressure groups in developed countries advocate for public sector climate-risk reporting, particularly in controlling and reducing environmental pollution (Lodhia & Sharma, 2019). On the other hand, public sector climate-risk reports from sub-Saharan African countries mainly address social investment programmes in sectors such as food security, education and water and sanitation (He, 2022). Finally, public sector climate-risk reporting in sub-Saharan African countries places little emphasis on human capital development, including welfare and creating equal opportunities for workers (Farisyi et al., 2022).

5.3 Towards a Conceptual Framework for Climate-Risk Reporting and Assurance Practices in Sub-Saharan Africa

As the IPSASB published the first Sustainability Reporting Standard (IPSASB SRS™) Exposure Draft (ED) at the end of October 2024, sub-Saharan Africa and other regions are expected to respond and give their views on the draft IPSASB standards (IPSASB, 2024). Sub-Saharan Africa needs several vital considerations when responding to the IPSASB's draft sustainability standards due to the continent's unique climate change challenges and opportunities. Countries in sub-Saharan Africa must ensure that the IPSASB standards are tailored to the local context and do not conflict with cultural norms when public sector institutions track and report their environmental, social and economic performance (Republic of Zimbabwe, 2023). By contextualizing the IPSASB standards, sub-Saharan African public sector institutions can improve the preparation of climate-risk disclosures targeting local audiences, enhancing greater confidence among key actors in climate-risk reporting (African Union, 2018). Further, the regional governments must conduct a comprehensive materiality assessment to categorize the key climate-risk problems facing sub-Saharan African public sector institutions. Materiality assessment is vital for regional governments to prioritize important sustainability concerns, efficiently distribute resources and contextualize the IPSASB standards to reflect the continent's key climate-risk aspects (Mezzanotte, 2023).

In adopting the IPSASB standards, the sub-Saharan African governments must consider data availability and quality. Countries in sub-Saharan Africa may contribute to addressing the challenges related to data availability and quality in the region by contextualizing the standards to suit the local environment, allowing contextualized methodologies and the accurate collection and reporting of the data that reflects the region's climate risk (World Bank, 2023). Moreover, sub-Saharan African public sector institutions lack professionals with the requisite technical skills and knowledge in financial reporting (Igwe et al., 2023). Regional countries can contribute to localizing IPSASB standards to suit the sub-Saharan African context so that the local staff can be equipped through capacity-building programmes to track and report climate-related risks and opportunities facing public sector institutions (He, 2022). Finally, in adopting the IPSASB standards, sub-Saharan African countries must help develop reporting standards that are tailored and relevant to addressing the continent's climate risks and opportunities (Erin et al., 2022). In particular, countries in sub-Saharan Africa may contribute towards inclusive reporting, which can be fostered by ensuring that climate-risk reporting and materiality practices reflect the principles and values of inclusivity and equity, acknowledging the needs and perspectives of various actors, including poor and vulnerable people.

The findings from this review permitted the construction of a conceptual framework for enhancing public sector climate-risk reporting and assurance practices in sub-Saharan Africa, as presented in Fig. 2. Allocating sufficient budgets is vital. Countries progressing well in public sector climate-risk reporting and assurance practices ensure adequate budgetary support and do not rely on international financial support from institutions such as the World Bank and IMF (for example, Australia) (Li & Lee, 2023). Robust legal and institutional frameworks are also important to promote public sector climate-risk reporting and assurance practices. Additionally, human and institutional capacity building needs to be built to successfully enhance climate-risk reporting and assurance practices in the public sector in Africa. Importantly, the involvement of diverse actors interested in sustainability issues, such as the government, donors, civil society organizations, think tanks and the private sector, needs to be involved and harnessed, particularly to mobilize the required technical, material and financial resources. Lastly, good data management governance is critical to ensure that climate change-related data are reliable and trustworthy. Data ownership and use rules are often inadequate in most developing countries in Africa and elsewhere worldwide, causing problems of data misuse.

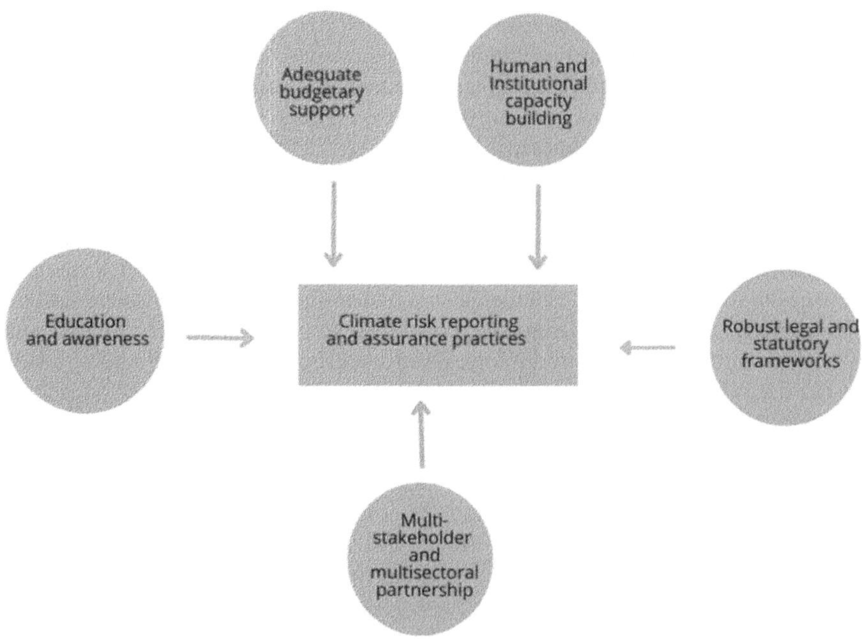

Fig. 2. Conceptual Framework for Enhancing Public Sector Climate-Risk Reporting and Assurance Practices in Sub-Saharan Africa. *Source:* Authors' construction based on findings.

6. DISCUSSION AND CONCLUSION

To successfully develop and implement public sector climate-risk reporting and assurance practices in Africa, efforts must be made to build robust legal and statutory frameworks. Findings from the literature show that many African countries lack specific and robust legal and policy frameworks for public sector climate-risk reporting and assurance practices. The inability of the governments to enforce mandatory disclosures is the main barrier to climate-risk reporting and assurance practices in the public sector. Few countries, particularly in the Global North, have seen significant developments in enacting specific legal frameworks to promote mandatory climate disclosures, including the United Kingdom and New Zealand. The lack of statutory and policy landscape in most African countries is impeding climate-risk reporting and assurance, with most governments lacking clear strategies, standards and reporting guidelines that are particularly tailored for public sector institutions. It is crucial for developing countries, particularly in Africa, to craft mandatory bold legal frameworks for climate-risk reporting and assurance practices in the public sector.

This review's findings suggest a lack of multistakeholder and multisectoral partnerships among the sub-Saharan African stakeholders involved in climate-risk reporting and assurance practices. The fragmentation and lack of coordination and harmonization of these diverse actors make climate-risk reporting and assurance practices challenging. Establishing a central coordination entity that brings diverse stakeholders could help to avoid duplication efforts and conflicts in climate-risk reporting and assurance practices. Multistakeholder and multisectoral partnerships are vital for sub-Saharan Africa's sustainable path towards a low-carbon economy by enhancing climate-risk reporting and assurance practices in the public sector. However, it is crucial to develop a framework for stakeholder collaboration, define clear goals and objectives, promote information sharing and standardize climate-risk reporting and assurance practices.

The review also suggests that most public sector institutions in African countries lack adequate budgetary resources, which may hinder climate-risk reporting and assurance practices. Public sector institutions consider climate-risk reporting and assurance costly because the process requires financial and material resources such as new technologies and specialized software, which are usually costly to acquire. African countries need approximately USD 2.8 trillion to transition to net zero, part of this amount going to scenario analysis and climate-risk assessment between 2021 and 2030. However, there is a considerable climate finance gap, considering the region only receives USD 30 billion annually (AEO, 2023). African governments must allocate adequate financial resources to transition to a low-carbon economy through promoting climate-risk reporting and assurance practices in the public sector. Harnessing the role of the private sector and international financial institutions like the World Bank and IMF is crucial to mobilize technical and financial resources.

Additionally, African public sector institutions lack human and institutional capacity to enhance climate risks and assurance practices. The lack of human capacity can be attributed to the excessive brain drain facing most public sector institutions, with skilled personnel leaving for better employment outside government. Similarly, the weak institutional capacity of African public sector institutions can be attributed to poor funding. It is thus important to roll out human and institutional capacity-building programmes through training programmes covering climate-risk reporting and assurance. Capacity building can also be enhanced through exchange programmes with advanced countries in climate-risk reporting and assurance practices.

Finally, a lack of education and awareness on climate-risk reporting and assurance practices was also identified as a challenge facing most stakeholders in Africa, particularly policymakers and leaders of public sector institutions. The lack of awareness results in a lack of commitment and motivation towards climate-risk reporting by government leaders and public sector institutions, which may negatively impact the adoption, timeliness and accuracy of climate-risk reporting and assurance (Alshbili et al., 2020). It is essential to roll out education and awareness programmes on climate-risk reporting and get buy-in from diverse stakeholders working in different sectors to know what information is important to disclose during climate-risk reporting. Dissemination of information through workshops, conferences, information, communication and technological (ICT) materials will help raise awareness and increase commitment to climate-risk reporting and assurance by policymakers and leaders of African public sector institutions.

To conclude, this chapter on climate-risk reporting and assurance practices, drawing lessons and input from sub-Saharan African nations, significantly contributes to accounting and finance for numerous reasons. Focusing on sub-Saharan African countries provides an important perspective often overlooked in developing climate-risk reporting standards and guidelines currently used by the private sector. Contributing a perspective from developing countries by paying attention to their experiences and challenges gives IPSASB insights into unique contexts and circumstances that will influence successful climate-risk reporting practices in the public sector in developing countries. This holistic approach to understanding how climate-risk reporting standards in the public sector should be framed allows IPSASB and other key stakeholders to develop all-inclusive and relevant frameworks across diverse socio-economic and political contexts. This research found that African countries face challenges in implementing climate-risk reporting and assurance in the public sector. These include a lack of legal framework on mandatory, voluntary disclosure, poor coordination and harmonization, weak human and institutional capacity, inadequate budgetary support and limited education and awareness. To enhance climate-risk reporting and assurance in Africa's public sector, it is crucial to develop robust legal frameworks, promote multistakeholder and multisectoral partnerships, ensure adequate financial support, ensure human and institutional human capacity building and roll out education and awareness. Finally, the chapter will become valuable in ensuring the democratization of climate-risk reporting, allowing an equitable and representative approach to developing climate-risk reporting standards in the public sector.

REFERENCES

Abhayawansa, S., & Adams, C. (2021). Towards a conceptual framework for non-financial reporting inclusive of pandemic and climate risk reporting. *Meditari Accountancy Research, 30*(3), 710–738.

African Economic Outlook (AEO). (2023). *Mobilising private sector financing for climate and green growth in Africa.* https://www.afdb.org/en/documents/african-economic-outlook-2023

African Union. (2018). *High-level meeting on public financial management and IPSASB strategy and workplan.* https://au.int/en/pressreleases/20180503/high-level-meeting-public-financial-management-kicked-today

Alsahali, K. F., & Malagueño, R. (2022). An empirical study of sustainability reporting assurance: Current trends and new insights. *Journal of Accounting & Organizational Change, 18*(5), 617–642.

Alshbili, I., Elamer, A. A., & Beddewela, E. (2020). Ownership types, corporate governance and corporate social responsibility disclosures: Empirical evidence from a developing country. *Accounting Research Journal, 33*(1), 148–166.

An, Y., Davey, H., & Harun, H. (2017). Sustainability reporting at a New Zealand public university: A longitudinal analysis. *Sustainability, 9*(9), 1529.

Assis, J. P. L., Imoniana, J. O., Kassai, J. R., Cornacchione, E. B., & Reginato, L. (2023). Relationships between corporate social responsibility, sustainability assurance, and adoption of integrated reporting in public sector. *Creative Education, 14*(11), 2239–2264.

Bashtovaya, V. (2014). CSR reporting in the United States and Russia. *Social Responsibility Journal, 10*(1), 68–84.

Bhatia, A., & Tuli, S. (2018). Sustainability reporting: An empirical evaluation of emerging and developed economies. *Journal of Global Responsibility, 9*(2), 207–234.

Bodle, K. A., Cybinski, P. J., & Monem, R. (2016). Effect of IFRS adoption on financial reporting quality: Evidence from bankruptcy prediction. *Accounting Research Journal, 29*(3), 292–312.

Boiral, O., Heras-Saizarbitoria, I., & Brotherton, M. C. (2019). Assessing and improving the quality of sustainability reports: The auditors' perspective. *Journal of Business Ethics, 155*, 703–721.

Braasch, A., & Velte, P. (2023). Climate reporting quality following the recommendations of the task force on climate-related financial disclosures: A focus on the German capital market. *Sustainable Development, 31*(2), 926–940.

Brüggemann, T., Bokelmann, L., & Dörkßen, K. (2022). How sustainability reporting of banks aligns with the Paris Agreement – A critical analysis of the financial sector's reporting regulations in the European Union. *Management Studies, 12*(1), 1–8.

Buallay, A. M. (2020). Sustainability reporting and bank's performance: Comparison between developed and developing countries. *World Review of Entrepreneurship Management and Sustainable Development, 16*(2), 187–203.

Buallay, A. M. (2022). Relevant theories to sustainability reporting. *International Perspectives on Sustainability Reporting*, 61–76.

Buallay, A., Fadel, S. M., Alajmi, J., & Saudagaran, S. (2021). Sustainability reporting and bank performance after financial crisis: Evidence from developed and developing countries. *Competitiveness Review: An International Business Journal, 31*(4), 747–770.

Bui, B., Houqe, M. N., & Zaman, M. (2021). Climate change mitigation: Carbon assurance and reporting integrity. *Business Strategy and the Environment, 30*(8), 3839–3853.

Cappellieri, F., Lombardi, R., Pizzo, M., & Vinciguerra, R. (2024). Environmental reporting in public sector organizations: A review of literature for the future paths of research. *Financial Accountability & Management, 41*, 159–199.

Carattini, S., Heutel, G., & Melkadze, G. (2023). Climate policy, financial frictions, and transition risk. *Review of Economic Dynamics, 51*, 778–794.

Chaka, M. (2018). Sustainability reporting in South Africa: A descriptive and comparative analysis. *Journal of Gender, Information and Development in Africa (JGIDA), 7*(2), 159–184.

Ching, H. Y., & Gerab, F. (2017). Sustainability reports in Brazil through the lens of signaling, legitimacy and stakeholder theories. *Social Responsibility Journal, 13*(1), 95–110.

Chua, W. F., James, R., King, A., Lee, E., & Soderstrom, N. (2022). Task force on climate-related financial disclosures (TCFD) implementation: An overview and insights from the Australian accounting standards board dialogue series. *Australian Accounting Review*, *32*(3), 396–405.

Clayton, A. F., Rogerson, J. M., & Rampedi, I. (2015). Integrated reporting vs. sustainability reporting for corporate responsibility in South Africa. *Bulletin of Geography. Socio-Economic Series*, *29*, 7–17.

Dameri, R. P., & Ferrando, P. M. (2022). Value creation disclosure: The international integrated reporting framework revisited in the light of stakeholder theory. *Meditari Accountancy Research*, *30*(3), 739–761.

Dutta, P., & Dutta, A. (2021). Impact of external assurance on corporate climate change disclosures: New evidence from Finland. *Journal of Applied Accounting Research*, *22*(2), 252–285.

Ens, E., & Johnston, C. (2020). *Scenario analysis and the economic and financial risks from climate change*. https://www.econstor.eu/bitstream/10419/227814/1/1700106546.pdf

Erin, O. A., & Ackers, B. (2024). Corporate board, assurance and sustainability reporting practices: A focus on selected African countries. *Journal of Accounting & Organizational Change*.

Erin, O., Adegboye, A., & Bamigboye, O. A. (2022). Corporate governance and sustainability reporting quality: Evidence from Nigeria. *Sustainability Accounting, Management and Policy Journal*, *13*(3), 680–707.

Farisyi, S., Musadieq, M. A., Utami, H. N., & Damayanti, C. R. (2022). A systematic literature review: Determinants of sustainability reporting in developing countries. *Sustainability*, *14*(16), 1–18.

Fernandez-Feijoo, B., Romero, S., & Ruiz, S. (2018). Financial auditor and sustainability reporting: Does it matter?. *Corporate Social Responsibility and Environmental Management*, *25*(3), 209–224.

Gamage, P., & Sciulli, N. (2017). Sustainability reporting by Australian universities. *Australian Journal of Public Administration*, *76*(2), 187–203.

Girón, A., Kazemikhasragh, A., Cicchiello, A. F., & Panetti, E. (2021). Sustainability reporting and firms' economic performance: Evidence from Asia and Africa. *Journal of the Knowledge Economy*, *12*(4), 1741–1759.

Habib, A., Bhuiyan, M. B. U., & Hasan, M. M. (2019). IFRS adoption, financial reporting quality and cost of capital: A life cycle perspective. *Pacific Accounting Review*, *31*(3), 497–522.

He, X. (2022). Sustainability reporting: A nuanced view of challenges. *Social and Environmental Accountability Journal*, *42*(3), 240–243.

He, X. (2023). Sustainability and accountability in public sector: A legitimacy perspective. *Social and Environmental Accountability Journal*, *43*(1), 84–88.

Hegazy, M. A. A., & Kamareldawla, N. M. (2021). Key audit matters: Did IAASB unravel the knots of confusion in audit reports decisions? *Managerial Auditing Journal*, *36*(8), 1025–1052.

Ho, S., Sidhu, B. K., & Yang, F. (2023). The response of Australian firms to AASB 138 disallowing the recognition of internally generated identifiable intangibles. *Accounting & Finance*, *63*(3), 3609–3641.

Hossain, M. M. (2018). Sustainability reporting by Australian local government authorities. *Local Government Studies*, *44*(4), 577–600.

Hughes, O. E. (2017). *Public management and administration*. Bloomsbury Publishing.

Igwe, M. N., Khatib, S. F., & Bazhair, A. H. (2023). Sustainability reporting in Africa: A systematic review and agenda for future research. *Corporate Social Responsibility and Environmental Management*, *30*(5), 2081–2100.

Junior, R. M., Best, P. J., & Cotter, J. (2014). Sustainability reporting and assurance: A historical analysis on a world-wide phenomenon. *Journal of Business Ethics*, *120*, 1–11.

Kitsikopoulos, C., Schwaibold, U., & Taylor, D. (2018). Limited progress in sustainable development: Factors influencing the environmental management and reporting of South African JSE-listed companies. *Business Strategy and the Environment*, *27*(8), 1295–1301.

Laswad, F., & Redmayne, N. B. (2015). IPSAS or IFRS as the framework for public sector financial reporting? New Zealand preparers' perspectives. *Australian Accounting Review*, *25*(2), 175–184.

Li, A., & Lee, E. C. (2023). Commentary: Climate-related risks disclosures in the notes to financial statements: Descriptive evidence from Australia. *Australian Accounting Review*, *33*(3), 230–236.

Lin, S., Riccardi, W. N., Wang, C., Hopkins, P. E., & Kabureck, G. (2019). Relative effects of IFRS adoption and IFRS convergence on financial statement comparability. *Contemporary Accounting Research*, *36*(2), 588–628.

Lodhia, S. K., & Sharma, U. (2019). Sustainability accounting and reporting: Recent perspectives and an agenda for further research. *Pacific Accounting Review*, *31*(3), 309–312.

Lyrio, M. V. L., Lunkes, R. J., & Taliani, E. T. C. (2018). Thirty years of studies on transparency, accountability, and corruption in the public sector: The state of the art and opportunities for future research. *Public Integrity*, *20*(5), 512–533.

Marx, B., & Van Dyk, V. (2011). Sustainability reporting at large public sector entities in South Africa. *South African Journal of Accounting Research*, *25*(1), 103–127.

Mezzanotte, F. E. (2023). Corporate sustainability reporting: Double materiality, impacts, and legal risk. *Journal of Corporate Law Studies*, *23*(2), 633–663.

Moloi, T., Marwala, T., Moloi, T., & Marwala, T. (2020). The legitimacy theory and the legitimacy gap. *Artificial Intelligence in Economics and Finance Theories*, 103–113.

Muserra, A. L., Papa, M., & Grimaldi, F. (2020). Sustainable development and the European Union policy on non-financial information: An Italian empirical analysis. *Corporate Social Responsibility and Environmental Management*, *27*(1), 22–31.

Page, M. J., McKenzie, J. E., Bossuyt, P. M., Boutron, I., Hoffmann, T. C., Mulrow, C. D., & Moher, D. (2021). Updating guidance for reporting systematic reviews: Development of the PRISMA 2020 statement. *Journal of Clinical Epidemiology*, *134*, 103–112.

Petera, P., & Wagner, J. (2015). Global reporting initiative (GRI) and its reflections in the literature. *European Financial and Accounting Journal*, *10*(2), 13–32.

Pirozzi, M. (2019). Stakeholders, who are they. *PM World Journal*, *8*(9), 1–10.

Republic of Zimbabwe. (2023). *The 2024 national budget statement*. Government Printers.

Rezaee, Z., Homayoun, S., Rezaee, N. J., & Poursoleyman, E. (2023). Business sustainability reporting and assurance and sustainable development goals. *Managerial Auditing Journal*, *38*(7), 973–996.

Sethi, S. P., Rovenpor, J. L., & Demir, M. (2017). Enhancing the quality of reporting in corporate social responsibility guidance documents: The roles of ISO 26000, global reporting initiative and CSR-sustainability monitor. *Business and Society Review*, *122*(2), 139–163.

Songi, O., & Dias, A. K. (2019). Sustainability reporting in Africa. *Business Ethics*, *279*, 536–550.

Stolowy, H., & Paugam, L. (2023). Sustainability reporting: Is convergence possible? *Accounting in Europe*, *20*(2), 139–165.

Tasdemir, C., & Gazo, R. (2018). A systematic literature review for better understanding of lean driven sustainability. *Sustainability*, *10*(7), 2544.

Tauringana, V. (2021). Sustainability reporting challenges in developing countries: Towards management perceptions research evidence-based practices. *Journal of Accounting in Emerging Economies*, *11*(2), 194–215.

The International Public Sector Accounting Standards Board (IPSASB). (2024). *IPSASB strategy and work program 2024-2028*. https://www.ipsasb.org/publications/login/69699

The International Public Sector Accounting Standards Board (IPSASB). (2022). *Handbook of international public sector accounting pronouncements*. https://www.ipsasb.org/publications/login/59225

Tilt, C. A., Qian, W., Kuruppu, S., & Dissanayake, D. (2021). The state of business sustainability reporting in sub-Saharan Africa: An agenda for policy and practice. *Sustainability Accounting, Management and Policy Journal*, *12*(2), 267–296.

Tumwebaze, Z., Bananuka, J., Kaawaase, T. K., Bonareri, C. T., & Mutesasira, F. (2022). Audit committee effectiveness, internal audit function and sustainability reporting practices. *Asian Journal of Accounting Research*, *7*(2), 163–181.

United Nations Framework Convention on Climate Change (UNFCCC). (2015). *United Nations' Paris Agreement*. https://unfccc.int/sites/default/files/resource/parisagreement_publication.pdf

United States Environmental Protection Agency (US EPA). (2024). *Climate-related financial risks and opportunities*. https://www.epa.gov/climateleadership/climate-related-financial-risks-and-opportunities

Uyar, A., Karmani, M., Kuzey, C., Kilic, M., & Yaacoub, C. (2022). Does governance quality explain the sustainability reporting tendency of the public sector? Worldwide evidence. *International Journal of Public Administration*, *45*(13), 931–947.

Uyar, A., Kuzey, C., & Kilic, M. (2021). Sustainable stock market and sustainability reporting propensity of the public sector: Mediating role of the private sector. *International Journal of Public Administration*, *44*(4), 322–335.

Wallage, P. (2000). Assurance on sustainability reporting: An auditor's view. *Auditing: A Journal of Practice & Theory*, *19*(s-1), 53–65.

Wambwa, D., Mundike, J., & Chirambo, B. (2024). Assessing financial assurance instruments for climate change mitigation and adaptation: A comparative study of Zambia and South Africa. *Scientific African*, *25*(1), 1–13.

World Bank. (2023). *Mauritius public expenditure review from resilience to performance: modernizing fiscal policies to boost Mauritius's growth post-pandemic*. https://documents1.worldbank.org/curated/en/099112323101025381/pdf/P176975023a29404f0850b02f95174298e8.pdf

Zharfpeykan, R., & Askarany, D. (2023). Sustainability reporting and organisational factors. *Journal of Risk and Financial Management*, *16*(3), 163.

A DYNAMIC, SURVIVORSHIP BIAS-FREE VIEW ON SCIENCE-BASED TARGETS: RESEARCH OPPORTUNITIES CONCERNING PRIVATE AND LISTED FIRMS

Thomas Kaspereit

University of Luxembourg, Luxembourg

ABSTRACT

The Science-Based Targets initiative (SBTi) presents numerous research opportunities, though empirical-archival studies remain scarce due to data access limitations. This chapter introduces a comprehensive, survivorship bias-free dataset of firms committed to or having set Science-Based Targets (SBTs), constructed from monthly snapshots of the SBTi dashboard (2015–2024) via the Internet Archive (Wayback Machine). This dataset, matched with S&P Capital IQ, provides granular insights into the target-setting process, including commitment, submission, validation and removal stages, offering a unique research setting due to SBTi's evolving transparency policies. Since February 2023, SBTi has adopted a 'name-and-shame' policy, flagging firms that withdraw or miss submission deadlines, in contrast to previous silent removals. This shift allows the examination of factors affecting firms' adherence to or withdrawal from climate commitments, such as peer influences and leadership traits within industries. Additionally, the dataset addresses challenges in firm identification, leveraging a fuzzy-matching process to link SBTi firms with S&P Capital IQ

Climate Risks Reporting Practices and Assurance
Advances in Environmental Accounting & Management, Volume 13, 113–143

ISSN: 1479-3598/doi:10.1108/S1479-359820250000013014

data, resulting in an 83.3% successful match rate and 8,298 matched firms. This method counters attrition inherent in current SBTi data. The research potential enabled by this dataset spans questions on industry dynamics, firm-level determinants of climate commitment, economic drivers and consequences.

Keywords: Science-Based Targets initiative (SBTi); greenhouse gas emission reduction; carbon emissions; emission reduction targets; dynamic data collection; survivorship-bias free data; sustainability; Paris Agreement

1. INTRODUCTION

The Science-Based Targets initiative (SBTi) is a collaborative effort that helps firms set emission reduction targets aligned with the Paris Agreement. The initiative involves organizations such as the Carbon Disclosure Project (CDP), the United Nations Global Compact, the World Resources Institute (WRI) and the World Wide Fund for Nature (WWF). The data disclosed on the initiative's website offer numerous research opportunities; however, empirical-archival research on the topic has been limited. Only a handful of working papers from high-profile research groups (Bolton & Kacperczyk, 2024; Freiberg et al., 2021) and publications in reputable academic journals exist (Bendig et al., 2023; Bolay et al., 2024; Romito et al., 2024). I argue that this discrepancy between research potential and output is due to challenges related to accessing data on when firms join or withdraw from the initiative. To address these challenges, I present a monthly, survivorship-free dataset of firms, matched with S&P Capital IQ, that have committed to or set Science-Based Targets (SBTs). My objective is to ensure that this dataset will enable researchers to explore questions that may have previously seemed infeasible or too costly – due to the demands of data collection and cleaning.

SBTs provide a rich research environment, as they encompass managerial decisions – both actions and inactions – across multiple stages of the greenhouse gas (GHG) reduction target-setting process. This includes target validation and removal decisions made by the non-governmental SBTi. The SBTi itself experiences varying degrees of public support and criticism over time, which affects its perceived legitimacy (Tilsted et al., 2023). For instance, in December 2023, Reclaim Finance, a non-governmental organization and think tank focused on sustainable finance, criticized the SBTi for 'dumping science' by weakening its net-zero standards for financial institutions, thereby allowing banks and investors to continue financing fossil fuel projects (Burley & Shreiber, 2023).

The target-setting process typically involves four steps, of which the first and last are observable to the public: (1) firms commit to setting a target that is aligned with the Paris Agreement; (2) within 24 months of committing, firms submit their targets to the SBTi; (3) the SBTi provides feedback and may request revisions; and (4) after final approval by the SBTi, the target is officially set. Once firms commit to setting targets, they immediately appear on the SBTi dashboard, along with information about the type of target-setting commitment. Target types can broadly be categorized by their time horizons: near-term targets (by 2030) and long-term targets (such as 'net zero' by 2050). There are also distinctions in the level of reduction committed, such as whether the target aligns with a 1.5°C or a 'well below 2.0°C' pathway. While the SBTi dashboard provides no updates when a firm submits its targets or during the approval process (steps 2 and 3), it acknowledges the final setting of targets. If a firm fails to submit and does not get its targets approved within 24 months, two outcomes are possible, depending on when this occurs. Before February 2023, firms were silently removed from the dashboard, leaving no record in the downloadable Excel file from the SBTi website. However, starting in February 2023, the SBTi began flagging firms that withdraw or are overdue on submitting near-term targets as 'commitment removed', while keeping them in the data. This policy has been extended to long-term targets starting in March 2024. This is a fascinating research setting, as the regime has shifted from a silent removal process to a transparent 'name-and-shame' approach. Firms can still submit their targets after being flagged and, upon approval, switch their status from 'commitment removed' to 'target set'.[1]

The primary challenge for researchers using SBTi data stems from the lack of archival data and SBTi's unresponsiveness to data requests.[2] The fact that, until February 2023, removals were performed silently, and the SBTi does not provide historical archives of its dashboard, presents a major challenge for research aimed at understanding why firms fail to meet their commitments or the consequences of dropping a commitment versus ultimately setting a target. Unsurprisingly, existing research focuses on the determinants of target commitment and setting, rather than the target removal process (Bolton & Kacperczyk, 2024).

However, as the saying goes, the internet never forgets – and this holds true for target commitments and removals as well. The main contribution of this chapter is the construction and description of a dataset based on monthly snapshots from the Internet Archive (Wayback Machine) of the SBTi dashboard, dating back to its inception in September 2015 and extending up to September 2024, thereby covering a full nine-year history. I anticipate that this dynamic and survivorship-bias free view on the target-setting process will enable researchers to address a wide range of relevant questions, such as whether peer effects exist between committing and withdrawing firms, and if so, whether there are industry leaders and followers. What management or firm characteristics determine leadership in this area? What are the economic factors driving these actions or inactions? These are just a few research ideas, which I will develop further and more systematically in the subsequent sections.

A secondary but significant challenge with SBTi data is the lack of consistent firm identifiers. The SBTi records firms by the names they provide, which often makes name-matching with financial databases difficult. These names may not even correspond to the firms' legal entity names but instead represent doing-business-as designations or product names. For example, the German firm 'Intelligent Apps GmbH' committed and validated targets under their brand name 'FREENOW', which is the name of their ride-hailing application. No purely text-based matching algorithm would reliably link such names. To address this issue, I match firm names in the SBTi data with those in S&P Capital IQ, a financial database that includes doing-business-as designations for both private and public firms. I complement the database provider's automatic matching algorithm with a fuzzy-matching process to compare SBTi firm names against the entire S&P Capital IQ universe. Then, I conduct thorough manual checks of any imperfect matches and fill gaps in SBTi firm coverage manually. This laborious process results in 9,417 matched firm names, leaving only 1,885 unmatched firm names in the SBTi dataset. Thus, the overall matching success rate exceeds 83.3%.[3] These 9,417 matched firm names belong to 8,298 distinct legal entities as defined by S&P Capital IQ's Entity ID. The overall revenues of matched firms range up to 29.2 trillion US-dollar and the market capitalization of the public firms up to 57.0 trillion US-dollar. The population is composed of an almost equal mixture of private and public firms in the recent years, while listed firms dominate in the earlier years. 15.6% of firms are headquartered in the United Kingdom and 13.5% in the United States. Industrial and consumer discretionary are the most represented industries. Using only the currently available information on the SBTi website, a dataset could miss up to a quarter of the firms that participated in the initiative during its early years. My data collection methodology corrects for this potential source of survivorship bias.

The remainder of this chapter is structured as follows. In the following section, I outline existing empirical-archival research on SBTs. In Section III, I describe the data collection, matching and cleaning processes. In Section IV, I develop research ideas that could be addressed using the newly created dataset. Section V concludes this chapter.

2. PRIOR EMPIRICAL-ARCHIVAL RESEARCH USING SBTi DATA

To obtain a systematic overview of best practices in SBT data collection and research questions that have already been addressed, I conduct a systematic literature review of all empirical-archival studies found within the first 100 results of each Google Scholar search using the terms *Science-Based Targets*, *Science-Based Targets capital markets* or *Science-Based Targets determinants*. This results in 18 studies, whose literature review and reference list sections I scan for relevant titles, yielding 2 additional studies, totalling 20 studies of diverse academic quality (i.e. ranging from publications in high-quality peer-reviewed journals and working papers from high-profile research groups to student theses with interesting research questions, some with obvious methodological limitations) as displayed in Table 1. I discuss 10 studies in more detail, selected based on my assessment of the high quality of the publication outlets or the reputation of the research groups. This choice is subjective, which is why I display short quotes on the main results of all 20 studies in Table 2. To maintain focus on the quantitative literature, my review excludes otherwise noteworthy qualitative studies, such as Berger-Schmitz et al. (2023) and Privato et al. (2024).

The most general, and thus most relevant, studies on the determinants and effects of committing to or setting SBTs are Bolton and Kacperczyk (2024), Bendig et al. (2023) and Freiberg et al. (2021).

Bolton and Kacperczyk (2024) combine data from Trucost, FactSet and SBTi (and, for other tests, from the Carbon Disclosure Project – CDP) over the period 2015–2019 to show that firms making commitments subsequently reduce their emissions. The authors do not specify how they obtained data on SBTs in their working paper. Upon email request, they explained that they also relied on the

Table 1. Literature Overview on Empirical Archival Studies Using SBT (Highlighted Are the Studies That Are Discussed in Detail; Citation Count From Google Scholar as of 23 October 2024).

No.	Authors (Year)	Publication Outlet	Citations	Period of SBT Data	Private Firms	Firms With SBT	Data Source for SBTs	Surv Bias	Dependent Variable	SBTi variables (C = committing) (S = Setting)	Financial Database
(1)	Ben-Amar et al (2024)	*Bus. Strat. Environ.*	0	2019	No	99	CDP	No	Stock returns	C & S (jointly)	Eikon
(2)	Bendig et al. (2023)	*J. Ind. Ecol.*	33	2015–2020	No	465	SBTi snapshot end of 2020	Yes	Return on assets, Tobin's Q	C & S (jointly)	Eikon
(3)	Berg et al. (2024)	Working paper	2	2016–2021	No	616	SBTi snapshot likely from 2021	Yes	Emissions, emission intensity	C & S (separately)	Unknown
(4)	Bharali Saikia and Maji (2024)	*Int. J. Law Manag.*	0	2019–2023	No	7	SBTi snapshot March 2023	No	Tobin's Q	S	ACE
(5)	Bjørn et al (2022)	*Curr. Clim. Change Rep.*	78	2015–2021	Yes	1,039	SBTi snapshot December 2021	Yes	None	S	None
(6)	Bolay et al (2024)	*J. Clean. Prod.*	0	2020	Yes	17%	CDP	No	Target progress	S	None
(7)	Bolton and Kacperczyk (2024)	Working paper	119	2015–2019	No	455	SBTi snapshot and historical snapshots from the internet archive likely from 2021	No	Science-based targets; Future emissions	C & S (separately)	FactSet, I/B/ES
(8)	Dahlstroem et al. (2023)	Working paper	0	2017–2022	No	757	SBTi snapshot likely from 2022	Yes	Stock return	C & S (separately)	Eikon
(9)	Freiberg et al (2021)	Working paper	48	2016–2019	No	1752	CDP	No	Science-based targets; Target ambitiousness	S	Bloomberg
(10)	Gehrke et al (2024)	Working paper	0	2015–2022	No	15.%	CDP and SBTi	?	Emissions, emission intensity	C & S (jointly)	Eikon

(Continued)

Table 1. *(Continued)*

No.	Authors (Year)	Publication Outlet	Citations	Period of SBT Data	Private Firms	Firms With SBT	Data Source for SBTs	Surv Bias	Dependent Variable	SBTi variables (C = committing) (S = Setting)	Financial Database
(11)	Giesekam et al (2021)	*Sustainability*	94	2015–2020	Yes	915	SBTi snapshot Jun 2020	Yes	Future emissions	C & S (separately)	Orbis
(12)	Guerrero-Escobar et al (2023)	Working paper	0	2015–2022	No	1,379	SBTi snapshots May 2021 and May 2022	Yes	Stock return, volatility	C & S (separately)	Bloomberg
(13)	Kacperczyk and Peydró (2024)	Working paper	172	2015–2018	No	28	SBTi snapshot likely from 2018 SBTi and historical snapshots from the internet archive	No	Emissions, emission intensity of borrowers	C	Compustat Capital IQ
(14)	Kaltenhauser (2023)	*Jun. Manag. Sci.*	0	2019–2021	No	<186	Media news	No	Science-based targets; Returns	C & S (jointly)	Eikon
(15)	Ko and Prakash (2024)	*npj Clim. Action*	0	2015–2023	No	188	SBTi snapshot Mar 2024	Yes	Stock return	C	CRSP, Compustat
(16)	Kuo and Chang (2021)	*Sustain. Prod. Consum.*	31	2016–2019	Yes	127	CDP	No	Carbon disclosure level	S	AsiaOne
(17)	Pindea Pérez (2023)	Master thesis	0	2015–2022	No	1,050	SBTi snapshot Mar 2023	Yes	Stock return, volatility, value-at-risk	C & S (jointly)	Eikon
(18)	Romito et al (2023)	*Bus. Strat. Environ.*	6	2015–2017	No	254	SBTi	Yes	Emissions, emission intensity	C & S (separately)	Eikon
(19)	Schuiling (2023)	Master thesis	0	2015–2021	No	962	SBTi snapshot May 2023	Yes	Emissions, ESG scores, environmental innovation	C & S (separately)	Eikon
(20)	Zhang (2022)	Master thesis	1	2018–2019	No	143	CDP	No	Emissions, emission intensity	S	Eikon

Table 2. Key Findings in the Literature.

No.	Authors (Year)	Results (Citation From the Abstract or Conclusion Section)
(1)	Ben-Amar et al (2024)	Using a sample of 336 US-based companies, our findings show that science-based targets are positively related to crash-period returns and negatively related to severity of loss
(2)	Bendig et al. (2023)	Our findings indicate a positive association between CCP and CFP for firms engaging in SBTs, implying a positive relation between decarbonization efforts and financial results
(3)	Berg et al (2024)	When controlling for assurance, we do not find evidence that SBTi target-setters reduce their future emissions. Instead, firms that obtain assurance reduce their future carbon intensity by 3.3%
(4)	Bharali Saikia and Maji (2024)	There is a negative relationship between corporate carbon emissions and financial performance. The findings support the 'win-win' hypothesis and confirm that reducing carbon emissions can improve the financial performance of Indian firms. Furthermore, the SBTi moderate the carbon emission and firm performance nexus
(5)	Bjørn et al (2022)	Descriptive study and review of prior literature
(6)	Bolay et al (2024)	Companies with more ambitious targets progress less than others, except when the ambitious targets are approved by the Science-Based Targets initiative
(7)	Bolton and Kacperczyk (2024)	While the companies that make commitments subsequently reduce their emissions, the effect on overall emissions of companies (including those that do not commit) has been small; the companies that commit, and those that make the most ambitious commitments, tend to have lower emissions
(8)	Dahlstroem et al. (2023)	Based on a sample of 757 SBTi committed international firms and a control group consisting of 748 peers as non-committed firms over the period 2018–2022, we find a positive SBTi transition premium
(9)	Freiberg et al (2021)	We find that firms with a track record of setting and achieving ambitious carbon targets are more likely to set science-based targets. Firms are also more likely to set science-based targets if they perceive climate change-related risks and have carbon-intensive operations. Using a difference-in-differences research design that compares the science and non-science targets of a firm, we find that targets become more difficult when firms adopt the science-based standard for the target, consistent with the standard increasing target difficulty and inconsistent with firms relabelling their existing targets. The increase in target difficulty is accompanied by more investment in carbon-reduction projects and higher expected emissions and monetary savings from these projects
(10)	Gehrke et al (2024)	One main finding is that firms with a science-based target achieve 4%–15% lower carbon emissions
(11)	Giesekam et al (2021)	Though the majority of targets assessed were on track and, in some cases, had already been achieved, just under half of the companies assessed were falling behind on one or more of their targets
(12)	Guerrero-Escobar et al (2023)	We find no evidence that committing or setting a target yields higher returns, while the impacts on price volatility are negative but short-lived
(13)	Kacperczyk and Peydró (2024)	Firms with higher carbon footprint previously borrowing from committed banks subsequently receive less bank credit. Affected firms also lower their total debt, leverage, size, and real investments, and increase their liquid assets

(Continued)

Table 2. *(Continued)*

No.	Authors (Year)	Results (Citation From the Abstract or Conclusion Section)
(14)	Kaltenhauser (2023)	The results reveal a significant correlation between a variety of determinants and a net-zero target announcement (e.g., industry profile, firm size) and show a significant negative capital market response irrespective of a target's individual attributes
(15)	Ko and Prakash (2024)	Our analysis of S&P 500 companies' quarterly stock prices for 2010–2023 finds little evidence that SBTi verification (of any type) increases stock prices
(16)	Kuo and Chang (2021)	The empirical results show that setting SBT or adopting ICP for carbon reduction have significantly positive effects on enhancing firms' CMR, respectively
(17)	Pindea Pérez (2023)	It has been found that there is a negative relationship when the financial variable is stock return. While when volatility and financial risk are measured, there is no statistically significant effect
(18)	Romito et al (2023)	The results showed that firms' participation led to lower levels of GHG emissions compared to similar non-participating counterparts, especially when they committed to the initiative with the intention to follow the proposed indications
(19)	Schuiling (2023)	The SBTi did not have any significant effect on emission no matter if we look at total emissions, scope one or scope two emissions, showing that setting the targets did not influence company action. ESG and Environmental Innovation Scores on the other hand were slightly negatively influenced, which could result from the SBTi's stricter regulations, time lags or the financial strain approval fees put on firms
(20)	Zhang (2022)	A difference-in-differences (DID) model is used in this study, which shows that firms setting SBTs reduce their absolute GHG emissions by about 5% and their carbon intensity by 8–10%

Internet Archive (Wayback Machine) to fill data gaps. As my later analysis will show, obtaining historical snapshots is important to avoid survivorship bias because firms silently are removed from the SBTi list of committed firms, either temporarily or permanently. The main finding of Bolton and Kacperczyk (2024) is that firms making commitments subsequently reduce their emissions, albeit with a small measured effect. Furthermore, firms that commit tend to be those with lower emissions in the first place.

Bendig et al. (2023) conduct an association study on the effects of decarbonization and financial performance, restricting their sample to firms that 'engage' (either commit to or set SBTs). They find a positive relationship between decarbonization efforts and financial results. Their consideration of whether a firm engages with SBTi is based on a snapshot of SBTi data from the end of 2020.

In an attempt to obtain panel data on SBTs that do not suffer from survivorship bias, Freiberg et al. (2021) consult CDP survey data on whether firms commit to or set SBTs. Freiberg et al. (2021, pp. 19–20) describe their data collection as follows: 'Starting in 2016, a new field was added to the CDP survey that allows us to identify emissions reduction targets as science-based. This new field asked "Is this a science-based target?" and permitted the following responses: “Yes”; “No, but we are reporting another target that is science-based”; “No, but we anticipate setting one in the next two years”; “No, and we do not anticipate setting one in the next two years”; and “Don’t know”. Although it is possible that a firm could identify a target as being science-based in its CDP response when it is not, we cross-checked the CDP responses with a listing of firms with approved science-based targets from the SBTi and noted only nine discrepancies that were due to mismatched company names or identifiers’. As the authors correctly state, the validity of the CDP questionnaire hinges on the accuracy of the responses provided by the firms. While I share the authors’ optimism regarding the validity of the responses provided by their sample of 1,752 listed firms in the early period, I am less optimistic about the more than 20,000 private and listed firms that respond to the CDP nowadays and the more than 8,000 firms that commit to or set SBTs. The consistency between CDP responses and SBTi data is a research topic on its own, for which the dataset I develop and describe in this chapter would be needed. Based on anecdotal evidence, we know that inferring SBTi status from CDP data introduces type II errors, as some listed firms did not participate in the CDP survey but were listed as SBT-committed firms on the SBTi dashboard.[4] I anticipate that the prevalence of private firms not responding to the CDP but committing to SBTs is comparatively higher, as putting one’s firm name on a list is an almost costless action, while responding to a comprehensive questionnaire is a more complex and thus costlier task. The results in Freiberg et al. (2021) indicate, among other findings, that firms with a track record of setting and achieving ambitious carbon targets are more likely to set science-based targets. These results are challenged by Berg et al. (2024), who find that, when controlling for assurance, there is no evidence that SBTi target-setters reduce their future emissions.

An important aspect of research on SBTs is whether firms committing to or setting targets differ from peers in terms of accounting or stock market performance. Especially for any study addressing the latter research question, an unbiased dataset that contains only information available at the time is required. Testing portfolio strategies with any survivorship or hindsight bias is considered inadmissible (Garcia & Gould, 1993). Nonetheless, Dahlström et al. (2023) use a snapshot from the SBTi dashboard as of early 2020 to define a treatment group (SBT-setting firms) and a control group (SBT-committing but not target-setting firms). Their estimation involves data from 2018 onward, and the results show that there is an SBTi adoption premium. Ben-Amar et al. (2024) show that the stock returns of US firms with SBTs in place or committed to setting SBTs had higher returns during the COVID-19 crisis.

Further studies on the consequences of target-setting or commitment to target-setting lend support to the hypothesis that emissions or emissions intensities decrease after joining the SBTi list of firms (Bolay et al., 2024; Romito et al., 2024) or even trigger changes in bank lender preferences toward less carbon-intensive clients (Kacperczyk & Peydró, 2024).

With the exceptions of Bolton and Kacperczyk (2024) and Kacperczyk and Peydró (2024), the studies in Tables 1 and 2 have in common that they either use snapshots of SBTi data – a data collection strategy that is potentially vulnerable to survivorship bias when firms silently drop from the list during the earlier years, before the flagging as 'commitment removed' was introduced by the SBTi – or rely on CDP questionnaire data, which is incomplete and possibly suffers from data input errors by the responding firms.

3. CREATING A SURVIVORSHIP BIAS-FREE SBTi DATASET

3.1 Overview on Procedural Steps

The data collection process consists of three key elements: (1) scraping all available snapshots of the SBTi dashboard website on the Internet Archive (Wayback Machine); (2) creating a matching list between the firm names found in those snapshots and S&P Capital IQ, including manual checking of machine-matched firm names; and (3) aligning the data onto a monthly timeline, i.e. creating a balanced dataset to identify gaps and manually research their causes. If any gap results from an error in the name-matching procedure, this error is corrected manually; if it arises from another reason, such as a firm disappearing from S&P Capital IQ due to bankruptcy or acquisition, the reason is recorded and not considered a silent dropping from the SBTi list. Researchers interested in investigating the phenomenon of firms dropping commitments to set SBTs will likely want these events separated from any other reason for a firm's disappearance. In other words, a silent dropping from the SBTi dashboard is only relevant if the respective firm continues to exist and the dropping is not confounded by other reasons for disappearance.

3.2 Scraping SBTi Data

I use a Python script with the Selenium and Beautiful Soup libraries to scrape all 1,379 snapshots (archived versions of a website that are stored by the Internet Archive) of the website 'sciencebasedtargets.org/companies-taking-action' in the Internet Archive. The Internet Archive takes snapshots at irregular intervals. Fig. 1 shows a screenshot of the overview of available snapshots over time. The Internet Archive reports 3,620 available snapshots, for 2,241 of them the data tables of the dashboard were not saved to the archive, potentially because the bot did not wait long enough for the table to load.

Except for the very early years of the SBTi, when data was stored in single-page HTML tables that can be read with Beautiful Soup, the data is generally held in multi-paginated, JavaScript-based tables that must be scraped page-by-page using Selenium. This process, while extremely time-intensive due to the long loading times of pages and IP-blocking/throttling, is remarkably stable, i.e. it runs without interruption and, in my experience, never misses any data. The last snapshot is available from 25 June 2024, after which SBTi introduced a CAPTCHA that prevents the Internet Archive from storing snapshots of the dashboard.[5]

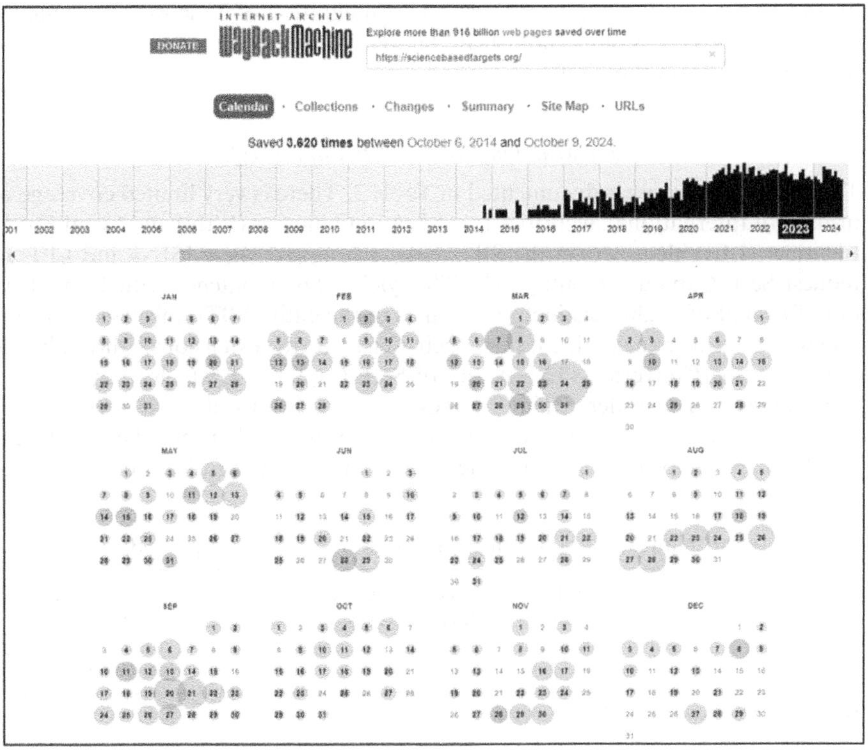

Fig. 1. Screenshot From the Internet Archive (as of 23 October 2024).

In addition to the data from the website snapshots, I download the MS Excel files that SBTi offered for download alongside the data tables. These MS Excel files are stored by the Internet Archive considerably less frequently, i.e. 11 files during the period from 30 November 2021 to 5 June 2024. From 25 June 2024 onward, I archived these tables with a frequency of one download per week on Fridays because, according to information provided by SBTi, updates occur on Thursdays. In doing so, I maintain a survivorship bias-free, up-to-date data structure even after the introduction of the CAPTCHA in June 2024.

3.3 The Choice of S&P Capital IQ

My choice of S&P Capital IQ as the referential database to create a unique firm identifier for the SBTi firms is motivated by careful consideration of its features and those of alternative research database products. Compared to Bloomberg, Orbis (Bureau Van Dijk), FactSet and Eikon (Refinitiv), S&P Capital IQ stands out in terms of its broad coverage of listed and private firms, its coverage of financial data (accounting and stock price data), its integration of Trucost data (since 2016, Trucost has been a product of Standard & Poor's with cross-matched firm identifiers) and its moderate cost.[6] The integration of Trucost is particularly appealing, as this is an established database for carbon emission data that includes data from the CDP.

3.4 Matching With S&P Capital IQ

The matching process is documented in Table 3. There is very limited coverage of firms with International Securities Identification Number (ISIN) and Legal Entity Identifier (LEI) identifiers in the SBTi data. I prioritize these ISINs and LEIs to request S&P Capital IQ Entity IDs. This yields 2,690 matches with Capital IQ out of a total of 11,302 distinct firm names in the entire SBTi universe. I run the remaining firm names, including their legal form extensions, through the SPG_IdentifierConverter_v1.xlsm tool of S&P Capital IQ, which fuzzy-matches firm names and considers doing-business-as designations alongside legal entity names. This yields 3,178 perfect matches. Since the residual matches are fuzzy, i.e. there are minor or even major deviations in the matched legal entity names,

Table 3. Firm Name Matching of SBTi Data With S&P Capital IQ.

	Step 1: ISIN/LEI Matching	Step 2: Fuzzy matching SPG_IdentifierConverter_v1	Step 3 Fuzzy matching reclink2.ado	Sum
Distinct firm names in SBTi data	11,302			
- thereof: matches based on ISIN/LEI	**2,690**			2,690
= remaining unmatched firm names for Step 2	8,612	⇒ 8,612		
- thereof: perfect name matches		**3,178**		3,178
- thereof: approved fuzzy matches		**2,629**		2,629
= remaining unmatched firms for Step 3		2,805	⇒ 2,805	
- thereof: approved fuzzy matches			**920**	920
= total number of matched firm names				9,417
Matched modified firm names				8,352
- reductions due to manual corrections after reviewing gaps and disappearances				50
- short appearances and disappearances between the start and end of the month				4
= total number of matched firm names after corrections				8,298

they require manual checking. I perform this manual checking by also considering the country recorded in the SBTi data versus the headquarter country recorded in S&P Capital IQ, and the industry that firms self-report to SBTi versus what is recorded in S&P Capital IQ. Whenever necessary, I conduct in-depth research on firm histories to understand name changes and merger and acquisition transactions to judge whether a firm name in SBTi refers to the same entity as the suggested match in S&P Capital IQ. I remain conservative, i.e. I require certainty of a correct match beyond reasonable doubt to manually approve a fuzzy match. This procedure leads to 2,629 approved fuzzy matches. For the remaining unmatched firm names, I run another fuzzy matching procedure using the user-written Stata command reclink2.ado (Wasi & Flaaen, 2015) and the Foundation data file, which lists all firm names in S&P Capital IQ. This final step results in 920 additional manually checked matches. The total number of matches is 9,417, associated with 8,352 unique S&P Capital IQ Entity IDs. The excess of firm names over unique identifiers is due to the same firm reporting different names; sometimes these are nuances in legal entity designations, while in other cases they are significant name changes or switches between legal entity names and doing-business-as designations.

I pay particular attention to firms that presumably disappear from the SBTi list. First, I manually check any firm that temporarily disappears. Often, this phenomenon can be traced back to the matching algorithm failing to find a match because a firm temporarily appears under a different name. I correct these cases, which leads to an overall reduction of 50 distinct S&P Capital IQ Entity IDs. In other cases, the firm commitment was indeed silently removed. To ensure that I properly distinguish between these fundamentally different reasons for absence, I also search Google for any information I can find on this firm in connection with SBTi. A typical pattern indicating true absence is finding an announcement of SBTi in an earlier year, for example, 2021, but no evidence that the firm ever set a target, and no mention in later sustainability reports regarding SBTi. Sometimes, the information found in sustainability reports after disappearance from the SBTi list is subtle: firms state that their targets are oriented toward or aligned with SBT guidelines, but avoid mentioning that these targets have been approved by SBTi or that the firm is still committed to having them approved. Often, direct reference to SBTi is avoided, while the firm uses the general term 'science-based', which technically leaves open the question of to which branch of climate science the firm is referencing.

Finally, there are four instances where legal entities appear only between the start and end of a month. These 'mayflies' are cases where firms decided to shift the target quickly to a different level in the corporate tree or corrected the name reported to the SBTi to reflect the correct level within the corporate tree at which the target is situated. Since my dataset has a monthly frequency, these instances fall through the gaps.

In total, the dataset contains 8,298 S&P Capital IQ-matched firms. Researchers are naturally interested in knowing how many of these firms are private versus listed. Since listing status can change over time, I track the availability of the data point 'market value of equity' in S&P Capital IQ to proxy for listing status. For 2,576 firms, I observe market value of equity at some point during the nine years of data coverage. The residual 5,722 firms remained private throughout the period covered by the dataset.

4. EVOLUTION OF SBTi COMMITMENTS AND TARGETS OVER TIME

4.1 Primer on SBTi Policy Changes

To understand the new dataset, it is imperative to review some important policy changes on the part of SBTi. Until January 2023, firms that did not submit targets within 24 months of making a commitment were silently removed from the dashboard. Since that time, SBTi has kept such firms on the dashboard but marks them as 'commitment removed' if they fail to submit their targets within the allotted time.

The 24-month deadline applies only to target submission, meaning that more than 24 months can elapse between target commitment and either commitment removal or target setting, as the target approval process itself may take several months. It is important to understand what happens if a firm submits within the 24-month deadline, but the approval process extends beyond this period and/or approval is not granted on the first attempt, requiring the application to be sent back for revision. For the period between April 2020 and January 2023, when the second version of the 'Protocol to Manage Expired Commitments' was effective (SBTi, 2020), this case was clearly defined: the firm would be removed from the list while preserving the possibility of getting back on it after having its revised targets ultimately approved. The wording of this scenario is less clear in the new policy effective from January 2023, which states that firms are flagged as 'commitment removed' if their commitment expired (24-month period) and they 'did not reach successful validation of their targets according to their commitment' (SBTi, 2022). When read together with the policy of 2020, it would be logical to assume that after a first unsuccessful attempt at validation extending beyond the 24-month period, the firm would be flagged as 'commitment removed' until successful resubmission and approval. I wonder, however, if SBTi would follow through with such a strict approach, as flagging a firm as 'commitment removed' despite an ongoing approval process could have legal implications and pose a litigation risk for SBTi – without having evaluated this aspect in depth, I envisage that a firm could challenge the non-approval in court and claim compensation for damage done to its reputation.

The 24-month deadline is subject to multiple exceptions, which depend on when the firm commits, i.e. which version of the three policies for commitment expiries (SBTi, 2018, 2020, 2022) is in place at the time of committing, and also which of the three policies is effective at the time the commitment expires. Table 4 provides an overview containing key quotes from the three versions of the policy and my summary assessment.

Table 4. Expiring Commitment Policies.

Version of Policy	Effective Date	Quotes/Summary Assessments
1	6-Dec-18	'[. . .], if a company shows **good faith** to develop a science-based target or where companies are waiting for a sector development to be completed (e.g. financial institutions), **the 24-month requirement may be waived. [**. . .] under certain circumstances, extensions can be discussed [. . .]' 'For companies in **sectors without a science-based target setting methodology, no action** will be taken' '[. . .], an **extension of up to six months** can be offered, provided that the company agrees to submit targets for official validation within this period' 'For committed companies that have **submitted targets** for official validation within the 24-month period and **have not fulfilled the SBTi criteria**, **an extension of up to twelve months** can be granted, provided that the company agrees to re-submit their target within this period' 'Any request for extensions beyond the time frames indicated in this Protocol will be approved by the Steering Committee of the SBTi on a **case-by-case basis**'
		Summary assessment: Commitment extensions of 6 months, 12 months, or longer could be awarded at the **discretion of the SBTi.**
2	15-Apr-20	'**All companies** committed to the SBTi before April 15th, 2020 **that have not been offered an extension will be granted 12 months** to complete the four step process of the Call to Action, if needed' 'Under **special circumstances** the SBTi may grant companies **additional time** to publish their targets' 'Companies that have publicly committed to set SBTs through the SBTi and joined the Business Ambition for 1.5°C campaign will have until the end of their existing commitment period to set targets. An **extension up to 12 months** may be offered' '**No action** to be taken for any company in a **sector without a science-based target setting methodology**; companies classified as Financial Institutions or Oil and Gas, as per the definitions provided by the SBTi, will have 24 months to submit targets for validation from the date the methodologies become available'
		Summary assessment: Automatic commitment extensions of **12 months for essentially all firms**; no deadline for financial firms and oil and gas firms. Further prolongations possible **'under special circumstances'.**

(Continued)

Table 4. *(Continued)*

Version of Policy	Effective Date	Quotes/Summary Assessments
3	31-Jan-23	'**No extensions will be granted on a case-by-case basis'.** 'Companies with **previously granted extensions** will have those extensions **honored'** 'Companies with commitments that expire before the new policy enters into force [31 January 2023] will **automatically be granted a one-off six-month grace period** to fulfill their commitment. [...] with the deadline for target submission of **31 July 2023'** **Business Ambition for 1.5C:** **Corporates: 31 Jan 2024** **Financial Institutions: 24 months from Financial Institutions Net-Zero launch [not yet launched]**
		Summary assessment: no more catch-all clauses such as 'case-by-case', 'special circumstance', or 'good faith' that would allow SBTi to extend commitment periods at their discretion. First **commitment removals foreseen for 31 July 2023**. For firms that joined the **Business Ambition for 1.5C campaign** between June 2019 and October 2021, removals are expected to occur soon **after January 2024.**

Versions 1.0 and 2.0 are governed by a set of automatic and loosely defined subjective criteria under which SBTi can offer commitment period extensions. In essence, it was at the discretion of SBTi, on a case-by-case basis, whether a firm was granted an extension. The tone became slightly more decisive in Version 2.0 ('under special circumstances') relative to the prior version ('showing good faith'). A fundamental shift occurred with Version 3.0, which was released in November 2022 and became effective on 31 January 2023. It explicitly abandoned case-by-case decisions and introduced two fixed deadlines (apart from legacy extensions):

- *31 July 2023* for any firms that have surpassed the 24-month commitment period without submitting targets for approval.
- *31 January 2024* for any firms that joined the SBTi via its Business Ambition for 1.5°C campaign, which firms could sign up for during the period from June 2019 to October 2021.

  With this new policy, which also became effective for firms that joined the SBTi earlier under the old versions, the SBTi changed the information retained on its dashboard. While Versions 1.0 and 2.0 reassured firms that no announcement of removal would be made and that they would silently disappear from the dashboard, Version 3.0 threatens to flag removed firms as 'commitment removed'. In return, SBTi offered legacy firms a withdrawal period from the announcement of the policy up until 31 January 2023:
- *In the time window from November 2022 to 31 January 2023*, firms learned about the new policy and could withdraw silently from their commitment without being flagged as 'commitment removed'.

This is an interesting feature of the target-setting process, as vigilant managers could have anticipated the implications of this regime shift and minimized damage to their firms by silently withdrawing rather than remaining flagged as 'commitment removed' indefinitely or until the target was finally approved. There was also no downside to a silent removal, as this would have still left open the option to submit targets later. In fact, the data show an increase in silently removed firms in February 2023, from 68 to 79. In July 2023, 'commitment removed' flags for near-term targets surged from 7 to 35, and then rose to 114 in December 2024. For long-term targets, the jump occurred in March 2024, from 0 to 245, while near-term removals reached 208. Who were the handful of managers who anticipated that it would be better to withdraw early? Why did other managers miss this opportunity and get trapped in the status of 'commitment removed'? Were they less attentive? Did they overestimate their ability to successfully set targets? Fig. 2 displays the timeline of commitment removal policies together with the three key months when a noticeable impact of these policy changes is visible on the dashboard. While changes in the dashboard are happening continuously, the months of February 2023 (silent withdrawals before lock-in), June 2023 (removal of some commitments not from the Business Ambition for 1.5°C campaign), December 2023 (further removals) and March 2024 (removal of many commitments from the Business Ambition for 1.5°C campaign) appear to show the clearest impact of the policy changes.

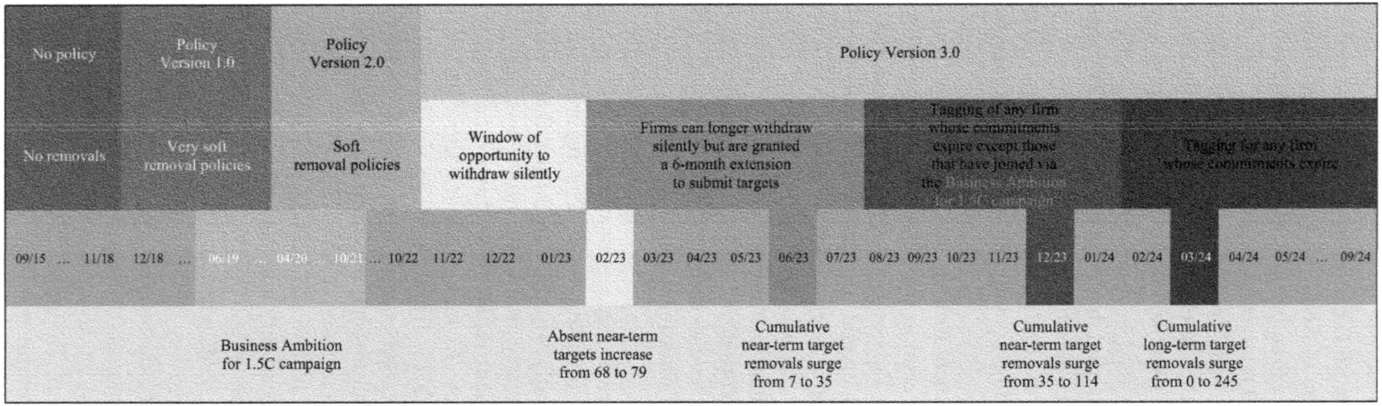

Fig. 2 Timeline of Expiring Commitment Policies. *Note:* Policy versions refer to the version of the 'Protocol to manage expired commitments' (SBTi, 2018, 2020) and the 'Commitment Compliance Policy' (SBTi, 2022).

4.2 Data Structure

The newly created dataset has a strongly balanced monthly structure, with a time series for each firm that has appeared on the SBTi dashboard at least once and for which the matching algorithm, including manual verification, finds an S&P Capital IQ Entity ID. This yields 109 months (September 2015–September 2024) × 8,298 unique Entity IDs = 904,482 observations. The two panels in Table 5 provide breakdowns by countries and sectors for the 8,298 firms. Firms from the United Kingdom are overrepresented (15.6%) relative to those from the United States (13.5%). I attribute this to some home bias, as the offices of the SBTi are in London. Of course, other more nuanced explanations, such as differences in regulations or culture, are possible and should be the subject of future research.

Based on the information scraped from the SBTi dashboard, I determine the status of the near-term and long-term (net zero) targets for each observation. The status categories are: (1) Has not yet committed to anything; (2) Committed with intermittent absence (silent removal); (3) Final absence (silent removal; no target set as of September 2024); (4) Final absence due to other reasons, e.g. disappearance of the firm or removal of oil and gas firms due to lacking standards; (5) Commitment removed; (6) Set; and only for long-term targets: (7) Has never committed to a long-term target; (8) Will commit to a long-term target later. These categorizations enable me to draw the three graphs in Fig. 3.

The first graph in Fig. 3 displays the cumulative number of firms appearing on the SBTi dashboard as either having committed to setting a target or having directly set a target (committing is not mandatory; firms can directly submit targets for approval). 'Cumulative' here means that these sub-graphs are monotonically increasing, i.e. the disappearance of firms is disregarded. To assess the success of the matching procedure with S&P Capital IQ graphically, I show the evolution of matched firms plus the number of unmatched firm names. Assuming that each unmatched firm name represents a unique firm (a conservative assumption), the distance between the dotted line and the solid black line for near-term target firms

Table 5. Country (Left-Hand Side) and Sector Composition (Right-Hand Side) of Firms in the Dataset.

Panel A: Country	Share (%)	Panel B: Sector	Share (%)
United Kingdom	15.62	Industrials	28.47
United States	13.52	Consumer discretionary	14.87
Japan	10.23	Information technology	10.73
Germany	6.50	Consumer staples	10.25
France	5.27	Materials	10.23
Sweden	4.62	Financials	6.54
China	3.82	Health care	5.40
India	3.63	Other	4.59
Netherlands	3.15	Real estate	3.68
Denmark	2.75	Utilities	2.03
Other	30.9%	Energy	0.28

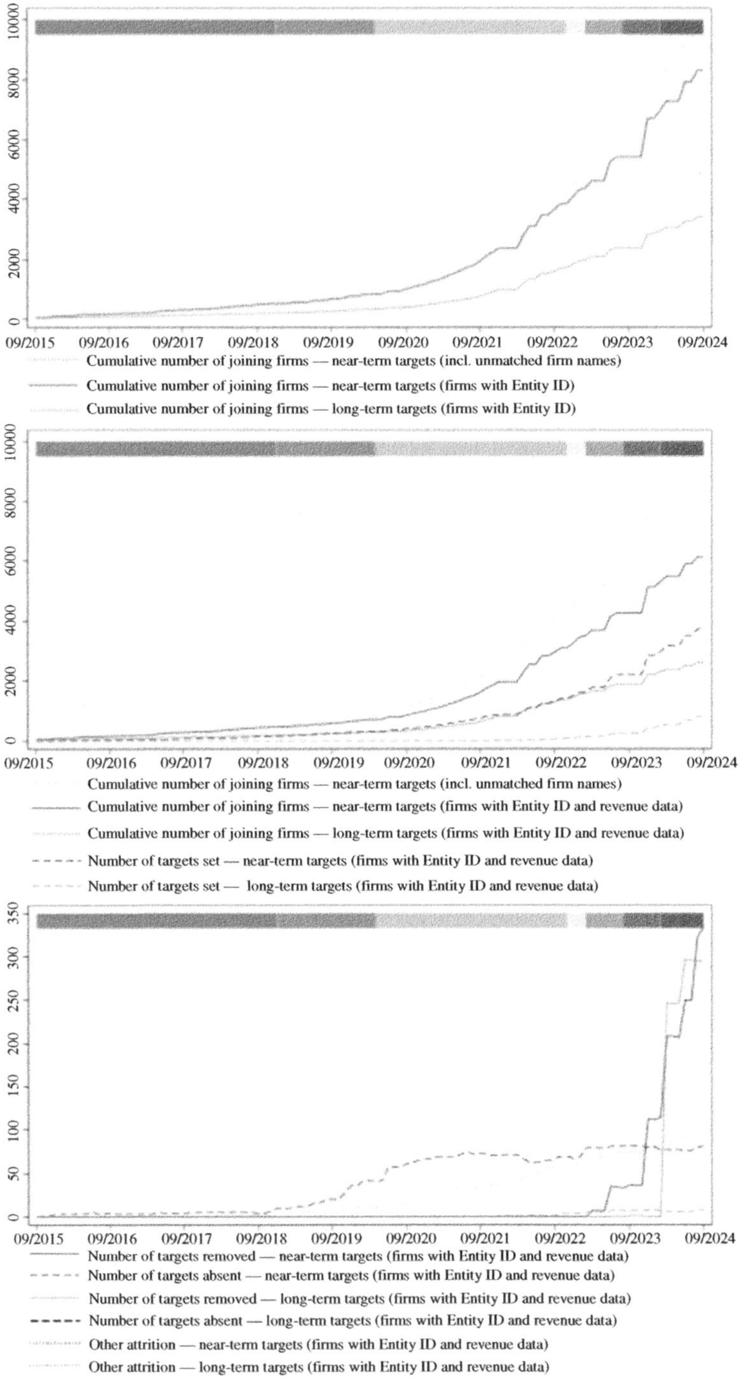

Fig. 3. Evolution of Firms With SBT Commitments, Set Targets and Target Removal (Colours Indicate the Strictness of Expiring Commitment Policies (SBTi, 2018, 2020, 2022) as Displayed in Fig. 2).

represents the matching gap, which remains moderate at any point in time. Interestingly, there is a plateau of new firms joining the SBTi dashboard from July 2023 to November 2023, which coincides with the introduction of Version 3.0 of the policy for expiring commitments, marking a fundamental shift from silently removing firms that failed to set a target to tagging them permanently as 'commitment removed'. I am curious, and this could be the subject of future research, whether this plateau is of a purely technical nature, i.e. the SBTi halted additions to the dashboard because it knew it was about to release the new policy, or whether firms could have still joined the dashboard but experienced a hold-up due to the new policy and the uncertainty surrounding its implementation.

The second graph in Fig. 3 differs from the first in that it restricts the analysis to firms with revenue data in S&P Capital IQ at some point in time. The idea is to disregard ultra-small firms that lack the basic information required for any empirical setup. S&P Capital IQ is comprehensive in that it includes records of legal entities with no disclosure requirements for financial information, which explains the high matching success with SBT data. Additionally, the second graph demonstrates the success rate of transitioning from committing to setting a target to having the target approved and set. For near-term targets, the graph of set targets (dashed black line) runs at slightly less than half the level of the cumulative number of joining firms (solid black line). The approval rate is substantially lower for long-term targets (gray dashed line vs. gray solid line) and is around one-third.

The third graph in Fig. 3 displays several aspects of attrition in SBTi data. The analysis remains restricted to firms that fulfil the minimum requirements to enter any empirical-archival study, i.e. availability of revenue data and a successful match with S&P Capital IQ. The solid black and gray lines represent the explicit tagging of firms as 'commitment removed' following the introduction of Version 3.0 of the policy for handling expiring commitments. These removals amount to 333 for near-term targets and 296 for long-term targets. With the introduction of the new policy, survivorship bias should no longer be an issue for recent sample periods. However, the third graph also shows two other types of attrition that can impact any study using data from earlier periods. These two types are silently removed targets (target absenteeism; black dashed line for near-term targets and gray dashed line for long-term targets) and other attrition as known in the accounting and finance literature, e.g. firms disappearing due to mergers and acquisitions or the end of going concern for economic reasons. In that category, I also include 17 firms from the oil and gas sector, which were removed by SBTi in early 2023 due to a lack of a sector-specific standard. This is a qualitatively different removal compared to firms not submitting a target within the commitment period (SBTi, 2023). The other attrition reaches 105 and 101 firms for near-term and long-term targets, respectively.

Figs. 4 and 5 show the evolution of the previous graphs in terms of revenue and market capitalization, respectively. The takeaway from these graphs is that target removal is more substantial when assessed in economic terms. For both revenue and market capitalization, the impact is on the order of magnitude of 10%; for example, 6.7 trillion US dollars of market capitalization experienced a 'commitment removed' event by September 2024. The total market capitalization of any firm that had ever joined the SBTi dashboard at that time was 57 trillion

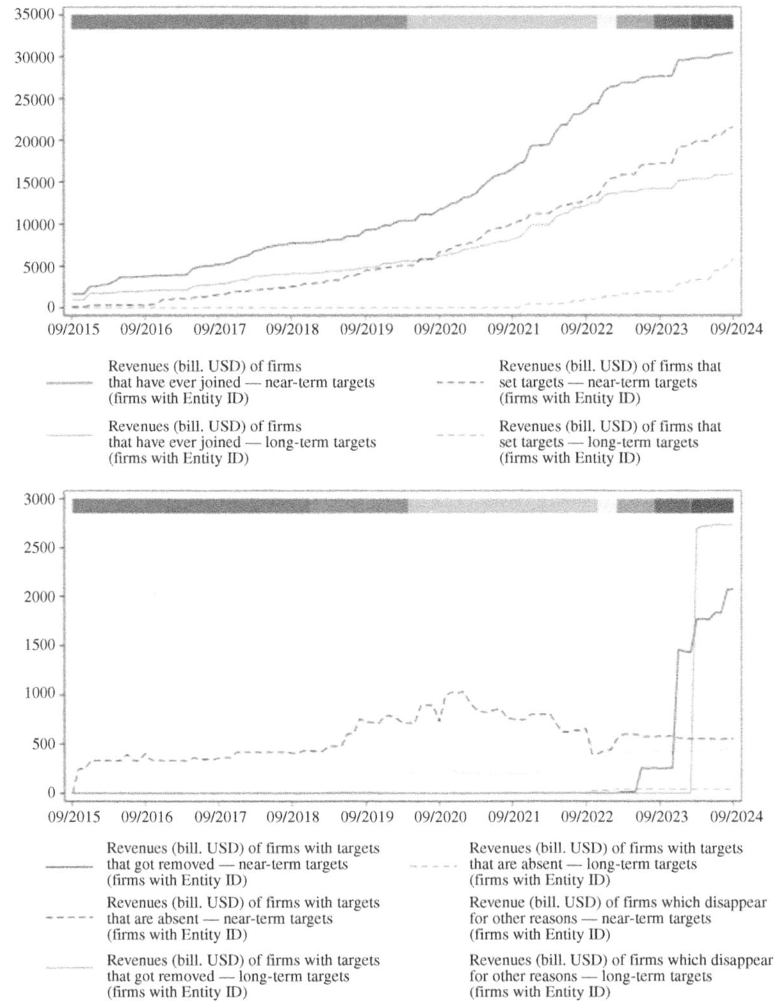

Fig. 4. Evolution of Revenues of Firms With SBT Commitments, Set Targets and Target Removal (Colours Indicate the Strictness of Expiring Commitment Policies (SBTi, 2018, 2020, 2022) as Displayed in Fig. 2).

US dollars, thus the ratio of commitment removal exceeds 10%. This ratio was considerably lower in Fig. 3 when assessing the number of firms. I conclude that big firms were disproportionately affected by the new commitment removal policy, whether self-inflicted or an inherent feature of the commitment-making and removal process (e.g. smaller firms are less likely to commit but more likely to directly submit targets).

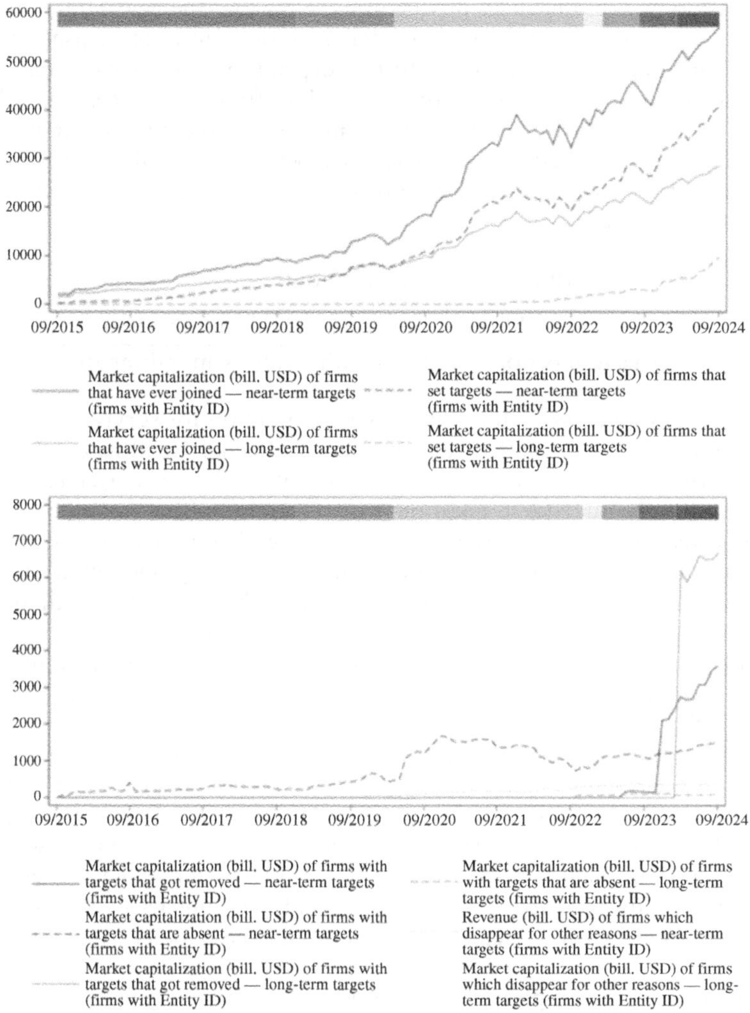

Fig. 5 Evolution of Market Capitalization of Firms With SBT Commitments, Set Targets and Target Removal (Colours Indicate the Strictness of Expiring Commitment Policies (SBTi, 2018, 2020, 2022) as Displayed in Fig. 2).

4.3 How Severe Is Attrition and the Potential Survivorship Bias in SBTi Dashboard Data?

The literature review in Section 2 has revealed that recent studies using SBTi data either use snapshot data from the dashboard or rely on CDP. While the former strategy potentially introduces survivorship bias, the latter risks not capturing SBT commitments fully or accurately. I argue that my new dataset overcomes survivorship bias and includes private firms. Now that the new dataset has been built, it allows me to quantify the potential attrition of firms in snapshotted SBTi dashboard data. The magnitude of attrition depends on two points in time: (1) the point in time when a researcher draws the data from its source, which I label 'month_obtained', and (2) the point in time (or sample period) for which the researcher conducts their analysis, which I label 'month_analysis'. I then define attrition as the percentage of missing observations due to non-representation at the time of data retrieval:

$$\text{Attrition}\left[\text{month\_obtain}, \text{month\_analysis}\right] = 1 - \frac{\text{observed firms for month\_analysis[month\_obtain]}}{\text{true number of firms for month\_analysis}\left[\text{month\_analysis}\right]} \tag{1}$$

Attrition is a necessary but not sufficient condition for survivorship bias, as bias implies that the result of an analysis is affected by attrition. In econometric terms, this occurs when the likelihood of attrition is correlated with the error term in the analysis in question. For research on SBT commitment, there are good reasons to assume that attrition also fulfils this criterion, as dropping a commitment is a managerial (in)decision, which, in my opinion, is at least as important as committing itself and is likely to be correlated with outcome variables such as financial performance, which have been dependent variables in prior research (see Table 1). Fig. 6 visualizes the attrition a researcher would face if relying exclusively on single snapshot data from the SBTi dashboard.

The graph in Panel A in Fig. 6 shows that attrition can reach up to 25.3%, which is attained for the combination of January 2021 as 'month_obtained' and November 2021 as 'month_analysis'. The fact that this peak occurs about a year after the outbreak of the COVID-19 pandemic might suggest the explanation that some firms did not follow through with the target-setting processes during the pandemic crisis and were silently removed from the dashboard. The impact of the COVID-19 pandemic on emission reduction targets may thus be another avenue for future research.

Surprisingly, the graph in Panel B in Fig. 6 shows a very similar proportion of attrition when the perspective is restricted to firms for which market value of equity data is available for at least one month during the sample period. I had expected that attrition and vulnerability to survivorship bias would be substantially lower. The fact that this is not the case can be explained by the high share of listed firms joining the initiative in the early years of the SBTi, as displayed in Fig. 7. Thus, any attrition measured relative to these early years captures the attrition of listed firms. In addition – but this notion would still need to be established by proper empirical testing in future research – listed firms are more likely to be scrutinized by the SBTi, while smaller unlisted firms might fly under the radar or not commit in the first place but directly submit targets.

(a)

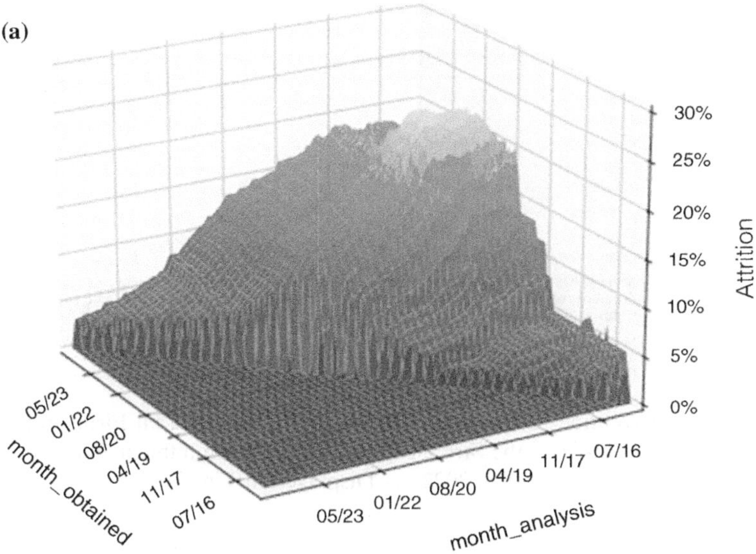

(b)

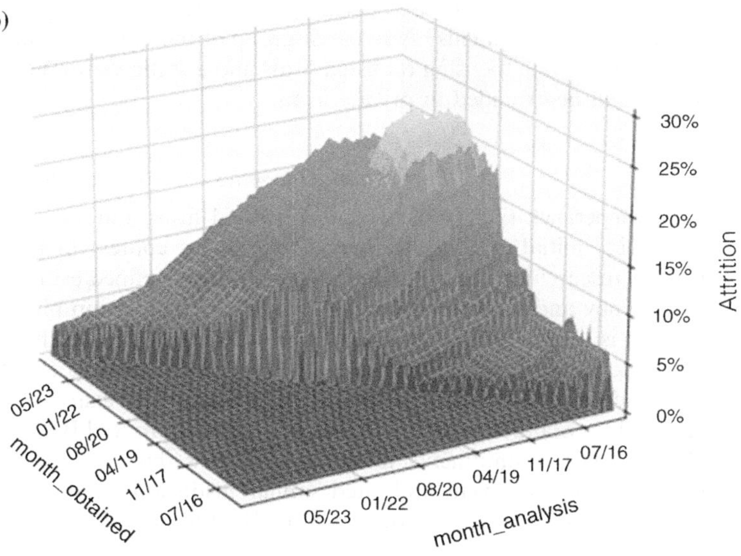

Fig. 6. Attrition for all Firms (Panel A) and Listed Firms (Panel B).

5. OPPORTUNITIES FOR FUTURE RESEARCH

5.1 Determinants of Commitment Removals

The newly created dataset offers a multitude of research opportunities. The most obvious one, in my opinion, is the analysis of which factors correlate with the

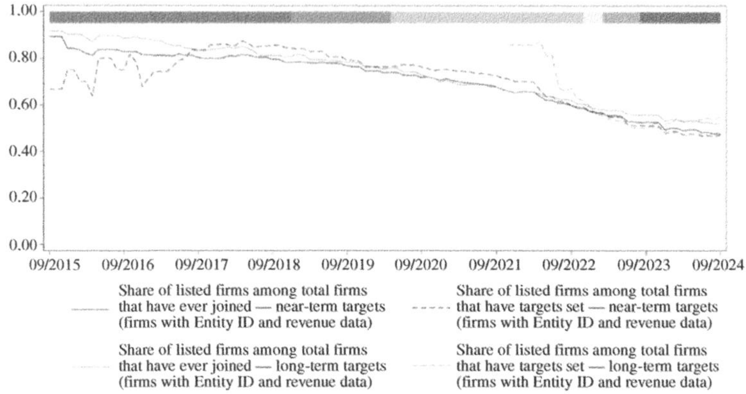

Fig. 7. Evolution of the Share of Listed Firms Among all Firms in the Dataset (Colours Indicate the Strictness of Expiring Commitment Policies (SBTi, 2018, 2020, 2022) as Displayed in Fig. 2).

removal of commitment. Are there managerial traits or governance characteristics (e.g. compensation tied to environmental performance) that explain the removal versus target submission in the aftermath of the fundamental shift in the policy for expiring commitments? A research group at the University of Cagliari is investigating this while focusing on listed firms and a static view (Wasli, 2024). This project could be extended to private firms.

5.2 Peer Group Dynamics

Bolton and Kacperczyk (2024), using data on listed firms and an annual data structure, provide initial evidence of peer effects in the context of target commitments. This research can be expanded to private firms, refined using data with monthly frequency and rerun on a dataset free from survivorship bias. Particularly promising is the analysis of individual firms' peer group leadership in terms of committing to or removing a commitment. What implications does it have for peers when leading firms set targets or withdraw them? For example, in 2023, four major banks – Standard Chartered, HSBC, ABN Amro and BNP Paribas – each withdrew their commitments in separate actions, but the business press picked this up as a joint event and cited similar justifications, such as targets preventing the financing of still-needed fossil fuels (Wilkes, 2023).

5.3 Shifting the Targets Up and Down the Corporate Tree, and Doing-Business-As Designations

While performing the manual corrections, particularly while checking whether gaps in the data represent true absenteeism of a previous commitment or can be explained by other phenomena, I realized that firms, more often than I would have expected, shift target commitments up or down the corporate hierarchy or make commitments at a lower corporate level even though there is already a commitment at a higher level. I have not yet fully understood this phenomenon, but I can envision that there may be more behind it than simple inaccuracies in reporting legal entity names to SBTi. For example, firms might use targets at lower levels as test balloons and elevate them to higher levels if they lead to desired outcomes. A more negative interpretation could be that firms commit to setting targets at lower levels, using them as marketing instruments, knowing that failure to set or comply with these targets would not have a direct backlash at the group level. My thoughts go in a similar direction with regard to doing-business-as designations. Since these designations are not fixed but tied to brands and businesses, if a brand reaches the end of its life cycle, the firm is no longer truly bound to its commitment. This is an aspect that could be of interest to research in the domain of marketing.

5.4 SBTi's Own Legitimacy

The SBTi itself is subject to criticism, and its perception and perceived legitimacy vary over time. A major discussion arose over whether it should allow the use of carbon certificates to offset Scope 3 emissions (SBTi, 2024). It would be intriguing to capture the initiative's own perceived legitimacy by analyzing the sentiment of news streams related to SBTi announcements and correlating it with firms' commitment and target-setting behaviour. From this, researchers could learn about the trade-offs faced by such an important non-governmental organization, which lists the Bezos Earth Fund, the IKEA Foundation and Bloomberg Philanthropies, among others, as its main funding sources.

5.5 Climate Change and Constitutional Law

Constitutional law often incorporates aspects of climate change targets as non-fixed governmental commitments, i.e. vague guidance for legislators that is hardly enforceable through legal actions. However, in some jurisdictions, courts have derived fixed commitments from such high-level articles, granting plaintiffs relief on very specific aspects. For example, in a landmark ruling in 2021, Dutch courts ordered Shell to reduce its carbon emissions by 45% by 2030 compared to 2010 levels.[7] The plaintiffs' arguments were based on high-level articles in the Dutch Civil Code and the European Convention on Human Rights (e.g. the right to life). An interesting research question is whether these landmark decisions lead to more or less commitment to carbon emission reductions at the corporate level.

5.6 Replications

The analysis of the newly created dataset has revealed that data drawn as a snapshot from the SBTi website can suffer from attrition of up to 25%, even for a sample of listed firms. Prior research by Easton et al. (2022a, 2022b) has shown how attrition can profoundly impact empirical results. Thus, the results of the studies discussed in Section 2 could be replicated and verified using the newly created dataset to check whether attrition indeed leads to survivorship bias in these settings.

6. CONCLUSION

The SBTi and its multi-stage process of first committing to set a target, and then either setting, withdrawing from, or getting removed from a commitment, create a rich research environment. This richness is amplified by the dynamic evolution of the SBTi's expiring commitment policies from 'silent removal' to tagging as 'commitment removed', resembling a name-and-shame scheme. Why is research in this domain still relatively underdeveloped, with few published papers in peer-reviewed field journals and a handful of outstanding working papers that, despite their overall high quality, rely on outdated data? My explanation for this is the lack of a comprehensive historical database with firm identifiers that link SBTi data to financial data.

In this chapter, I outline how such a database can be constructed. The costs are significant. I started this project in mid-June 2024 and finished it in mid-October 2024, dedicating half of my working time to it. Thus, the overall working time was about two months. To enable individual researchers to estimate their own costs for setting up this database, it is important to understand that I incurred no material learning costs; at the time of starting, I was already familiar with coding techniques and could draw on many years of experience from similar projects where firm names needed to be matched to financial databases. Therefore, depending on a researcher's experience level and coding skills, I estimate the cost of constructing such a dataset to be between two and six months of intensive work (full-time equivalents). Unfortunately, I am not permitted to make the dataset publicly available, as the S&P Capital IQ Entity ID represents proprietary data of Standard & Poor's. My request to publish a list of firm names alongside Entity IDs was denied by the data vendor.

Given these significant costs and the fact that I am not allowed to publish the newly created dataset, I invite researchers to collaborate on joint projects. This would require that the collaborator's institution has a licence to access S&P Capital IQ. Alternatively, my institution can host visiting researchers if they bring their own funding.[8] I would be delighted to receive applications by email, stating the research idea and how it can be executed using the newly created dataset.[9]

FUNDING NOTICE

This research was funded in whole, or in part, by the Luxembourg National Research Fund (FNR), grant reference [16661455].

NOTES

1. When accessing the current version of the SBTi dashboard (https://sciencebasedtargets.org/target-dashboard), a pop-up window with the following message appears: 'The dashboard shows organizations that have had greenhouse gas (GHG) emissions reduction targets validated as science-based by the SBTi. It also shows organizations that have committed to set science-based targets, as well as those that have had their commitments removed in accordance with our Commitment Compliance Policy. The information in the dashboard is updated every Thursday, with commitment removals taking place once a month, ordinarily on the first Thursday of the month'.

2. Within another research project, my co-author requested archival data from SBTi and received no response.

3. It exceeds 83.3% because the 1885 unmatched firm names likely include variations of the same entity written differently.

4. I thank Nouha Wasli from the University of Cagliari for compiling the list of the following examples: CAF Group, Globant España S.A. and Byggmax Group AB. This list is not exhaustive.

5. CAPTCHA stands for 'completely automated public Turing test' to tell computers and humans apart. It refers to various authentication methods that validate users as humans, not bots, by presenting a challenge that is simple for humans but difficult for machines (https://www.ibm.com/topics/captcha).

6. I am not allowed to disclose the terms of my institution's contract with Standard & Poor's. Nevertheless, I can state that the annual fees are likely affordable for any academic institution in an economically developed environment. In addition, Standard & Poor's allows an unlimited number of users in our research department without charging extra fees.

7. https://climatecasechart.com/non-us-case/milieudefensie-et-al-v-royal-dutch-shell-plc/

8. The process of hosting holders of EU passports is straightforward. The process for holders of other passports is less so, but still feasible.

9. Interested researcher can use the 'Pitching Research' form of Faff (2021).

REFERENCES

Bendig, D., Wagner, A., & Lau, K. (2023). Does it pay to be science-based green? The impact of science-based emission-reduction targets on corporate financial performance. *Journal of Industrial Ecology*, *27*(1), 125–140.

Ben-Amar, W., Comyns, B., & Martinez, I. (2024). Firm commitments on climate change: Effects of science-based targets on financial outcomes during the COVID-19 crisis. *Business Strategy and the Environment*, *33*, 7768–7787.

Berg, F., Huidobro, J. O., & Rigobon, R. (2024). On the importance of assurance in carbon accounting. https://papers.ssrn.com/sol3/papers.cfm?abstract_id=4734240. Accessed on October 17, 2024.

Berger-Schmitz, Z., George, D., Hindal, C., Perkins, R., & Travaille, M. (2023). What explains firms' net zero adoption, strategy and response? *Business Strategy and the Environment*, *32*(8), 5583–5601.

Bharali Saikia, M., & Maji, S. G. (2024). Corporate carbon emissions, science-based targets initiatives and firm performance: Evidence from India. *International Journal of Law and Management*. https://doi.org/10.1108/IJLMA-05-2024-0161

Bjørn, A., Tilsted, J. P., Addas, A., & Lloyd, S. M. (2022). Can science-based targets make the private sector Paris-aligned? A review of the emerging evidence. *Current Climate Change Reports*, *8*(2), 53–69.

Bolay, A.-F., Bjørn, A., Patouillard, L., Weber, O., & Margni, M. (2024). What drives companies' progress on their emission reduction targets? *Journal of Cleaner Production*, *468*, 143124.

Bolton, P., & Kacperczyk, M. T. (2024). *Firm commitments*. Accessed on 16 October 2024.

Burley, H., & Shreiber, P. (2023). *Science based target initiative dumps science with massive fossil finance loopholes*. https://reclaimfinance.org/site/en/2023/12/08/science-based-target-initiative-dumps-science-with-massive-fossil-finance-loopholes/. Accessed on October 16, 2024.

Dahlström, P., Lööf, H., Sahamkhadam, M., & Stephan, A. (2023). Asset pricing of carbon emission disclosure. https://www.oru.se/globalassets/oru-en/schools/hh/finecon-2023-presentations/sahamkadam—asset-pricing-of-carbon-emission-disclosure.pdf. Accessed on October 17.

Easton, P. D., Kapons, M. M., Kelly, P., & Neuhierl, A. (2022a). Attrition bias and inferences regarding earnings properties; evidence from compustat data. https://www8.gsb.columbia.edu/ceasa/sites/ceasa/files/Easton%20Kapons%20Kelly%20Neuhierl%2020200818.pdf. Accessed on December 2, 2022.

Easton, P. D., Kapons, M. M., Kelly, P., & Neuhierl, A. (2022b). Attrition bias in studies using CRSP/compustat merged data. https://papers.ssrn.com/sol3/papers.cfm?abstract_id=3040354. Accessed on December 19, 2022.

Faff, R. (2021). Pitching Research(R). https://papers.ssrn.com/sol3/papers.cfm?abstract_id=2462059. Accessed on October 28, 2024.

Freiberg, D., Grewal, J., & Serafeim, G. (2021). Science-based carbon emissions targets. https://papers.ssrn.com/sol3/papers.cfm?abstract_id=3804530. Accessed on October 17, 2024.

Garcia, C. B., & Gould, F. J. (1993). Survivorship bias. *Journal of Portfolio Management*, *19*(3), 52.

Giesekam, J., Norman, J., Garvey, A., & Betts-Davies, S. (2021). Science-based targets: On target? *Sustainability*, *13*(4), 1657.

Guerrero Escobar, S., Hernández-del-Valle, G., Hernandez, M., & de-la-Mora, P. (2023). The stock market effects of committing and setting GHG targets: Evidence from the science-based initiative. https://papers.ssrn.com/sol3/papers.cfm?abstract_id=4518351. Accessed on October 17, 2024.

Kacperczyk, M. T., & Peydró, J.-L. (2024). Carbon emissions and the bank-lending channel. https://papers.ssrn.com/sol3/papers.cfm?abstract_id=3915486. Accessed on October 17, 2024

Kaltenhauser, J. (2023). Determinants and capital market consequences of net zero targets. *Junior Management Science*, *8*(2), 404–430.

Ko, I., & Prakash, A. (2024). Stock markets, corporate climate pledges, and the Science-Based Target Initiative. *NPJ Climate Action*, *3*(1), 69.

Kuo, L., & Chang, B.-G. (2021). Ambitious corporate climate action: Impacts of science-based target and internal carbon pricing on carbon management reputation-Evidence from Japan. *Sustainable Production and Consumption*, *27*, 1830–1840.

Pineda Pérez, B. (2023). The science based targets initiative: Its impact on the financial results and the determinants to join. https://kth.diva-portal.org/smash/record.jsf?pid=diva2%3A1773388&dswid=8577. Accessed on October 17, 2024.

Privato, C., Johnson, M. P., & Busch, T. (2024). Raising the bar: What determines the ambition level of corporate climate targets? *Climatic Change*, *177*(145).

Romito, S., Vurro, C., & Pogutz, S. (2024). Joining multi-stakeholder initiatives to fight climate change: The environmental impact of corporate participation in the science based targets initiative. *Business Strategy and the Environment*, *33*(4), 2817–2831.

SBTi. (2018). *Protocol to manage expired commitments*. https://sciencebasedtargets.org/resources/legacy/2020/04/Protocol-to-manage-expired-commitments.pdf. Accessed on October 17, 2024.

SBTi. (2020). *Protocol to manage expired commitments*. https://sciencebasedtargets.org/resources/files/Protocol-to-manage-expired-commitments.pdf. Accessed on October 17, 2024.

SBTi. (2022). *Science based targets initiative commitment compliance policy*. https://sciencebasedtargets.org/resources/files/Commitment-Compliance-Policy.pdf. Accessed on October 17, 2024.

SBTi. (2023). *Oil and gas*. https://sciencebasedtargets.org/sectors/oil-and-gas#company-commitments-removed-from-the-sb-ti-website-under-the-policy-update. Accessed on October 16, 2024.

SBTi. (2024). *Statement from the SBTi board of trustees on use of environmental attribute certificates, including but not limited to voluntary carbon markets, for abatement purposes limited to scope 3*. https://sciencebasedtargets.org/news/statement-from-the-sbti-board-of-trustees-on-use-of-environmental-attribute-certificates-including-but-not-limited-to-voluntary-carbon-markets-for-abatement-purposes-limited-to-scope-3. Accessed on October 18, 2024.

Schuiling, V. (2023). Change in ESG-firm behaviour after the adoption of SBTi. https://studenttheses.uu.nl/handle/20.500.12932/45316. Accessed on October 17, 2024.

Tilsted, J. P., Palm, E., Bjørn, A., & Lund, J. F. (2023). Corporate climate futures in the making: Why we need research on the politics of science-based targets. *Energy Research & Social Science*, *103*, 103229.

Wasi, N., & Flaaen, A. (2015). Record linkage using stata: Preprocessing, linking, and reviewing utilities. *STATA Journal*, *15*(3), 672–697.

Wasli, N. (2024). Determinants of removals of sciene based targets. Unpublished working paper – Presented at the *Journal of Management and Governance paper developement workshop on 30 November 2024*.

Wilkes, T. R. (2023). Exclusive: Four banks quit initiative assessing climate targets. *Reuters*. https://www.reuters.com/sustainability/four-banks-quit-initiative-assessing-climate-targets-sources-2023-11-29/. Accessed on October 18, 2024.

Zhang, H. (2022). The impact of science-based targets on GHG emissions and financial performance. https://researchdirect.westernsydney.edu.au/islandora/object/uws:70082/datastream/PDF/view. Accessed on October 17, 2024.

VALUATION, ACCOUNTING AND CLIMATE RISK

Su Li, Tony van Zijl and Roger Willett

Victoria University of Wellington, New Zealand

ABSTRACT

This chapter investigates whether climate risk influences accounting-based equity valuation by observing how investors adjust their relative valuation weights on different accounting variables when facing climate risk. A novel log-linear valuation model is adopted in this chapter. The valuation weights are measured by the elasticities of market prices to the book value of equity and earnings. The authors estimate elasticities using data on a sample of 213,846 annual observations on listed US firms over the period 1971–2022, and the authors use the annual global anomaly temperature over the period to measure climate risk. The authors find that climate risk is associated with the elasticities of book value of equity and earnings at both the US country-wide and industry levels of analysis. The association of climate risk with the elasticity of book value is positive, but the association with the elasticity of earnings is negative. The authors also find that the association varies across industries and appears to be long run rather than short run. The authors conduct several robustness tests and the results support our baseline results.

Keywords: Climate risk; elasticity; global anomaly temperature; long-run risk; valuation

1. INTRODUCTION

The economic consequences of climate risk arising from global warming have been extensively investigated in a variety of disciplines. Economic literature investigates how climate risk influences national income, agricultural output and industrial outputs (Carleton & Hsiang, 2016; Dell et al., 2014; Stern, 2008; Tol, 2009, 2018, 2024). However, the measures, such as national income, suffer the criticism of backward-looking information. Because capital markets contain

Climate Risks Reporting Practices and Assurance
Advances in Environmental Accounting & Management, Volume 13, 145–179

ISSN: 1479-3598/doi:10.1108/S1479-359820250000013016

forward-looking information, the burgeoning strand of studies in finance, called climate finance, shifts the research focus to how capital markets price climate risk (see Hong et al., 2020; Giglio et al., 2021 for a review). This strand of the literature highlights that equity valuation in the context of climate risk is a core and challenging research topic because of the extreme high uncertainty and complexity in climate risk, the heterogeneous beliefs about the maturity of climate risk and the lack of investment decision tools for investors (Bernstein et al., 2019; Bolton & Kacperczyk, 2023; Krueger et al., 2020; Stroebel & Wurgler, 2021). Investors' equity valuation processes have potentially important implications for dealing with climate change because they can work as an incentive to transit economies toward a net-zero emissions economy (Giglio et al., 2021).

It is well-known that accounting information plays an important role in the equity valuation process. Moreover, accounting-based valuation is one of the most interesting research topics in accounting and finance (Core et al., 2003). Accounting literature has explored the effect of climate risk on firms' earnings at the industry, firm and establishment levels (Addoum et al., 2020, 2023; Huang et al., 2018) and finds a complex non-linear relationship between climate risk and firms' financial performance (Broadstock et al., 2018; Griffin et al., 2024). However, these studies do not explicitly reveal the valuation role of accounting variables in the context of climate risk (Huang et al., 2022) and the fact that both earnings and firm values covary under the influence of climate risk provides insufficient evidence for the valuation explanation. In this chapter, we extend the literature by investigating whether and how climate risk influences accounting-based equity valuation. Specifically, we test whether climate risk drives investors to adjust their valuation weights placed on individual accounting variables within the value relevance framework. At the same time, we aim to demonstrate whether climate risk is incorporated into stock prices through the accounting information channel based on a common premise in accounting literature that accounting numbers play a critical role in transferring risk-related information to the stock market (Beaver et al., 1970; Penman & Zhang, 2020).

A better understanding of the valuation effect of climate risk from an accounting perspective will not only benefit investors but also provide useful insights for accounting standard setters and other environmental regulators. Prior studies show that investors divert more attention to accounting information during times of uncertainty (Dickinson et al., 2018; Schaberl, 2016), implying that accounting information will play a more important role in equity valuation in the context of climate change. Currently, firms provide insufficient information about firms' climate risk for investors' investment decisions (Ilhan et al., 2023). To resolve this issue, academic researchers (e.g. Brooks & Schopohl, 2021) and professional institutions (e.g. SEC, 2010, 2024 and Task Force on Climate-related Disclosure (TFCD, 2017) mainly advocate to enhance the disclosure of climate-related information in firms' annual reports, but other aspects of accounting information have received less attention. Recently, an emerging subject, called 'Accounting for Climate Change', highlights that climate-related risk and opportunity also influence the recognition and measurement of accounting elements, such as impairment on assets, provisions and contingent liabilities, and even the 'going concern' assumption.[1] However, current accounting standards do not explicitly require firms to consider these issues when calculating their accounting numbers, which gives rise to the concern about the reliability and the value relevance of accounting numbers under the influence of climate risk. Therefore, our study shifts the research focus from disclosure to the bottom-line numbers and aims to provide empirical evidence for/against the above concern based on a novel log-linear accounting valuation model.

In this study, we mainly adopt global temperature to measure climate risk for the following reasons. First, global temperature is regarded as a good summary measure for the high dimensional climate system (Hsiang & Kopp, 2018) and can capture comprehensive aspects of exposure to climate risk (Li et al., 2024). Global warming provides a scenario involving significant uncertainty, specifically long-run uncertainty, and heterogeneity of beliefs about future cash flows (Bernstein et al., 2019). Baker and Bloom (2013) argue that it is the degree of uncertainty rather than the expectation stemming from the uncertainty that influences managers' and investors' decisions. Global temperature is a proper measure to capture the degree of uncertainty. Second, the literature has revealed the valuation effects of global warming. In climate economic literature, national income or its growth usually are expressed as a function of the global surface and air temperature (Dell et al., 2012; Tol, 2018). The macroeconomic effects of global warming, in turn, have valuation effects on assets (Bansal et al., 2016; Bansal & Ochoa, 2012). Third, by adopting global temperature, we can observe the heterogeneous responses from the common global shocks (Dell et al., 2014). Such a phenomenon cannot be observed by using any type of firm-level climate-risk measures. The characteristic of common shocks has important implications for studies on climate change because climate change and its effects are a global phenomenon (Auffhammer, 2018; Stern, 2008), impose aggregate risk to the economy and financial system (Giglio et al., 2021) and exhibit global externality (Nordhaus, 2019). Fourth, while carbon emissions are one of the most popular climate-risk measures, Hong et al. (2019) state that climate change risk should not be constricted to carbon exposures. Stern (2008) emphasizes that it is the stock of greenhouse gases (GHGs) in the atmosphere that results in global warming. Bolton and Kacperczyk (2023) find that carbon premium does not reflect physical climate risk.

Within the value relevance framework, we predict that climate change leads investors to review their expectations about future dividends and to adjust the valuation of firms according to the principles set out in Gordon (1962). Hence it is expected that climate change will influence the value of the coefficients on different accounting variables in the valuation model. The fluctuations of the coefficients on accounting variables with measures of climate risk provide evidence of the role of accounting variables in transferring risk information into the stock price. Therefore, the paper reveals a new dimension to the information content of accounting variables.

Following Kothari and Shanken (2003), our study adopts a two-stage research design by using a sample of 213,846 firm-year observations for US firms over the period 1971–2022. Since different industries may have different vulnerabilities to climate risk, our tests are conducted at both country and industry levels. Our research is built on the seminal paper by Ball and Brown (1968) on the relationship between accounting information and stock price. In value relevance studies, the estimated association between accounting variables and share prices provides evidence revealing the information content of the corresponding accounting variables (Kormendi & Lipe, 1987; Lipe, 1986) and capturing the equity valuation process (Holthausen & Watts, 2001). The time series patterns of the value relevance of individual accounting variables can indicate the effect of external shocks. An important goal of capital market studies in accounting is to identify these shocks (Kothari, 2001).

In the first stage of the analysis, we perform cross-sectional regressions using a novel log-linear model to estimate the elasticities of market value with respect to the book value of equity and earnings for each year of our sample period. This describes the time series patterns of the estimated coefficients at both the country and the industry level. The estimated coefficients from cross-sectional regression reflect the long-run accounting–market relationship, which motivates us to explore their relationship with the long-run component of climate risk. We conjecture that the estimated coefficients subsume the mitigated and adaptive actions originating from the long-run effects of climate change. The time series patterns of the value relevance of individual accounting variables can indicate the effect of external shocks.

However, the convincing interpretation relies on the correctly specified valuation models (Falta & Willett, 2013; Kothari & Shanken, 2003; Onali et al., 2017). The widely adopted linear additive models, either level form (e.g. Barth et al., 1998) or return form (e.g. Easton & Harris, 1991), suffer from some econometric issues. Therefore, we adopt the log-linear model developed by Falta and Willett (2013) and Lubberink and Willett (2021). There are fundamental logical reasons that justify elasticities as being more valid measures of the response coefficients of accounting variables to changes in market capitalization than the coefficients produced by the usually adopted additive-linear models of the market-accounting relation (e.g. Aczel, 1966; Roberts, 1984). In addition, empirically, the distributions of both market values and the magnitudes of accounting variables are closely approximated by the lognormal, rather than the Gaussian approximation, with the consequence that the log-linear model also provides highly reliable coefficient estimates of the market–accounting relation. A specification which is immune from the issue of related omitted variables is especially crucial for our study. Kothari and Shanken (2003) find that aggregate growth and discount rate effects influence the estimated coefficients through the effect of correlated omitted variables. In such a situation, interpreting the estimated coefficients as the market's valuation process becomes too strong and possibly incorrect. Studies demonstrate that global warming captures both the growth and discount rate effects (Bansal et al., 2016).

Consistent with Boonlert-U-Thai and Schaberl (2022) and Lubberink and Willett (2024), in the log-linear model, we take logs of all the variables in the model so that the value relevance of accounting variables can be measured by the measurement of elasticities. Elasticity reflects the proportionate change in market value in response to a proportionate change in an accounting variable and is thus consistent with traditional value relevance studies, capturing the mapping of accounting information into the stock price.

In the second stage, we conduct time series regressions of the accounting variable elasticities on a measure of climate risk to test for the impact of climate risk on the elasticities. The time series approach is very common in macro accounting literature. The signs and magnitudes of the association between climate risk and elasticities provide evidence showing that climate risk is transmitted into stock markets through the accounting system. In our baseline tests, we use annual global anomaly temperature as the measure of climate risk. The direct consequences of continuous global warming are that natural catastrophes, such as floods, storms and droughts, become more frequent and severe (Stern, 2008). By adopting a temperature measure, we can obtain a much longer sample period than with other measures of climate risk, such as carbon emissions or an environmental, social and governance (ESG) index, and hence include the long-run effect of climate risk in our analysis.[2] Following Bansal et al. (2016); Bansal and Ochoa (2012); Dell et al. (2008); and Dell et al. (2012), we use the year-to-year fluctuations as the identification strategy. Global temperature is viewed as exogenous and random by meteorological scientists (Pindyck, 2007), which makes the identification effect stronger (Dell et al., 2014). Exogeneity and randomness, along with the long time series period, make the time series approach compelling because the fixed effects from some confounding variations are not required if climate shocks are truly exogenous (Auffhammer & Mansur, 2014).

Our results demonstrate a positive impact of climate risk on the book value of equity, and a negative impact on earnings, and are consistent with climate risk being incorporated into the market value of equities through the channel of accounting information. Moreover, our findings are also consistent with prior findings that investors tend to increase the relative valuation weight on the book value of equity but reduce the relative valuation weight on earnings under the pressure of risk (Barth et al., 1998; Boonlert-U-Thai & Schaberl, 2022; Hasan et al., 2024; Huang & Zhang, 2012). Specifically, the results for the US economy as a whole show that a 1°C increase in the global anomaly temperature is associated with an increase of 0.103 in the elasticity of book value and a decrease of 0.158 in the elasticity of earnings. Although the signs of these impacts are the same across different industries, the magnitudes vary across the industries. We also find that the impact of climate risk appears to be long run rather than short run.

In the robustness analysis, we adopt the Engle-Granger's two-step approach to investigate the co-integrating relationship between the dependent variables and explanatory variables in our second-stage time series regressions. The results enable us to rule out concerns that the time series regressions may reflect spurious regressions. Moreover, we also conduct a portfolio-level analysis to show that firms' sensitivity to climate risk contributes to the underlying mechanism which manifests relative value weights on book value of equity and earnings. The portfolio-level analysis provides evidence supporting the baseline results.

Our study is closely related to Cheng and Micale (2022) and Hasan et al. (2024), which, to our knowledge, are the only two studies explicitly examining the impacts of climate risk on the value relevance of earnings and book value of equity by using firm-level climate-risk measures. The former uses the ESG index, and the latter uses the measure based on earnings conference calls, but obtains the opposite results. Different from the two studies, we test the equity valuation effects of climate risk at the aggregate level, that is, the US economy as a whole and industry level. While it is common in the fields of economics and finance, accounting literature only recently started to pay some attention to aggregate-level analysis. Ball and Sadka (2015) state that traditional firm-level studies on accounting information–market value relationships fail to consider the diversification effect from holding diversified portfolios so the measured association does not reflect investor welfare. They call for aggregate-level accounting studies, which can evaluate accounting information under the welfare economic framework. Therefore, our study echoes Ball and Sadka's (2015) argument. Following the tradition of aggregate-level studies, we adopt the time series analysis in the second stage of our tests to identify the valuation effects of climate risk. It should be noted that in this chapter, we reveal the associations, rather than the causal relationships, between climate risk and the value relevance of accounting variables. As with all association studies, the results in our study do not rule out other potential macroeconomic drivers, such as inflation (Binz et al., 2023) and monetary policy (Gallo et al., 2016).[3]

This chapter contributes to the following strands of the literature. First, it contributes to the climate finance literature. A key research topic in this branch of studies is whether climate risk is priced in capital markets and whether climate-risk premium exists. Our study adds to the literature by highlighting the role of accounting information in valuing climate risk. Moreover, we focus on the bottom-line numbers rather than disclosure, which has been extensively explored (e.g. Ben-Amar et al., 2024). In this chapter, we observe the heterogeneous responses to the common global shocks by utilizing global temperature while prior studies attempt to identify the heterogeneous responses to heterogeneous climate exposure as measured by firm-level climate-risk variables. While prior studies reveal that climate risk can be incorporated into stock price through various channels, such as labour productivity and investor mood, our study shows that accounting information system is a potential channel.

Second, the study adds to the literature on the value relevance of accounting from multiple perspectives. An important goal of capital market studies in accounting is to test whether the underlying economic factors that affect stock prices are incorporated into the data generating process of accounting variables and influence the value relevance of individual accounting variables (Kothari, 2001). Dunham and Grandstaff (2022) point out that the research on identifying economic factors is still understudied and remains highly interesting today. Prior studies have examined the effects of factors such as changes in market growth expectations and discount rates (Kothari & Shanken, 2003), changes in the macroeconomic environment (Barth et al., 2023; Collins et al., 1997; Core et al., 2003) and changes in financial distress risk (Barth et al., 1998). In this chapter, we view climate risk as the potential underlying economic driver because climate change and its impact on the environment has become a serious concern worldwide and is viewed as an important source of economic risk.

With respect to methodology, our paper uses the log-linear model to overcome the econometric issues involved in traditional additive-linear models. A key issue in value relevance studies is how to specify the market value-accounting information relationship. Collins et al. (1999) state that the valuation models are a powerful tool to examine the value relevance of accounting numbers in accounting research. However, in contrast to prior studies, which estimate the slope of coefficients based on a linear relationship model, our study uses a log-linear model to specify the market-accounting relation that produces elasticities as the regression coefficients on individual accounting variables. The measurement of elasticities provides a better understanding of the role of the accounting system in reflecting the global scale of climate risk and adds new empirical evidence for adopting the novel valuation model.

Third, in the environmental accounting literature, researchers investigate the valuation effects of climate change or environmental performance based on a variant of the Ohlson (1995) model.[4] While we also construct our research design based on Ohlson's (1995) model, our study differs from the prior studies because we focus on whether the climate-risk measure influences the value relevance of individual accounting variables rather than the value relevance of a climate-risk measure itself. The theoretical foundation for prior studies is the so-called 'other information' in Ohlson (1995) but the theoretical foundation in this chapter is that accounting numbers play a role in transferring information about risk to stock price. Because of this, we adopt a different research design from those in other studies. From this perspective, our study makes a significant leap over existing literature.

The rest of this chapter is organized as follows. Section 2 reviews the relevant literature and develops our hypotheses. Section 3 describes the research design. Section 4 reports the baseline results. Section 5 reports results based on portfolio analysis. Section 6 presents the results of the robustness analysis. Section 7 discusses the findings and presents our conclusion.

2. LITERATURE REVIEW AND DEVELOPMENT OF HYPOTHESIS

2.1 The Literature on the Value Relevance of Accounting Information

While the evolution of the value relevance of accounting variables studies also provides support for our studies, we mainly focus on the literature about the different roles of accounting variables in the equity valuation process.[5] This branch of studies observes the complementary relationship between the value relevance of the book value of equity and earnings and provides different explanations about the roles of individual accounting variables in the valuation process. It is natural to expect that climate risk may have similar effects on the value relevance of individual accounting variables. In the value relevance literature, a variety of individual accounting variables has been explored. Our study focuses on the book value of equity and earnings because they are 'two primary accounting summary measures' (Barth et al., 2023, p. 5) and two inputs in theoretical valuation models, (e.g. Ohlson (1995)).

Ohlson (1995) indicates that the book value of equity and earnings play a different role in equity valuation. The book value of equity reflects the present value of expected future normal earnings (Kothari & Shanken, 2003) and earnings reflect a firm's future abnormal earnings (Barth et al., 1998). Huang and Zhang (2012, p. 270) point out that 'investors rely on the balance sheet more when they face greater uncertainty about future earnings'. Therefore, we expect that climate risk will influence the relative valuation weights of individual accounting variables and drive investors to put a higher weight on the book value of equity.

Kormendi and Lipe (1987) investigate the magnitude of earnings response coefficients and argue that the magnitude indicates the information on the time-series properties of earnings and the discount rates relevant to the valuation of shares and equals the present value of the current and expected future equity benefits arising from a $1.00 earnings innovation. In their study, earnings are assumed to capture investors' revision of future cash flows. Imhoff and Lobo (1992) argue that ex-ante uncertainty in earnings influences the earnings response coefficients. However, they state that if the uncertainty represents the fundamental uncertainty about a firm's future cash flows, the earnings response coefficients will increase. If the uncertainty represents noise in the process generating the earnings signal, the earnings response coefficients will decrease. The observed earnings response coefficients are the equilibrium outcome of the two effects.

Collins et al. (1997) find that the value relevance of earnings declined during the period from 1953 to 1993, but the value relevance of the book value of equity compensates for the decline in the value relevance of earnings. They attribute the results to both the transitory components in earnings and the value of abandonment options contained in the book value of equity. While Burgstahler and Dichev (1997) agree that the valuation weights of the book value of equity and earnings are complementary in the valuation model, they state that the relation should be non-additive, rather than additive as suggested by Ohlson (1995). However, the role of the book value of equity in valuation is difficult to fully capture. For example, Jiang and Stark (2013) find that the valuation weight on the book value of equity reduces for loss firms with high R&D intensity based on the sample of UK firms.

Barth et al. (1998) find that concerns about firms' financial condition increase the valuation importance of the book value of equity but decrease the valuation importance of earnings because the book value of equity plays a role in capturing future abnormal earnings and involving abandonment options. Moreover, they highlight that the phenomenon varies across industries because of differences in the extent of unrecognized intangible assets held in each industry. Kothari and

Shanken (2003, p. 71) argue that 'recognising how different factors influence the estimated slope is crucially important in economic interpretations of the results from value-relevance research'. They reveal that the growth and the discount rate are the economic factors that drive the relative valuation importance of individual accounting variables, which results in the significant time series difference between the valuation importance of the book value of equity and earnings. They also find that the valuation importance of earnings is negatively impacted by growth and the discount rate.

2.2 The Literature on Climate Risk

The climate finance literature provides evidence that climate risk can be viewed as a source of systematic risk and is incorporated into stock prices. Bolton and Kacperczyk (2021) examine the relation between carbon emissions and share returns and find that the levels of carbon emissions and change in emissions from the three channels have a significantly positive impact on share returns. By using a factor-based asset pricing model, Görgen et al. (2020) demonstrate that the constructed carbon-based risk factors reflect the systematic variation in returns and are orthogonal to other common risk factors. The authors conclude that the constructed factors are of relevance for asset pricing and that market participants assess the carbon risk in their valuation process.

The climate finance research also reveals the specific characteristics of climate risk. A characteristic of climate risk is its high level of uncertainty. Sautner et al. (2023b) list various sources of uncertainty relating to climate change: carbon emissions, temperature trends, regulatory intervention and the success of developments toward lower-carbon technologies. An economic consequence of the high uncertainty is that it is difficult to insure against climate risk (Engle et al., 2020). Another characteristic of climate risk is that it is highly complex and multi-faceted. Sautner et al. (2023a) decompose the total exposure into different components, including opportunity exposure (both upside and downside aspects), physical exposure, regulatory shocks and sentiment measures. These measures reflect climate change exposure from multiple perspectives. Climate change exposures are multifaceted, and different firms suffer from different aspects of exposure over time.

Assessment of climate change plays a crucial role in valuation (Hong et al., 2020) and awareness of carbon risk affects the carbon premium (Bolton & Kacperczyk, 2021). Studies find that climate change is an important factor influencing the valuation process of retail investors (Santi, 2023), institutional investors (Goetzmann et al., 2015) and analysts (Dehaan et al., 2017). Several surveys worldwide show that institutional investors view climate risk as a material risk in their investment decisions (Ilhan et al., 2023; Krueger et al., 2020). There is strong evidence showing that attention to climate change is increasing (Choi et al., 2020; Schlenker & Taylor, 2021) and this growing awareness of climate risk may influence how investors utilize different forms of accounting information in their valuation process.

Pankratz et al. (2023) find, based on a sample of 4,400 firms in 57 countries over the period from 1995 to 2017, that high temperature reduces revenue and operating income. Hugon and Law (2019) find that while there is a generally negative impact of warming temperatures on earnings, firms vary in their sensitivity to higher temperatures. Some firms are winners, but others are losers. Addoum et al. (2023) study the impact of extreme temperature at the industry level and find that extreme temperature harms some industries while it benefits other industries but fail to find similar evidence at the firm level. Other studies find that climate risk influences firms' cash flow (Brown et al., 2021; Hsu et al., 2023). However, there is a non-linear relationship between the measure of climate risk and firms' financial performance (Broadstock et al., 2018; Griffin et al., 2024).

Based on the literature above, we propose the following null hypotheses:

H1. Climate risk has no impact on market value.

H2. Climate risk has no impact on the relative valuation relevance of the book value of equity and earnings.

The literature on climate risk indicates that the responses to climate risk are heterogeneous across industries. Ilhan et al. (2021) point out that there is strong uncertainty in climate regulation, which includes the time, the approach and the effectiveness of climate policy. Moreover, the uncertainty in climate regulation is heterogeneous across firms even within an industry. Heterogeneity means that the same policy may have different effects on firms' equity value with respect to both its direction and magnitude. Sautner et al. (2023a) find several characteristics concerning exposure to climate change. First, exposures have industry patterns. For example, utilities mainly face opportunity and regulatory risk. Second, the measures reveal the variation across industries. The heterogeneity across firms within an industry shows that climate change has differing effects on firms within the industry. It also shows that different firms within an industry have different abilities to adjust towards a green economy. Third, the measures fluctuate but there is a general increasing trend. The authors find that about 70–97% of the variation is explained at the firm level. Therefore, investors need to diversify their investments across industries to hedge climate risk. Pankratz et al. (2023) find that the relationship between climate risk and firms' financial performance is affected by industrial and geographic heterogeneity. Based on the literature above, we propose the following null hypothesis:

H3. Climate risk has a uniform impact across industries.

In climate-risk studies, it is important to distinguish between the long-run and short-run effects of climate. First, the effects of long-run climate risk and short-run climate risk on firm performance are different. Second, the term structure of discount rates for long-run climate risk and short-run climate risk differs, which implies that they have different valuation consequences. Third, the effects of short-run climate risk may be masked by long-run climate risk due to adaptive behaviours. Bansal et al. (2016) and Kölbel et al. (2020) emphasize the long-run nature of climate risk as the impacts may spread over a long period, especially with mitigating and adapting activities (Dell et al., 2012). In this chapter, we also distinguish the different effects of long-run and short-run climate effects on equity valuation.

Based on the Epstein-Zin style utility function, Bansal et al. (2016) develop a temperature-augmented long-run risk (LRR-T) model, showing that warming temperature lowers the current wealth-to-consumption ratio, which, in turn, influences asset valuation. The Epstein-Zin style utility function implies that agents prefer early resolution of uncertainty. If agents have a preference for early resolution of uncertainty, they become concerned about uncertainty that is persistent over a long period (Bansal et al., 2019). Therefore, Bansal et al. (2016) argue that low-frequency temperature shifts (long-run component) have a significant impact on equity valuation, but that high-frequency temperature fluctuations (short-run component) are transient and the impacts on valuation are small and insignificant. It is the trend of global warming that increases the likelihood of breaching the threshold point of inducing damage. Bolton and Kacperczyk (2021) investigate the different effects of long-run and short-run carbon risk on stock returns by using emission levels to capture the long-run risk and change in emissions to capture the short-run risk, but they find that both the long-run and short-run risk are positively and significantly related to stock return. Bolton and Kacperczyk (2021) argue that the level of carbon emission is persistent and reflects a long-run risk and that changes in emissions reflect a short-run risk. Engle et al. (2020) note that the nature of long-run climate risk is difficult to hedge against. Hong et al. (2019) argue that while panel regression with location-fixed effects can be useful in identifying short-run temperature shocks, adaption is uncertain in the long run. The severity of damage from climate change cannot be captured through consideration of short-run effects only. However, there is evidence that long-term climate risk can be priced in the bond market through long-term bond issuances (Painter, 2020). Based on Bansal et al.'s (2016) temperature-augmented long-run risk (LRR-T) model, we propose the following null hypothesis:

H4. The effect of climate risk is the same in the short run and the long run.

3. RESEARCH DESIGN

3.1 Test Methodology

Our design has two stages. In the first stage, we use the following log-linear form of the relationship between accounting variables, and market value:

$$\log(M_{i,t}) = k + \beta_1 \log(|B_{i,t-1}|) + \beta_2 \log(|E_{i,t}|) + \beta_3 \log(|D_{i,t}|) + \beta_4 \log(|O_{i,t}|) + \epsilon_{i,t} \quad (1)$$

where M denotes the market price of a firm at the end of the third month following the fiscal year end; B_{t-1} denotes opening book value of equity; E_t denotes the earnings; D_t denotes common dividends; O_t denotes the residual that completes the clean surplus relation over time, and ϵ_t represents an exogenous error term, which is normal given that the lognormal model variables have been transformed into logs.[6] The relationship among the accounting variables by construction is a clean surplus:

$$B_t = B_{t-1} + E_t + D_t + O_t \quad (2)$$

In Eq. (1), we take absolute values of accounting variables before taking logs for these variables to avoid the issue that accounting variables, especially earnings, sometimes are negative and hence cannot be log-transformed. Moreover, taking absolute value implies that we are interested in the magnitude, not the sign, of the variables (Clout & Willett, 2016; Lubberink & Willett, 2021, 2024).

We estimate Eq. (1) for each year of the pooled sample and the sample of each industry. We use ordinary least squares (OLS) regression and focus on β_1 and β_2, the market elasticities with respect to the book value of equity and earnings, respectively. The distribution of the variables is much closer to being lognormal than normal and therefore OLS estimation of Eq. (1), being linear, provides confidence that the coefficient estimates in (1) are both logically valid and statistically reliable.

For stage 2, the econometric model is expressed as:

$$y_{jt} = v_{jt} + \gamma_j x_{jt} + \omega_{jt} \quad (3)$$

where y_{jt} represents in turn the estimated elasticities $\widehat{\beta_{1,j,t}}$ and $\widehat{\beta_{2,j,t}}$; x_{jt} represents our measure for climate risk. The coefficient of interest in this stage is γ_j. Consistent with stage 1, all the regressions in this stage are also conducted at both the US and industry levels. In our primary tests, we use global anomaly temperature as the measure of climate risk. In our robustness tests, we use the trend in the Palmer Drought Severity Index (PDSI). In the robustness analysis, we adopt the Engle-Granger's two-step approach to investigate the cointegration relationship between the dependent variables and explanatory variables in our second-stage time series regressions. The results enable us to rule out concerns that the time series regressions may simply be spurious.

3.2 Data

Our sample comprises US companies listed on the NYSE, Amex and NASDAQ over the period from 1971 to 2022. We extracted the annual accounting data from COMPUSTAT and the data on monthly stock price and the number of shares outstanding from Center for Research in Security Prices (CRSP). The data from the two datasets were merged through the 'CRSP/Compustat Merged Database – Linking Table' (CCM Link Table) provided by Wharton Research Data Services (WRDS). The accounting variables extracted were the book value of equity, net income and common dividends. The variable O_t was calculated following Eq. (2). We eliminated a small number of firm-year observations if their net income, book value of equity or market value was zero. For the large number of firm observations with no dividends, we replace zero values with one for ease of log transformation. Market value was calculated by multiplying the stock price by the number of shares outstanding with the variables being measured in millions of dollars. Table 1 Panel A provides descriptions of the market and accounting variables.

The firms in the total sample were categorized into 10 industries based on their two-digit SIC codes, resulting in the following industries: Agriculture (675 firm-year observations), Mining (9,382 firm-year observations), Construction (2,743 firm-year observations), Manufacturing (92,627 firm-year observations), Transport (18,611 firm-year observations), Wholesale (7,847 firm-year observations), Retail (14,285 firm-year observations), Finance (34,475 firm-year observations), Service (31,117 firm-year observations) and Non-classification (2,084 firm-year observations).[7] In the US-level analysis, we included the full sample. In the industry-level analysis, the Agriculture and Non-classification categories were not analyzed because of the small number of observations.

The climate change data used in the study were obtained from the website of the US National Oceanic and Atmosphere Administration (NOAA).[8] The global temperature data are calculated based on an area-weighted 5° × 5° latitude–longitude grid across land and ocean. The global anomaly temperature is the

Table 1. Variable Definitions.

Variable	Description
Panel A	
M	Market value. It is calculated as the stock price at the end of the third month of the fiscal year multiplied by the number of shares outstanding
B	Opening book value of equity. It equals the value of common equity of the last fiscal year
E	Net income
D	Common dividends
O	The residual value that completes the clean surplus relation: $B_t = B_{t-1} + E_t + D_t + O_t$
Panel B	
Variable	Description
Temperature	Global anomaly temperature extracted from the NOAA website
Long-run	The long-run component of annual global anomaly temperature by calculating the 3-year moving average of the annual global anomaly temperature
Short-run	The short-run component of annual global anomaly temperature by taking the first-order difference of annual global anomaly temperature
PDSI	Palmer Drought Severity Index (PDSI) from the NOAA website
Trend_PDSI	The long-run trend coefficient in an AR(1) model of PDSI

temperature deviation from the mean global temperature over the period 1901–2000, which is 13.9°C. Consistent with the market and accounting data, the time series period of the climate change variables was confined to the period from 1971 to 2022. To test the duration of climate risk, we calculated a long-run measure of climate risk (the three-year moving average of the annual global anomaly temperature) and a short-run measure (the first difference of the annual global anomaly temperature). In the robustness analysis we used the long-run trend coefficient in an AR(1) model of the PDSI, which was obtained from the website of the NOAA.[9] Table 1 Panel B describes the temperature variables.

4. RESULTS

4.1 Descriptive Statistics

Table 2 Panel A reports the descriptive statistics for the company data on the market value of equity and the four accounting variables: opening book value of equity, earnings, dividends and the clean surplus residual. Table 2 Panel B reports the descriptive statistics for the company data after taking logs. From the comparison of Panels A and B, it is evident that the distribution of the log-transformed data in Panel B is close to being Gaussian.

Table 2. Descriptive Statistics.

Variables	Mean	SD	25th	Median	75th	*N*
Panel A: Original Data						
M	2,581.355	20,629.989	25.560	122.521	699.393	213,846
B	870.116	6,056.335	14.749	64.999	304.150	213,846
E	111.837	1,188.565	−0.851	3.718	30.493	213,846
D	46.653	380.139	1.000	1.000	4.583	213,846
O	−11.368	1,085.127	−0.523	0.207	6.368	213,846
Panel B: Logged data						
Log(*M*)	4.953	2.338	3.241	4.808	6.550	213,846
Log(*B*)	4.304	2.165	2.791	4.229	5.755	213,846
Log(*E*)	2.447	2.250	0.907	2.394	3.936	213,846
Log(*D*)	0.883	1.828	0.000	0.000	1.522	213,846
Log(*O*)	0.243	4.732	−1.211	1.046	3.049	213,846
Panel C: Climate Variables						
Temperature	0.469	0.294	0.235	0.435	0.665	52
Long Run	0.453	0.284	0.240	0.413	0.650	52
Short Run	0.016	0.119	−0.080	0.035	0.115	52
PDSI	0.705	2.233	−0.477	0.602	2.190	52
Trend_PDSI	0.158	0.286	0.045	0.154	0.275	52

Note: The table summarizes the descriptive statistics of accounting and market variables. Panel A reports the results before taking logs of the variables. Panel B reports result after taking logs of the variables.

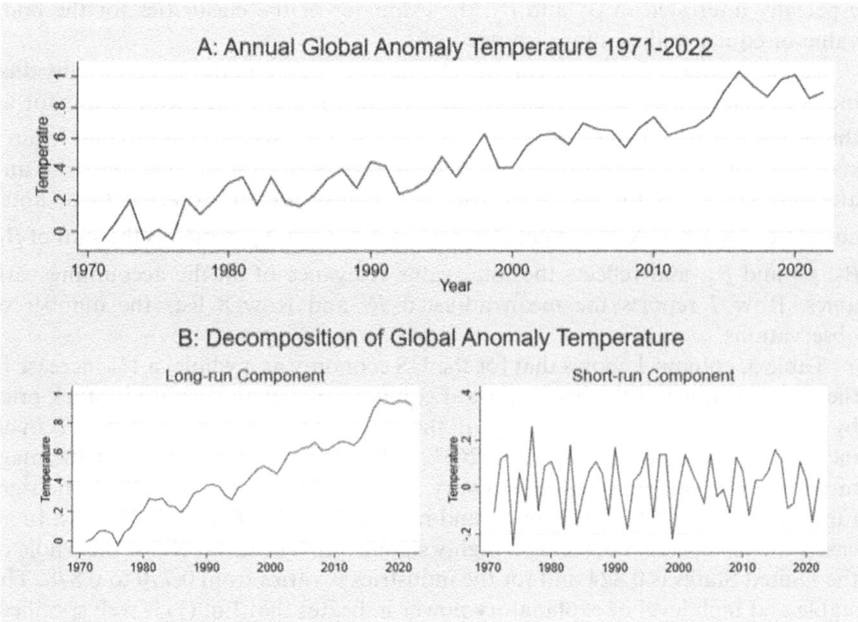

Fig. 1. The Global Anomaly Temperature and the Decomposition. *Note:* The figure depicts the time series pattern of global anomaly temperature (Panel A) and US anomaly temperature (Panel B) over the period 1971–2022. The global temperature (Panel A) is the average temperature across land and ocean. The abnormal temperature is calculated as the level temperature minus 13.9°C, which is the mean temperature over the period 1901–2000. In Panel B, the long-run component of global anomaly temperature (left side) is calculated by taking a 3-year moving average of the temperature, and the short-run component is calculated by taking the first-order difference in the temperature variable. The data are extracted from the NOAA website https://www.ncdc.noaa.gov/monitoring-references/faq/anomalies.php#anomalies.

Table 2 Panel C reports the descriptive statistics of the climate variables. Fig. 1, Panel A, shows the trend of the global anomaly temperature over the period 1971–2022, which shows the upward-sloping trend in the anomaly temperature. Panel B shows the decomposition of the global anomaly temperature into the long-run and short-run components.

4.2 Results for Stage 1

In stage 1 we generated the time series vector of estimated elasticities for the test in stage 2. The estimates were obtained by conducting annual OLS cross-sectional regressions of Eq. (1). The regressions explain about 80% of the variation in the log of the stock price. Among the estimated coefficients, we are especially interested in $\widehat{\beta_1}$ and $\widehat{\beta_2}$, the estimates of the elasticities for the book value of equity and earnings, respectively.

Table 3 reports the mean results. Columns 1–9 denote the US and individual industry results. For completeness, we show in rows 1–5 the mean results for all the estimated parameters of $\widehat{\beta_1}$, $\widehat{\beta_2}$, $\widehat{\beta_3}$, $\widehat{\beta_4}$ and $\widehat{\alpha}$. We also report the mean t statistics based on Newey-West standard errors corrected for heterogeneity and autocorrelation, as the residuals from the regressions are expected to be autocorrelated (Kothari & Shanken, 2003). Row 6 reports $\sum\widehat{\beta}$ which is the sum of $\widehat{\beta_1}$, $\widehat{\beta_2}$, $\widehat{\beta_3}$ and $\widehat{\beta_4}$, and reflects the total value relevance of all the accounting variables. Row 7 reports the mean adjusted R^2 and Row 8 lists the number of observations.

Table 3, column 1 shows that for the US economy as a whole, a 1% increase in the absolute value of the book value of equity results in an increase in stock price by about 0.526% and a 1% increase in the absolute value of earnings results in an increase in stock price by about 0.266%. The mean values reveal that the magnitudes of the estimated elasticities vary across industries but with the same sign, ranging from 0.505 to 0.642 for $\widehat{\beta_1}$ and ranging from 0.146 to 0.318 for $\widehat{\beta_2}$. In all cases, the results are, on average, highly significant. The mean R^2 for the whole of the United States is 0.824 and for the industries it varies from 0.770 to 0.878. The stable and high level of explanatory power indicates that Eq. (1) is well specified. Combining the evidence on the estimated coefficients and the explanatory power, we believe that the fluctuations among elasticities of the book value of equity and earnings are driven by exogenous economic factors, rather than measurement errors in these explanatory variables.

Fig. 2 depicts the time series pattern of the elasticities for the book value of equity, denoted by the solid line, and earnings, denoted by the dashed line, for both US and individual industries. We can see some obvious patterns in these graphs: (1) the value relevance of the book value of equity generally dominates that of earnings, and (2) the value relevance of the two accounting variables complements each other. Fig. 3 also suggests that our regression model is robust across the subsamples of firms at the industry level. Our results explain Core et al.'s (2003) claim that 'By itself, evidence on the regression model's explanatory power paints an incomplete picture of equity values over time. The coefficients in the regression model can change over time even when explanatory power is relatively constant. Similarly, changes in explanatory power do not necessarily imply that the coefficients in the regression model have changed' (p. 47).

Fig. 3 depicts the box plots to compare the variation of estimated elasticities of the book value of equity and earnings across industries and the US economy as a whole with Panel A demonstrating the results for book value of equity and Panel B demonstrating the results for earnings. Fig. 4 shows that the estimated elasticities vary across industries.

4.3 Results for Stage 2

Stage 2 provides evidence of the impact of climate risk. Table 4 reports the results from time series regressions in Panel A, and B when using $\widehat{\beta_1}$ and $\widehat{\beta_2}$, respectively,

Table 3. The Mean Value of the Estimated Results for the United States and Each Industry.

		US (1)	Mining (2)	Construction (3)	Manufacturing (4)	Transportation (5)	Wholesale (6)	Retail (7)	Finance (8)	Service (9)
1	$\widehat{\beta_1}$	0.526	0.585	0.642	0.520	0.505	0.610	0.563	0.524	0.526
	t	43.150	29.411	16.519	42.557	32.018	32.760	27.334	34.120	43.150
	t_newywest	33.881	23.275	13.602	34.057	27.239	29.142	22.765	27.709	34.881
2	$\widehat{\beta_2}$	0.266	0.146	0.178	0.270	0.303	0.268	0.318	0.265	0.233
	t	20.698	7.901	4.882	21.677	14.247	15.986	15.476	16.008	12.271
	t_newywest	16.042	6.557	3.886	16.727	11.903	14.048	12.407	13.268	9.256
3	$\widehat{\beta_3}$	0.118	0.188	0.153	0.137	0.088	0.133	0.086	0.153	0.131
	t	17.914	17.191	8.168	17.494	8.954	13.403	11.756	13.820	12.269
	t_newywest	13.622	14.453	6.901	13.206	7.571	10.891	9.669	10.485	9.444
4	$\widehat{\beta_4}$	0.100	0.084	0.065	0.111	0.074	0.063	0.099	0.059	0.144
	T	12.321	9.372	7.651	11.600	10.165	9.690	10.479	10.572	10.762
	t_newywest	8.953	7.374	6.471	8.504	7.996	7.927	7.718	7.905	7.852
5	$\widehat{\alpha}$	1.799	1.853	1.304	1.826	1.865	1.327	1.592	1.613	1.968
	t	34.475	22.355	10.947	33.675	29.087	17.961	20.355	28.079	33.914
	t_newywest	29.535	17.476	9.358	28.960	23.395	15.854	17.286	22.551	30.687
6	$\sum\widehat{\beta}$	1.008	1.004	1.057	1.035	0.966	1.065	1.062	0.999	1.047
7	R^2	0.824	0.826	0.799	0.832	0.862	0.823	0.820	0.878	0.770

Note: The table reports the mean results from the annual cross-sectional OLS regression of the multiplicative valuation model over the period 1971–2022. The empirical model is $\log(M_{i,t}) = \alpha+\beta_1\log(|B|_{i,t\text{-}1})+\beta_2\log(|E|_{i,t})+\beta_3\log(|D|_{i,t})+\beta_4\log(|O|_{i,t})+\epsilon_{i,t}$. Rows 1–5 denote the mean results of coefficients in the model, respectively. Row 6 denotes the sum of elasticities. Row 7 denotes R^2. Each column denotes the US or individual industry. Both the t statistics and Newy West t statistics are calculated based on the time series standard errors of the estimated elasticities. The Newy West t statistics correct the autocorrelation in each estimated coefficient.

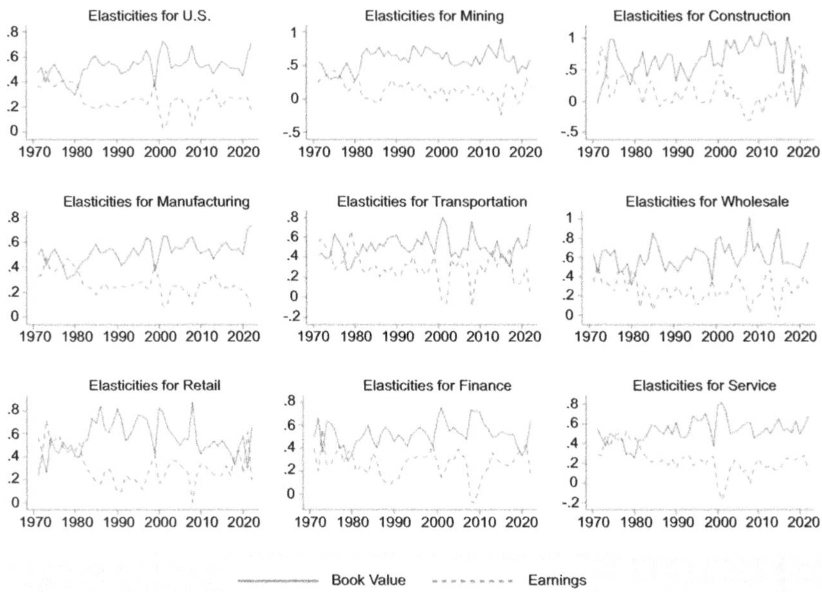

Fig. 2. Time Series Pattern of Elasticities for Book Value of Equity and Net Income. *Note:* The figure depicts the time series pattern of the estimated coefficients on book value and net income from 1971 to 2022. The x-axis denotes the year. The y-axis denotes the magnitude of estimated elasticity. The solid line represents the estimated coefficients on book value. The dashed line denotes the estimated coefficients on net income. Each panel represents US and individual industries. All coefficients are obtained by conducting annual cross-sectional regressions on the model: $\log(M_{i,t}) = \alpha + \beta_1\log(|B|_{i,t-1}) + \beta_2\log(|E|_{i,t}) + \beta_3\log(|D|_{i,t}) + \beta_4\log(|O|_{i,t}) + \epsilon_{i,t}$.

as the dependent variable and the global anomaly temperature as the explanatory variable. In each panel, columns 1–9 report the results for the US and each industry.

Panel A reports the estimation by using $\widehat{\beta_1}$ as the dependent variable. The coefficient for the United States demonstrates that a 1°C increase in the global anomaly temperature increases the elasticity of market value with respect to the book value of equity by 0.103 and the result is significant at the 1% level. The coefficients for individual industries range from −0.001 for Retail to 0.290 for Construction. The results are significant in all industries other than Transportation, Retail and Wholesale. The results for the elasticity for the book value of equity show that the temperature variable has a positive impact on the relation between book value and market value, suggesting that increasing climate risk causes investors to put higher valuation importance on the book value of equity.

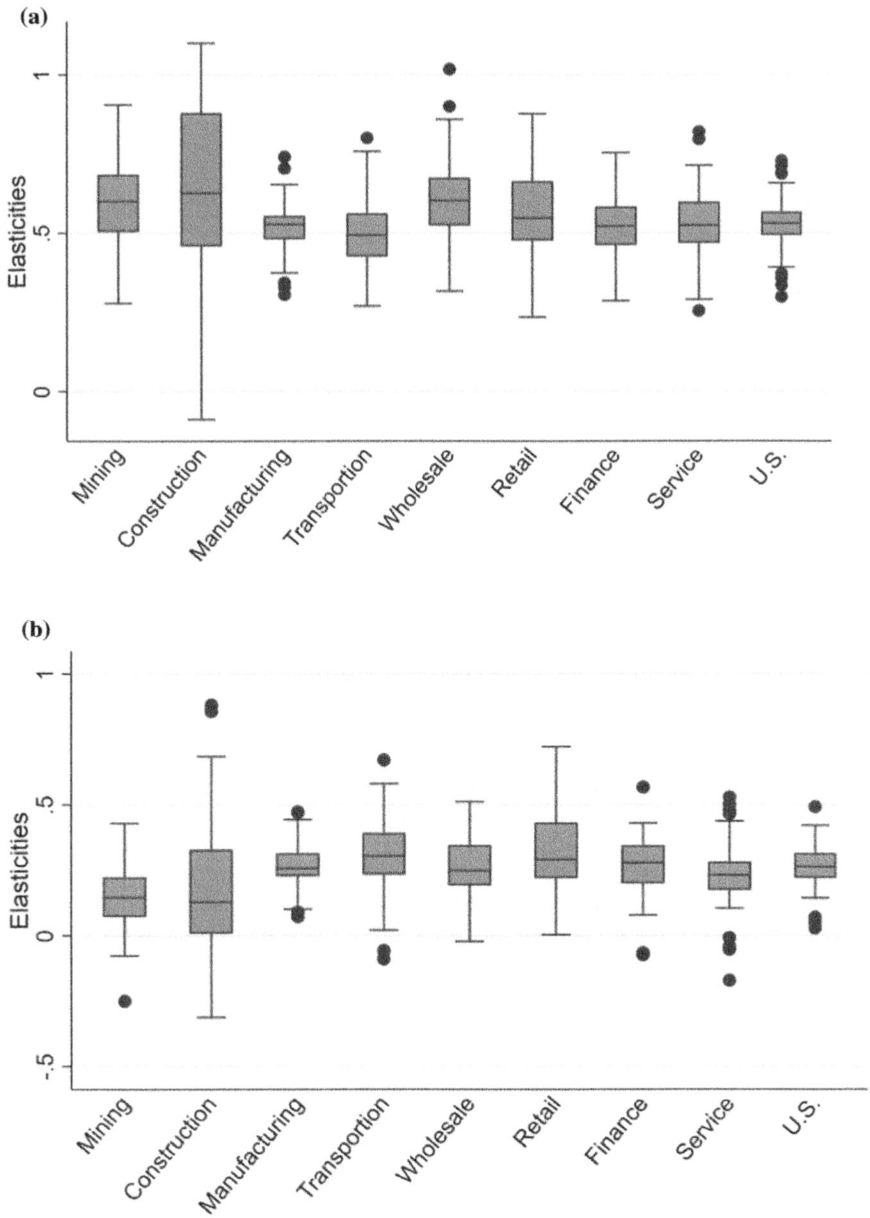

Fig. 3. Box Graphs of Elasticities for the Book Value of Equity and Net Income Across Industries and the United States. (a) Elasticities for the Book Value of Equity. (b) Elasticities for Earnings. *Note:* The figure depicts the box plots for the estimated elasticities of the book value of equity and earnings across industries and the US economy as a whole across the period from 1971 to 2022. Panel A demonstrates the elasticities of the book value of equity and Panel B demonstrates the elasticities of earnings.

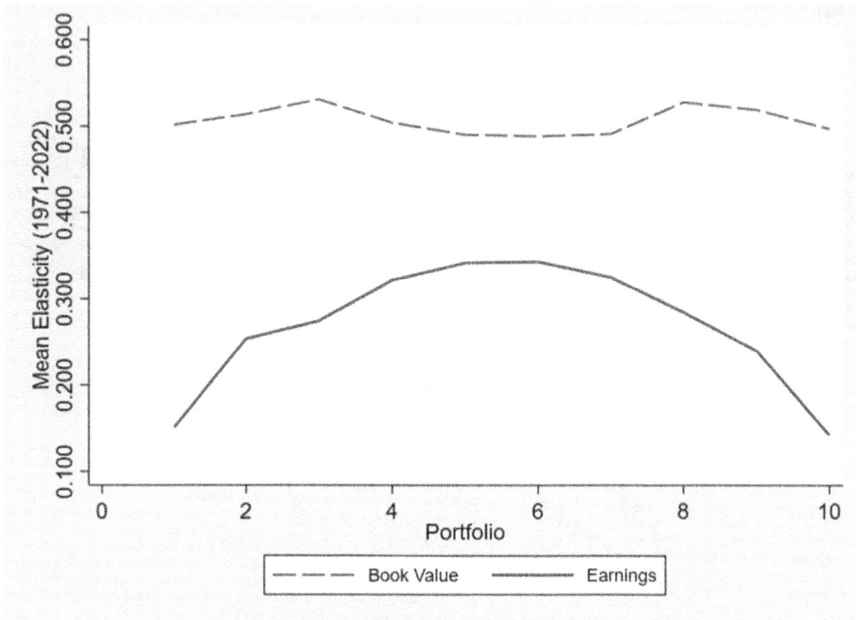

Fig. 4. Estimated Elasticities Among Portfolios Based on Temperature Sensitivity. *Note:* The figure depicts the mean of the estimated elasticities of the book value of equity and earnings over the period from 1971 to 2022 for individual portfolios, which are formed based on firms' temperature sensitivity. The x-axis denotes the individual portfolios from 1 to 10. The top and bottom portfolios are sensitive to climate change while the middle portfolios are insensitive to climate change. The y-axis denotes the mean of the estimated elasticities of individual accounting variables over the sample period. The dashed line (upper part of the graph) represents the mean elasticity of book value of equity. The solid line (lower part of the graph) represents the mean elasticity of earnings.

However, the magnitude of the increase varies across industries and does not apply to Transportation, Retail and Wholesale.

Panel B shows the results for the elasticity of earnings. A 1°C increase in the global anomaly temperature leads to a decrease of 0.158 in the elasticity of market value with respect to earnings for the United States and this result is significant at the 1% level. For individual industries, the impact of a 1°C increase in the climate-risk variable on the elasticity of earnings is negative and significant in all industries other than Wholesale and Finance. The coefficient varies from −0.163 for Manufacturing to −0.287 for Service. The results suggest that climate change negatively influences the relationship between earnings and market value, but the influence varies across industries.

The baseline results reject the null Hypotheses 1–3 thereby suggesting that accounting variables can provide value-relevant information about climate risk

Table 4. The Time Series Analysis Using Global Anomaly Temperature.

	(1) US	(2) Mining	(3) Construction	(4) Manufacturing	(5) Transportation	(6) Wholesale	(7) Retail	(8) Finance	(9) Service
Panel A:	Dependent variable = $\widehat{\beta_1}$								
Temperature	0.103***	0.190***	0.290**	0.147***	0.024	0.038	−0.001	0.106**	0.158**
	(2.463)	(2.650)	(2.210)	(3.951)	(0.399)	(0.547)	(−0.009)	(2.142)	(2.935)
R^2	0.114	0.130	0.094	0.249	0.003	0.006	0.000	0.089	0.155
Observations	52	52	52	52	52	52	52	52	52
Panel B:	Dependent variable = $\widehat{\beta_2}$								
Temperature	−0.158***	−0.224***	−0.237*	−0.163***	−0.187**	−0.048	−0.177***	−0.075	−0.287***
	(−3.475)	(−3.561)	(−1.901)	(−4.064)	(−2.432)	(−0.781)	(−2.496)	(−1.228)	(−4.734)
R^2	0.204	0.212	0.071	0.260	0.112	0.013	0.117	0.031	0.323
Observations	52	52	52	52	52	52	52	52	52

Note: The table reports the results from the time series OLS regressions of the estimated elasticities of net income and book value on the global anomaly temperature variable. The econometric model is $y_{jt} = v_{jt} + \gamma_j x_{jt} + \omega_{jt}$. Each column represents the result for the United States as a whole or the individual industries. Panels A and B report the regression results for $\widehat{\beta_1}$, and $\widehat{\beta_2}$, respectively, t-statistics are reported in the parentheses. *, ** and *** denote the significant level of 10%, 5% and 1%, respectively.

that is impounded into stock prices. The difference between the impact on book value of equity and earnings is consistent with the results of other studies. Furthermore, the impact of climate risk varies across industries.

4.4 Decomposition of the Global Temperature Into Long-Run and Short-Run Components

Table 5 reports the results from regressions when the long-run and short-run components of annual global anomaly temperature are used as explanatory variables to repeat the time series tests conducted in stage 1. Columns 1 and 3 report the results for the long-run component of global temperature and Columns 2 and 4 report the results for the short-run component of global temperature. Table 5 reveals that most of the results for the long-run component are significant at 0.01 or 0.05 level, but all the results for the short-run component are insignificant. Taking the results for the United States as an example it can be seen that for $\widehat{\beta_1}$, the coefficient on the long-run component of global temperature is 0.117 (t-statistic = 2.682) and the coefficient on the short-run component of global temperature is 0.054 (t-statistic = 0.518). For $\widehat{\beta_2}$, the coefficient on the long-run component of global temperature is −0.177 (t-statistic = −3.765) and the coefficient on the short-run component of global temperature is −0.043 (t-statistic = −0.361). This evidence is consistent with the long-run risk explanation of climate risk, showing that the impact of climate risk can persist over a long period.

5. PORTFOLIO ANALYSIS

To facilitate checking the robustness of the baseline results, we construct a measure to capture the temperature sensitivity of each firm. Based on the constructed measure, we sort the full sample into deciles each year. Firms in each portfolio have a

Table 5. Long-Run and Short-Run Components of Global Temperature.

	$\widehat{\beta_1}$		$\widehat{\beta_2}$	
	(1) Long-run	(2) Short-run	(3) Long-run	(4) Short-run
US	0.117***		−0.177***	
	(2.682)		(−3.765)	
		0.054		−0.043
		(0.518)		(−0.361)
Mining	0.202***		−0.235***	
	(2.676)		(−3.545)	
		0.093		−0.117
		(0.520)		(−0.713)
Construction	0.361***		−0.310**	
	(2.671)		(−2.413)	
		−0.421		0.463
		(−1.337)		(1.578)

Table 5. *(Continued)*

	$\widehat{\beta_1}$		$\widehat{\beta_2}$	
	(1) Long-run	(2) Short-run	(3) Long-run	(4) Short-run
Manufacturing	0.158***		−0.183***	
	(4.061)		(−4.429)	
		0.094		−0.040
		(0.946)		(−0.372)
Transportation	0.030		−0.214***	
	(0.481)		(−2.464)	
		0.093		−0.061
		(0.671)		(−0.320)
Wholesale	0.062		−0.079	
	(0.844)		(−1.238)	
		−0.083		0.149
		(−0.510)		(1.055)
Retail	0.008		−0.215***	
	(0.111)		(−2.934)	
		0.030		0.057
		(0.185)		(0.323)
Finance	0.128**		−0.095	
	(2.509)		(−1.496)	
		−0.079		0.080
		(−0.661)		(0.560)
Service	0.165***		−0.317***	
	(2.896)		(−5.074)	
		0.167		−0.077
		(1.241)		(−0.449)

Note: The table reports the results for the components of global temperature as the explanatory variable. Columns 1 and 3 repeat the time series OLS regressions in stage 2 to capture the impacts of the long-run component of global temperature on the coefficients $\widehat{\beta_1}$, and $\widehat{\beta_2}$ respectively. The long-run component of global temperature is calculated by taking a 3-year moving average of global anomaly temperature. Columns 2 and 4 repeat the time series regressions in stage 2 to capture the impacts of the short-run component of global temperature on the coefficients of $\widehat{\beta_1}$ and $\widehat{\beta_2}$ respectively. The short-run component of global temperature is calculated by taking first-order differences of global anomaly temperature. t-statistics are reported in parentheses. *, ** and *** denote the significant level of 10%, 5% and 1%, respectively.

different degree of vulnerability to climate change. Next, the log-linear valuation model is estimated annually for each portfolio, similar to the process in our baseline analysis. Regressions using the log-linear model with the portfolios capture the effect of climate change on the estimated elasticities relative to each portfolio and enable us to cross-check the long-run relation of accounting variables and climate change.

5.1 Measurement of Temperature Sensitivity

The measure of temperature sensitivity we use is based on Cuculiza et al. (2021). First, we extract the monthly global anomaly temperature over the sample period from the NOAA website. Second, we extracted the monthly stock return, market return and Treasury bill rate data from CRSP, and the library titled 'Fama-French Portfolio and Factors' in WRDS to obtain the monthly returns data for the full sample from 1971 to 2022. Third, we conduct the regressions of the 213,846 firm-year observation based on the following model:

$$r_{j,t} - r_{f,t} = \alpha_j + \beta_j\left(r_{m,t} - r_{f,t}\right) + \theta_j \text{Temp}_t + \epsilon_{j,t} \tag{4}$$

where j denotes firm and t denotes month. $r_{j,t}$ represents the holding period return of stock j in month t. The left-hand side of the expression is the excess return. $r_{m,t}$ is the market return and the amount in the bracket is the excess return of the market. Temp_t is the global anomaly temperature in a month t. θ_j is the coefficient of interest, which measures the climate sensitivity. For each firm each year, we use 12 months of data to conduct the regression of the above model, obtain the coefficients on global temperature for each firm each year, and compile the annual temperature sensitivity measure for each firm. Fourth, for each year, firms are sorted into deciles. The top and bottom portfolios are sensitive to climate change while the middle portfolios are insensitive. Fifth, we conduct annual regressions of the log-linear model for each portfolio, similar to the industry-level regressions in the baseline study. Finally, we calculate the mean of the estimated elasticities over the period from 1971 to 2022 for each portfolio.

5.2 Results

Fig. 4 depicts the results. The *x*-axis denotes the different portfolios: Portfolio 1 (the LHS) contains the firms with the most negative climate sensitivity. Portfolio 10 (the RHS) contains the firms with the most positive climate sensitivity. Portfolio 5 contains the firms that are least sensitive to climate change. The *y*-axis denotes the mean of estimated elasticities of individual accounting variables over the sample period.

The dashed line (upper part of the graph) represents the mean elasticity of book value of equity. It shows that the mean elasticity of the book value of equity is almost constant across individual portfolios and just fluctuates over a very narrow range. However, except for the top and bottom portfolios, the elasticities of book value decrease from both sides toward the middle portfolio, implying that investors tend to place less importance on the book value of equity when the climate sensitivity declines. For the top and bottom portfolios, climate sensitivity declines with the importance of book value. The solid line (lower part of the graph) represents the mean elasticity of earnings. It shows that the size of the elasticity of earnings increases from both sides when the climate sensitivity declines.

When comparing the two lines, it is seen that climate change has an opposite association with the elasticities of book value and earnings. Climate change increases (decreases) the relative valuation importance of book value (earnings), which is consistent with the baseline findings. The elasticity of book value is greater than the elasticities of earnings across individual portfolios. The finding is also consistent with the baseline results. An additional pattern in the results is that in top and bottom portfolios, the value relevance of both elasticities of book value and earnings decline, implying that extreme sensitivity to climate change renders both book value of equity and earnings less important in the valuation process.

6. ROBUSTNESS ANALYSIS

6.1 Co-integration Tests

Our baseline results show that climate risk, measured as global anomaly temperature, positively affects the elasticity of the book value of equity and negatively affects the elasticity of earnings over the period from 1971 to 2022. However, we need to address the possibility of spurious regression for the time series analysis conducted in stage 2. We observe that the time series pattern of global abnormal temperature contains an obvious trend. We also test and find that there exist unit roots in the relevant variables. In this subsection, therefore, we test to see whether the dependent variables and independent variables have a co-integration relationship, using the Engle and Granger (1987) two-stage approach.[10] First, we conduct the time series regressions for Eq. (3) and obtain the residuals. Next, we conduct unit root tests for the residuals. We apply both the Augmented Dickey–Fuller test and the Phillips–Perron test to examine the unit root in the residuals. The former is a parametric test and the latter is a non-parametric test. It is generally believed that the Phillips-Perron test has higher power than the Augmented Dickey–Fuller test.

Compared to the differencing and detrending approaches often utilized in this area of the accounting literature, the co-integration approach is useful because it enables the detection of long-run and equilibrium relationships among the non-stationary vectors of time series (Banerjee et al., 2003).

Table 6 reports the $Z(t)$ and p values for both the Augmented Dickey–Fuller test and the Phillips–Perron test. Columns 1–4 report the results when $\widehat{\beta_1}$ is the dependent variable and Columns 5–8 report the results when $\widehat{\beta_2}$ is the dependent variable. Collectively, the results in Table 6 strongly reject the null hypothesis that the time series of residuals contains a unit root. We conclude that $\widehat{\beta_1}$ and $\widehat{\beta_2}$ have an integrated relationship with global anomaly temperature. The above tests provide strong support for our baseline results.

6.2 Trend_PDSI

In this subsection, we use the PDSI as the proxy for climate risk to repeat the tests in Section 4.2. Following Hong et al. (2019), we obtain the long-term trend of PDSI to capture the effect of long-run climate risk. The results of this test provide additional evidence in support of the Bansal et al. (2016) argument. While we find

Table 6. Co-integration Tests.

	$\widehat{\beta_1}$				$\widehat{\beta_2}$			
	Augmented Dickey-Fuller		Phillips-Perron		Augmented Dickey-Fuller		Phillips-Perron	
	(1) $Z(t)$	(2) p Value	(3) $Z(t)$	(4) p Value	(5) $Z(t)$	(6) p Value	(7) $Z(t)$	(8) p Value
United States	−3.285	0.016	−3.748	0.004	−2.620	0.089	−3.401	0.011
Mining	−2.662	0.081	−3.774	0.003	−3.389	0.011	−4.897	0.000
Construction	−1.781	0.390	−4.485	0.000	−1.974	0.298	−3.576	0.006
Manufacture	−3.551	0.007	−3.843	0.003	−2.551	0.104	−3.296	0.015
Transport	−2.825	0.055	−4.143	0.001	−3.038	0.032	−4.391	0.000
Wholesale	−3.729	0.004	−5.251	0.000	−2.772	0.062	−5.137	0.000
Retail	−1.919	0.323	−4.593	0.000	−1.822	0.370	−3.950	0.002
Finance	−3.175	0.022	−4.258	0.001	−3.308	0.015	−4.274	0.001
Service	−2.439	0.131	−4.313	0.000	−1.937	0.315	−3.200	0.020

Note: The table reports the results of unit root tests on the time series residuals of $y_{jt} = v_{jt} + \gamma_j x_{jt} + \omega_{jt}$ for the coefficients $\widehat{\beta_1}$, and $\widehat{\beta_2}$. The unit root tests are used to examine the cointegrating relation between the explanatory variable and dependent variable in the time series model. For each coefficient, we apply both the Augmented Dickey–Fuller test and the Phillip–Perron test. We report both the test statistic $Z(t)$ and the corresponding p-value in the table.

supportive evidence for the Bansal et al. (2016) argument, our findings indicate there is a problem with the Hong et al. (2019) research design because they ignore the U shape of the PDSI.

Climate science finds that droughts have a close relation with global temperature. Palmer (1965) developed the PDSI, to measure the severity of droughts based on the information about temperature and moisture in the soil. The value of the PDSI ranges from −10 to 10, with −4 and below indicating extreme drought, 4 and above indicating extreme moisture, and −1.9 to 1.9 indicating normal.

We obtained data on the US PDSI from the National Center for Environmental Information (NCEI) of the US NOAA, which provides the monthly data starting from January 1895. For consistency with Hong et al. (2019), we extract the data from January 1900.

Following Hong et al. (2019), the long-term trend of PDSI is calculated based on an AR(1) model augmented with a linear deterministic time trend, which is expressed as

$$\mathrm{PDSI}_t = a + bt + c\mathrm{PDSI}_{t-1} + \epsilon_t \tag{5}$$

The parameter of interest is the trend coefficient b, which measures the long-run risk embodied in PDSI. In this section, we use the time series coefficient b as the proxy for climate risk to regress on the elasticities. The AR(1) model is estimated by using a rolling recursive approach starting from January 1900 up to the date over the period from 1971 to 2022. Hong et al. (2019) start from 1900 but consider the period from 1984 to 2014. We estimate the trend term using the monthly data and then average these into annual data to match with our elasticities data. To be consistent with the frequency of Trend_PDSI, the data for PDSI are also converted into annual data by taking an average of the monthly data. The descriptive statistics are reported in Table 2 Panel C. Fig. 5 depicts the time series pattern of PDSI and Trend_PDSI over the period from 1971 to 2022. The *x*-axis represents the year. The left *y*-axis represents the magnitude of PDSI and the right *y*-axis represents the magnitude of Trend_PDSI. PDSI is depicted using the dashed line and Trend_PDSI is depicted using the solid line. From the solid line, we can see that there is a significant trend for the United States toward more moisture soil conditions. The positive trend peaks in the middle of the 1990s.

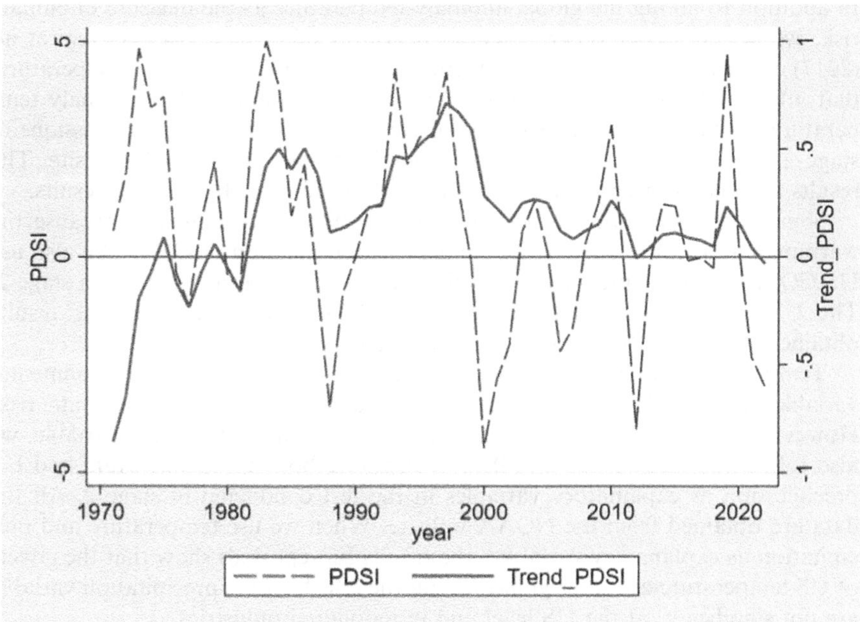

Fig. 5. Time Series US Patterns of Palmer Drought Severity Index (PDSI) and the Long-Term Trends of PDSI Over the Period From 1971–2022. *Note:* The figure depicts the time series pattern of the PDSI and the Long-Run Trends of PDSI over the period from 1971 to 2022. The data for PDSI is obtained from the NOAA website. The monthly data are annualized by taking the mean of monthly PDSI. The Long-Term Trend of PDSI is calculated based on the augmented AR(1) model by following Hong et al. (2019). The *x*-axis denotes the year. The left *y*-axis denotes the magnitude of PDSI, and the right *y*-axis denotes the magnitude of the Long-Term Trend of PDSI. The data are extracted from the NOAA website https://www.ncei.noaa.gov/access/monitoring/climate-at-a-glance/national/time-series/.

Hong et al. (2019) note that the positive trend group has larger downside beta and relative downside beta (the difference between the downside beta and CAPM beta) than the negative trend group. Therefore, we interpret the trend toward more moisture as a proxy for climate risk. If investors perceive the threat of climate risk, it is expected that there would be a positive association between the elasticities of the book value of equity and Trend_PDSI and a negative association between the elasticities of earnings and Trend_PDSI. This is different from Hong et al. (2019), which views the trend toward droughts as a source of climate risk. Table 7 shows that both the US economy as a whole and most industries have a positive relation between climate risk and the elasticities of book value of equity and a negative relation with elasticities of earnings. The results are consistent with our predictions and the baseline results.

6.3 Other Climate Change Variables

In addition to taking the global anomaly temperature as the measure of climate risk, we also consider other potential measures of climate risk. Balvers et al. (2017) claim that it is the local temperature, rather than the global temperature, that affects US stock returns. Therefore, we use the annual US anomaly temperature as the explanatory variable to repeat all the time series regressions in stage 2. The annual US data are also obtained from the NOAA website. The results obtained (unreported) are qualitatively similar to the baseline results.

Some studies investigate the valuation effect of CO_2 emissions because the warming temperature arises from the higher accumulation of GHG. We also use US CO_2 emission as the measure of climate risk to repeat all the tests in stage 2. The US CO_2 data are obtained from the World Bank website. The results obtained (unreported) are also similar to the baseline results.

Temperature is only one component of the large set of possible environmental variables to consider but it is regarded as a good indicator of climate risk. However, to avoid any potential estimation bias in the temperature variable, we also follow Addoum et al. (2020) to incorporate both US temperature and US precipitation as explanatory variables in the test conducted in stage 2. All the data are obtained from the NOAA website. When we use temperature and precipitation as explanatory variables, the results (unreported) show that the effects of US temperature are still significant, but the effects of the precipitation variable are not significant, at the US level and in individual industries.

7. DISCUSSION AND CONCLUSION

The evidence from our study supports the position that information about climate risk is incorporated into stock price through the channel of the accounting variables namely, book value of equity and earnings. Because of the continuing increase in global temperature, climate change, and the related climate risk have become matters of increasing concern around the world. Our results are complementary to other studies examining how the capital market reacts to climate risk. While these

Table 7. The Time Series Analysis Using the Long-Term Trend of PDSI (Palmer Drought Severity Index).

	(1) United States	(2) Mining	(3) Construction	(4) Manufacturing	(5) Transportation	(6) Wholesale	(7) Retail	(8) Finance	(9) Service
Panel A:	Dependent variable = $\widehat{\beta_1}$								
Trend_PDSI	0.105***	0.251***	0.145**	0.068*	0.093*	0.077	0.280***	0.018	0.23**
	(2.646)	(3.971)	(1.122)	(1.713)	(1.687)	(1.177)	(5.309)	(0.373)	(2.322)
R^2	0.130	0.251	0.026	0.059	0.057	0.029	0.375	0.003	0.103
Observations	52	52	52	52	52	52	52	52	52
Panel B:	Dependent variable = $\widehat{\beta_2}$								
Trend_PDSI	−0.114***	−0.211***	−0.418***	−0.108***	−0.218***	−0.188***	−0.288***	−0.042	−0.151**
	(−3.221)	(−3.529)	(−3.912)	(−2.594)	(−3.042)	(−3.655)	(−4.938)	(−0.723)	(−2.270)
R^2	0.181	0.209	0.246	0.125	0.165	0.221	0.342	0.011	0.099
Observations	52	52	52	52	52	52	52	52	52

Note: The table reports the results from the time series OLS regressions of the estimated elasticities of net income and book value on the Trend_PDSI. The econometric model is $y_{jt} = v_{jt} + \widehat{\gamma_j x_{jt}} + \omega_{jt}$. Each column represents the result for the United States as a whole or the individual industries. Panels A and B report the regression results for $\widehat{\beta_1}$ and $\widehat{\beta_2}$, respectively, t-statistics are reported in the parentheses. *, ** and *** denote the significant level of 10%, 5% and 1%, respectively.

studies reveal such channels as productivity, our study highlights the impact of accounting variables in the valuation process.

The key objective of accounting is to provide information that is useful to investors. Because information on climate risk has become increasingly important to investors today, our study also has a significant implication for the means of achieving the objective of accounting. Lev (2018) has criticized the shift from focus on the income statement to the balance sheet in the development of the Conceptual Frameworks adopted by both the Financial Accounting Standards Board and the International Accounting Standards Board as it has led to decreasing usefulness of accounting information. However, our results show that, in terms of conveying information on climate risk, the book value of equity plays a more important role than earnings in the process of valuation and thus our results support the direction taken by the standards setters.

We use elasticities of market price with respect to the book value of equity and earnings as measures of the valuation weight investors place on the accounting variables. In stage 1 of our tests, we estimate the elasticities by annual cross-sectional OLS regressions based on the multiplicative valuation model. Our sample period covers 1971–2022 and the tests are conducted not only on the US level but also at the industry level. The industry-level study helps us to reveal clearer effects of climate risk because estimates of population average effects may mask interesting and economically important variations (Addoum et al., 2023) due to the complex effects of climate risk. Our results reveal that the relative valuation importance of the book value of equity and earnings are complementary with each other and investors generally put higher valuation importance on the book value of equity. The results are consistent with prior studies, such as Barth et al. (1998), Burgstahler and Dichev (1997) and Collins et al. (1997). However, in contrast to these studies, which focus on the slope of coefficients in a linear relationship, our study focuses on elasticities.

In stage 2, we use the global anomaly temperature as the measure of climate risk to examine how climate risk influences the time series patterns of the estimated elasticities. We find that the global temperature is positively related to the elasticity of book value of equity but negatively related to the elasticities of earnings. We posit that the book value of equity reflects the aggregate of past information and earnings capture investors' expectations about the future. When investors become pessimistic about the future due to climate risk, they tend to put relatively higher valuation importance on the book value of equity and less on earnings. Our results are, to a large extent, consistent with the arguments from Sautner et al. (2023b). They classify the risk associated with climate change into three types: opportunity, regulator and physical shocks, and highlight that investors are not only concerned with the second moment of returns, which is the general measure of risk but are also concerned with higher-order moments reflecting extreme risks and opportunities. Moreover, investors may prefer different types of climate risk during different periods. Therefore, we posit that the trade-off between the second and higher-order moments results in the complementary movement of the elasticities for the book value of equity and earnings. Specifically, when investors are concerned more about the higher-order moment of risk, they will focus more on the book value of equity. Our robustness tests strongly support our baseline results.

NOTES

1. See https://oag.parliament.nz/2024/climate-change-accounting. Similarly, Penman (2024) studies how to use an accounting system to recognize and measure a firm's carbon emissions instead of focusing on how to disclose carbon emissions.

2. The value relevance studies tend to focus on the longer period of value relevance measures. For example, Binz et al. (2023) study the effect of inflation on the value relevance of accounting numbers based on datasets from 1926 to 2021 and argue that such an effect should be observed based on long-time series data to contain a sufficient amount of inflation variation. For the same reason, the longer period of temperature data will facilitate the identification of climate risk on the value relevance of accounting variables.

3. To identify the dominant factor among these alternative explanations is an open empirical question, which is beyond the scope of our study. The authors thank the reviewer for suggesting this question.

4. Please refer to Clarkson (2012) for an excellent review of this strand of the literature.

5. Readers who are interested in this branch of studies can refer to Barth et al. (2023), Section 2.

6. Linnainmaa and Roberts (2018) find that the clean-surplus principle was violated more frequently after the 1960s. Therefore, we add the residual variable, O_t, into the model to take into account the dirty surplus relation among accounting variables in practice.

7. Some studies exclude financial firms because the properties of accounting data are different from other industries. Some studies exclude utility firms because they are highly regulated. However, for completeness, we included both categories of firms. Another reason for considering the finance industry is the high engagement of the finance industry in fighting against climate risk and utilities are regarded as the industry with the highest CO_2 emissions (Bolton & Kacperczyk, 2021).

8. The data are extracted from https://www.ncei.noaa.gov/access/monitoring/global-temperature-anomalies#anomalies.

9. The data are extracted from https://www.ncei.noaa.gov/access/monitoring/climate-at-a-glance/national/time-series/.

10. Doornik and Hendry (2013) point out three types of non-stationarity. They are (1) integrated behaviour; (2) regime switches; and (3) 'inherent non-stationary owing to innovative human behavior or natural process' (p. 230). In this subsection, we mainly address the first type of non-stationarity.

REFERENCES

Aczel, J. (Ed.). (1966). *Lectures on functional equations and their applications, mathematics in science and engineering* (Vol. 19). Academic Press.

Addoum, J. M., Ng, D. T., & Ortiz-Bobea, A. (2023). Temperature shocks and industry earnings news. *Journal of Financial Economics*, *150*(1), 1–45. https://doi.org/10.1016/j.jfineco.2023.07.002

Addoum, J. M., Ng, D. T., & Ortiz-Bobea, A. (2020). Temperature shocks and establishment sales. *The Review of Financial Studies*, *33*(3), 1331–1366. https://doi.org/10.1093/rfs/hhz126

Auffhammer, M. (2018). Quantifying economic damages from climate change. *Journal of Economic Perspectives*, *32*(4), 33–52.

Auffhammer, M., & Mansur, E. T. (2014). Measuring climatic impacts on energy consumption: A review of the empirical literature. *Energy Economics*, *46*, 522–530. https://doi.org/10.1016/j.eneco.2014.04.017

Baker, S. R., & Bloom, N. (2013). *Does uncertainty reduce growth? Using disasters as natural experiments*. NBER Working Paper Series. https://doi.org/10.3386/w19475

Ball, R., & Brown, P. (1968). An empirical evaluation of accounting income numbers. *Journal of Accounting Research*, 159–178.

Ball, R., & Sadka, G. (2015). Aggregate earnings and why they matter☆. *Journal of Accounting Literature*, *34*(1), 39-57. https://doi.org/10.1016/j.acclit.2015.01.001

Balvers, R., Du, D., & Zhao, X. (2017). Temperature shocks and the cost of equity capital: Implications for climate change perceptions. *Journal of Banking & Finance*, *77*, 18–34. https://doi.org/10.1016/j.jbankfin.2016.12.013

Banerjee, A., Dolado, J. J., Galbraith, J. W., & Hendry, D. (2003). *Co-integration, error correction, and the econometric analysis of non-stationary data*. Oxford University Press.

Bansal, R., Kiku, D., & Ochoa, M. (2016). *Price of long-run temperature shifts in capital markets*. https://www.nber.org/system/files/working_papers/w22529/w22529.pdf

Bansal, R., Kiku, D., & Ochoa, M. (2019). *Climate change risk*. https://www.frbsf.org/wp-content/uploads/sites/4/Paper-5-2019-11-8-Kiku-1PM-1st-paper.pdf

Bansal, R., & Ochoa, M. (2012). *Temperature, aggregate risk, and expected returns*. NBER Working Paper, 17575 (pp. 10–11). http://www.nber.org/papers/w17575.pdf

Barth, M. E., Beaver, W. H., & Landsman, W. R. (1998). Relative valuation roles of equity book value and net income as a function of financial health. *Journal of Accounting and Economics*, *25*(1), 1–34. https://doi.org/10.1016/S0165-4101(98)00017-2

Barth, M. E., Li, K., & McClure, C. G. (2023). Evolution in value relevance of accounting information. *The Accounting Review*, *98*(1), 1–28. https://doi.org/10.2308/TAR-2019-0521

Beaver, W., Kettler, P., & Scholes, M. (1970). The association between market determined and accounting determined risk measures. *The Accounting Review*, *45*(4), 654–682. https://www.jstor.org/stable/244204

Ben-Amar, W., Herrera, D. C., & Martinez, I. (2024). Do climate risk disclosures matter to financial analysts? *Journal of Business Finance & Accounting*, *51*(7–8), 2153–2180. https://doi.org/10.1111/jbfa.12778

Bernstein, A., Gustafson, M. T., & Lewis, R. (2019). Disaster on the horizon: The price effect of sea level rise. *Journal of Financial Economics*, *134*(2), 253–272. https://doi.org/10.1016/j.jfineco.2019.03.013

Binz, O., Graham, J. R., & Kubic, M. (2023). Does inflation affect value relevance? A century-long analysis. https://ssrn.com/abstract=4467947. http://doi.org/10.2139/ssrn.4467947

Bolton, P., & Kacperczyk, M. (2021). Do investors care about carbon risk? *Journal of Financial Economics*, *142*(2), 517–549. https://doi.org/10.1016/j.jfineco.2021.05.008

Bolton, P., & Kacperczyk, M. (2023). Global pricing of carbon-transition risk. *The Journal of Finance*, *78*(6), 3677–3754. https://doi.org/10.1111/jofi.13272

Boonlert-U-Thai, K., & Schaberl, P. (2022). Value relevance of book values, earnings, and future earnings: Evidence by time, life cycle stage, and market uncertainty. *Asian Review of Accounting*, *30*(5), 648–668. https://doi.org/10.1108/ARA-03-2022-0070

Broadstock, D. C., Collins, A., Hunt, L. C., & Vergos, K. (2018). Voluntary disclosure, greenhouse gas emissions and business performance: Assessing the first decade of reporting. *The British Accounting Review*, *50*(1), 48–59. https://doi.org/10.1016/j.bar.2017.02.002

Brooks, C., & Schopohl, L. (2021). Green accounting and finance: Advancing research on environmental disclosure, value impacts and management control systems. *The British Accounting Review*, *53*(1), 100973. https://doi.org/10.1016/j.bar.2020.100973

Brown, J. R., Gustafson, M. T., & Ivanov, I. T. (2021). Weathering cash flow shocks. *The Journal of Finance*, *76*(4), 1731–1772. https://doi.org/10.1111/jofi.13024

Burgstahler, D. C., & Dichev, I. D. (1997). Earnings, adaptation and equity value. *Accounting Review*, 187–215. https://www.jstor.org/stable/248552

Carleton, T. A., & Hsiang, S. M. (2016). Social and economic impacts of climate. *Science*, *353*(6304), aad9837.

Cheng, M., & Micale, J. A. (2022). ESG risks and the value relevance of current and historical earnings. *Financial Markets, Institutions & Instruments*, *31*(5), 207–237. https://doi.org/10.1111/fmii.12162

Choi, D., Gao, Z., & Jiang, W. (2020). Attention to global warming. *The Review of Financial Studies*, *33*(3), 1112–1145. https://doi.org/10.1093/rfs/hhz086

Clarkson, P. M. (2012). The valuation relevance of environmental performance: Evidence from the academic literature. In S. Jones & J. Ratnatunga (Eds.), *Contemporary issues in sustainability accounting, assurance and reporting* (pp. 11–42). Emerald Group Publishing.

Clout, V. J., & Willett, R. J. (2016). Earnings in firm valuation and their value relevance. *Journal of Contemporary Accounting & Economics*, *12*(3), 223–240. https://doi.org/10.1016/j.jcae.2016.09.005

Collins, D. W., Maydew, E. L., & Weiss, I. S. (1997). Changes in the value-relevance of earnings and book values over the past forty years. *Journal of Accounting and Economics*, *24*(1), 39–67. https://doi.org/10.1016/S0165-4101(97)00015-3

Collins, D. W., Pincus, M., & Xie, H. (1999). Equity valuation and negative earnings: The role of book value of equity. *The Accounting Review*, *74*(1), 29–61. https://doi.org/10.2308/accr.1999.74.1.29

Core, J. E., Guay, W. R., & Van Buskirk, A. (2003). Market valuations in the new economy: An investigation of what has changed. *Journal of Accounting and Economics*, *34*(1–3), 43–67. https://doi.org/10.1016/S0165-4101(02)00087-3

Cuculiza, C., Kumar, A., Xin, W., & Zhang, C.. (2021). Climate change, analyst forecasts, and market behavior. https://ssrn.com/abstract=3781157. http://doi.org/10.2139/ssrn.3781157

Dehaan, E., Madsen, J., & Piotroski, J. D. (2017). Do weather-induced moods affect the processing of earnings news? *Journal of Accounting Research*, *55*(3), 509-550.https://doi.org/10.1111/1475-679X.12160

Dell, M., Jones, B. F., & Olken, B. A. (2008). *Climate change and economic growth: Evidence from the last half century*. https://www.nber.org/papers/w14132

Dell, M., Jones, B. F., & Olken, B. A. (2012). Temperature shocks and economic growth: Evidence from the last half century. *American Economic Journal: Macroeconomics*, *4*(3), 66–95.

Dell, M., Jones, B. F., & Olken, B. A. (2014). What do we learn from the weather? The new climate-economy literature. *Journal of Economic Literature*, *52*(3), 740–798.

Dickinson, V., Kassa, H., & Schaberl, P. D. (2018). What information matters to investors at different stages of a firm's life cycle? *Advances in Accounting*, *42*, 22–33. https://doi.org/10.1016/j.adiac.2018.07.002

Doornik, J. A., & Hendry, D. F. (2013). *PcGive 14 volume II: Modelling dynamic systems*. Timberlake Consultants Ltd.

Dunham, L. M., & Grandstaff, J. L. (2022). The value relevance of earnings, book values, and other accounting information and the role of economic conditions in value relevance: A literature review. *Accounting Perspectives*, *21*(2), 237–272. https://doi.org/10.1111/1911-3838.12280

Easton, P. D., & Harris, T. S. (1991). Earnings as an explanatory variable for returns. *Journal of Accounting Research*, *29*(1), 19–36. https://doi.org/10.2307/2491026

Engle, R. F., Giglio, S., Kelly, B., Lee, H., & Stroebel, J. (2020). Hedging climate change news. *The Review of Financial Studies*, *33*(3), 1184–1216. https://doi.org/10.1093/rfs/hhz072

Engle, R. F., & Granger, C. W. J. (1987). Co-integration and error correction: Representation, estimation, and testing. *Econometrica: Journal of the Econometric Society*, 251–276. https://doi.org/10.2307/1913236

Falta, M., & Willett, R. J. (2013). The impact of exponential growth variables on regression models of the market–accounting relation. *Journal of Accounting, Auditing & Finance*, *28*(3), 243–272. https://doi.org/10.1177/0148558X13491966

Görgen, M., Jacob, A., Nerlinger, M., Riordan, R., Rohleder, M., & Wilkens, M. (2020). Carbon risk. https://ssrn.com/abstract=2930897. http://doi.org/10.2139/ssrn.2930897

Gallo, L. A., Hann, R. N., & Li, C. (2016). Aggregate earnings surprises, monetary policy, and stock returns. *Journal of Accounting and Economics*, *62*(1), 103–120. https://doi.org/10.1016/j.jacceco.2016.04.003

Giglio, S., Kelly, B., & Stroebel, J. (2021). Climate finance. *Annual Review of Financial Economics*, *13*, 15–36. https://doi.org/10.1146/annurev-financial-102620-103311

Goetzmann, W. N., Kim, D., Kumar, A., & Wang, Q. (2015). Weather-induced mood, institutional investors, and stock returns. *The Review of Financial Studies*, *28*(1), 73–111. https://doi.org/10.1093/rfs/hhu063

Gordon, M. J. (1962). *The investment, financing, and valuation of the corporation*. RD Irwin.

Griffin, P. A., Lont, D. H., & Lubberink, M. J. P. (2024). The effects of extreme high temperature spells on financial performance. *The British Accounting Review*, 101383. https://doi.org/10.1016/j.bar.2024.101383

Hasan, I., Micale, J. A., & Rapaccioli, D. (2024). Climate change exposure and the value relevance of earnings and book values of equity. *Journal of Sustainable Finance and Accounting*, *1*, 100004. https://doi.org/10.1016/j.josfa.2024.100004

Holthausen, R. W., & Watts, R. L. (2001). The relevance of the value-relevance literature for financial accounting standard setting. *Journal of Accounting and Economics*, *31*(1–3), 3–75. https://doi.org/10.1016/S0165-4101(01)00029-5

Hong, H., Karolyi, G. A., & Scheinkman, J. A. (2020). Climate finance. *The Review of Financial Studies*, *33*(3), 1011–1023. https://doi.org/10.1093/rfs/hhz146

Hong, H., Li, F. W., & Xu, J. (2019). Climate risks and market efficiency. *Journal of Econometrics*, *208*(1), 265–281. https://doi.org/10.1016/j.jeconom.2018.09.015

Hsiang, S., & Kopp, R. E. (2018). An economist's guide to climate change science. *Journal of Economic Perspectives*, *32*(4), 3–32.

Hsu, P.-H., Li, K. A. I., & Tsou, C.-Y. (2023). The pollution premium. *The Journal of Finance*, *78*(3), 1343–1392. https://doi.org/10.1111/jofi.13217

Huang, H. H., Kerstein, J., & Wang, C. (2018). The impact of climate risk on firm performance and financing choices: An international comparison. *Journal of International Business Studies*, *49*(5), 633–656. https://doi.org/10.1057/s41267-017-0125-5

Huang, H. H., Kerstein, J., Wang, C., & Wu, F. (2022). Firm climate risk, risk management, and bank loan financing. *Strategic Management Journal*, *43*(13), 2849–2880. https://doi.org/10.1002/smj.3437

Huang, Y., & Zhang, G. (2012). An examination of the incremental usefulness of balance-sheet information beyond earnings in explaining stock returns. *Journal of Accounting, Auditing & Finance*, *27*(2), 267–293. https://doi.org/10.1177/0148558X11409153

Hugon, A., & Law, K. (2019). Impact of climate change on firm earnings: Evidence from temperature anomalies. https://ssrn.com/abstract=3271386. http://doi.org/10.2139/ssrn.3271386

Ilhan, E., Krueger, P., Sautner, Z., & Starks, L. T. (2023). Climate risk disclosure and institutional investors. *The Review of Financial Studies*, *36*(7), 2617–2650.

Ilhan, E., Sautner, Z., & Vilkov, G. (2021). Carbon tail risk. *The Review of Financial Studies*, *34*(3), 1540–1571.

Imhoff, Jr, E. A., & Lobo, G. J. (1992). The effect of ex ante earnings uncertainty on earnings response coefficients. *Accounting Review*, 427–439. https://www.jstor.org/stable/247734

Jiang, W., & Stark, A. W. (2013). Dividends, research and development expenditures, and the value relevance of book value for UK loss-making firms. *The British Accounting Review*, *45*(2), 112–124. https://doi.org/10.1016/j.bar.2013.03.003

Kölbel, J. F., Leippold, M., Rillaerts, J., & Wang, Q. (2020). *Does the CDS market reflect regulatory climate risk disclosures?* https://doi.org/10.5167/uzh-187908

Kormendi, R., & Lipe, R. (1987). Earnings innovations, earnings persistence, and stock returns. *Journal of Business*, 323–345. https://www.jstor.org/stable/2352874

Kothari, S. P. (2001). Capital markets research in accounting. *Journal of Accounting and Economics*, *31*(1–3), 105–231. https://doi.org/10.1016/S0165-4101(01)00030-1

Kothari, S. P., & Shanken, J. (2003). Time-series coefficient variation in value-relevance regressions: A discussion of Core, Guay, and Van Buskirk and new evidence. *Journal of Accounting and Economics*, *34*(1–3), 69–87. https://doi.org/10.1016/S0165-4101(02)00091-5

Krueger, P., Sautner, Z., & Starks, L. T. (2020). The importance of climate risks for institutional investors. *The Review of Financial Studies*, *33*(3), 1067–1111. https://doi.org/10.1093/rfs/hhz137

Lev, B. (2018). The deteriorating usefulness of financial report information and how to reverse it. *Accounting and Business Research*, *48*(5), 465–493. https://doi.org/10.1080/00014788.2018.1470138

Li, Q., Shan, H., Tang, Y., & Yao, V. (2024). Corporate climate risk: Measurements and responses. *The Review of Financial Studies*, *37*(6), 1778–1830.

Linnainmaa, J. T., & Roberts, M. R. (2018). The history of the cross-section of stock returns. *The Review of Financial Studies*, *31*(7), 2606–2649. https://doi.org/10.1093/rfs/hhy030

Lipe, R. C. (1986). The information contained in the components of earnings. *Journal of Accounting Research*, 37–64. https://doi.org/10.2307/2490728

Lubberink, M. J. P., & Willett, R. J. (2021). Specification of the market-accounting relation. https://ssrn.com/abstract=3976635. http://doi.org/10.2139/ssrn.3976635

Lubberink, M., & Willett, R. (2024). How sensitive are bank market values to regulatory adjustments of capital? *The International Journal of Accounting*, 2450014. https://doi.org/10.1142/S1094406024500148

Nordhaus, W. (2019). Climate change: The ultimate challenge for economics. *American Economic Review*, *109*(6), 1991–2014.

Ohlson, J. A. (1995). Earnings, book values, and dividends in equity valuation. *Contemporary Accounting Research*, *11*(2), 661–687. https://doi.org/10.1111/j.1911-3846.1995.tb00461.x

Onali, E., Ginesti, G., & Vasilakis, C. (2017). How should we estimate value-relevance models? Insights from European data. *The British Accounting Review*, *49*(5), 460–473. https://doi.org/10.1016/j.bar.2017.05.006

Painter, M. (2020). An inconvenient cost: The effects of climate change on municipal bonds. *Journal of Financial Economics*, *135*(2), 468–482. https://doi.org/10.1016/j.jfineco.2019.06.006

Palmer, W. C. (1965). *Meteorological drought*. Research paper no. 45 (p. 58). US Weather Bureau.

Pankratz, N., Bauer, R., & Derwall, J. (2023). Climate change, firm performance, and investor surprises. *Management Science*, *69*(12), 7352–7398.

Penman, S. H. (2024). Accounting for carbon. https://ssrn.com/abstract=4721974. http://doi.org/10.2139/ssrn.4721974

Penman, S., & Zhang, X. (2020). A theoretical analysis connecting conservative accounting to the cost of capital. *Journal of Accounting and Economics*, *69*(1), 101236. https://doi.org/10.1016/j.jacceco.2019.101236

Pindyck, R. S. (2007). Uncertainty in environmental economics. *Review of Environmental Economics and Policy*, *1*(1), 45–65.

Roberts, F. S. (1984). Measurement theory: With applications to decision-making, utility, and the social sciences. In *Encyclopedia of mathematics and its applications* (Vol. 7). Cambridge University Press.

Santi, C. (2023). Investor climate sentiment and financial markets. *International Review of Financial Analysis*, *86*, 102490. https://doi.org/10.1016/j.irfa.2023.102490

Sautner, Z., van Lent, L., Vilkov, G., & Zhang, R. (2023b). Pricing climate change exposure. *Management Science*, *69*(12), 7540–7561.

Sautner, Z., van Lent, L., Vilkov, G., & Zhang, R. (2023a). Firm-level climate change exposure. *The Journal of Finance*, *78*(3), 1449–1498. https://doi.org/10.1111/jofi.13219

Schaberl, P. D. (2016). Beyond accounting and back: An empirical examination of the relative relevance of earnings and "other" information. *Advances in Accounting*, *35*, 98–113. https://doi.org/10.1016/j.adiac.2016.08.004

Schlenker, W., & Taylor, C. A. (2021). Market expectations of a warming climate. *Journal of Financial Economics*. https://doi.org/10.1016/j.jfineco.2020.08.019

SEC. (2010, Feburary 2). *Final Rule. Commission guidance regarding disclosure related to climate change*. Release Nos. 33-9106; 34-61469; File No. S7-10-22. Securities and Exchange Commission. https://www.sec.gov/files/rules/interp/2010/33-9106.pdf

SEC. (2024, March 6). *Final rule. The enhancement and standardization of climate-related disclosures for investors*. Release Nos. 33-11275; 34-99678; FR-82. Securities and Exchange Commission. https://www.sec.gov/files/rules/final/2024/33-11275.pdf

Stern, N. (2008). The economics of climate change. *American Economic Review*, *98*(2), 1–37.

Stroebel, J., & Wurgler, J. (2021). What do you think about climate finance? *Journal of Financial Economics*, *142*(2), 487–498. https://doi.org/10.1016/j.jfineco.2021.08.004

TFCD. (2017, June). *Final report: Recommendations of the task force on climate related financial disclosures*. https://assets.bbhub.io/company/sites/60/2020/10/FINAL-2017-TCFD-Report-11052018.pdf

Tol, R. S. J. (2009). The economic effects of climate change. *Journal of Economic Perspectives*, *23*(2), 29–51.

Tol, R. S. J. (2018). The economic impacts of climate change. *Review of Environmental Economics and Policy*, *12*(1), 4–25.

Tol, R. S. J. (2024). A meta-analysis of the total economic impact of climate change. *Energy Policy*, *185*, 113922. https://doi.org/10.1016/j.enpol.2023.113922

Printed and bound by CPI Group (UK) Ltd, Croydon, CR0 4YY

21/09/2025

14739244-0002